VATICAN II

VATICAN II

THE ESSENTIAL TEXTS

Documents *edited by*
NORMAN TANNER, S.J.

Introductions from
POPE BENEDICT XVI *and* JAMES CARROLL
Prefatory Material from
EDWARD P. HAHNENBERG

IMAGE

New York

Library of Congress Cataloging-in-Public Data
Vatican Council (2nd : 1962–1965)
 [Documents of Vatican II. English. Selections]
 Vatican II : the essential texts / documents edited by Norman Tanner ; with essays from Pope Benedict XVI, James Carroll and Edward P. Hahnenberg.
   p. cm.
 Includes bibliographical references and index.
1. Vatican Council (2nd : 1962–1965) 2. Catholic Church—Doctrines.
I. Benedict XVI, Pope, 1927– II. Carroll, James, 1943– III. Hahnenberg, Edward P. IV. Title.
 BX8301962.A3 T36 2012
 262'.52--dc23

                              2011052077

ISBN: 978-0-307-95280-6
eISBN: 978-0-307-95293-6

Printed in the United States of America

Cover design by Laura Duffy
Cover photography by Richard l'Anson/Lonely Planet Images

10 9 8 7 6 5 4 3 2 1

First Image Books Edition

Contents

VATICAN II

INTRODUCTIONS

What Has Been the Result of the Council?
POPE BENEDICT XVI

The Beginning of Change
JAMES CARROLL

What Has Been the Result of the Council?

POPE BENEDICT XVI

What has been the result of the Second Vatican Council? Was it well-received? What, in the acceptance of the Council, was good and what was inadequate or mistaken? What still remains to be done? No one can deny that in vast areas of the Church the implementation of the Council has been somewhat difficult, even without wishing to apply to what occurred in these years the description that St. Basil, the great Doctor of the Church, made of the Church's situation after the Council of Nicaea: he compares her situation to a naval battle in the darkness of the storm, saying among other things: "The raucous shouting of those who through disagreement rise up against one another, the incomprehensible chatter, the confused din of uninterrupted clamouring, has now filled almost the whole of the Church, falsifying through excess or failure the right doctrine of the faith . . ."[1]

We do not want to apply precisely this dramatic description to the situation of the post-conciliar period, yet something from all that occurred is nevertheless reflected in it. The question arises: Why has the implementation of the Council, in large parts of the Church, thus far been so difficult?

Well, it all depends on the correct interpretation of the Council or—as we would say today—on its proper hermeneutics, the correct key to its interpretation and application. The problems in its implementation arose from the fact that two contrary hermeneutics came face to face and quarrelled with each other. One caused confusion, the other, silently but more and more visibly, bore and is bearing fruit.

On the one hand, there is an interpretation that I would call "a hermeneutic of discontinuity and rupture"; it has frequently availed itself of the sympathies of the mass media, and also one trend of modern theology. On the other, there is the "hermeneutic of reform," of renewal in the continuity of the one subject-Church which the Lord has given to us. She is a subject which increases in time and develops, yet always remaining the same, the one subject of the journeying People of God.

The hermeneutic of discontinuity risks ending in a split between the pre-conciliar Church and the post-conciliar Church. It asserts that the texts of the Council as such do not yet express the true spirit of the Council. It claims that they are the result of compromises in which, to reach unanimity, it was found necessary to keep and reconfirm many old things that are now pointless. However, the true spirit of the Council is not to be found in these compromises but instead in the impulses toward the new that are contained in the texts.

These innovations alone were supposed to represent the true spirit of the Council, and starting from and in conformity with them, it would be possible to move ahead. Precisely because the texts would only imperfectly reflect the true spirit of the Council and its newness, it would be necessary to go courageously beyond the texts and make room for the newness in which the Council's deepest intention would be expressed, even if it were still vague.

In a word: it would be necessary not to follow the texts of the Council but its spirit. In this way, obviously, a vast margin was left open for the question on how this spirit should subsequently be defined and room was consequently made for every whim.

The nature of a Council as such is therefore basically misunderstood. In this way, it is considered as a sort of constituent that eliminates an old constitution and creates a new one. However, the Constituent Assembly needs a mandator and then confirmation by the mandator, in other words, the people the constitution must serve. The Fathers had no such mandate and no one had ever given them one; nor could anyone have given them one because the essential constitution of the Church comes from the Lord and was given to us so that we might attain eternal life and, starting from this perspective, be able to illuminate life in time and time itself.

Through the Sacrament they have received, Bishops are stewards of the Lord's gift. They are "stewards of the mysteries of God" (I Cor 4:1); as such, they must be found to be "faithful" and "wise" (cf. Lk 12:41–48). This requires them to administer the Lord's gift in the right way, so that it is not left concealed in some hiding place but bears fruit, and the Lord may end by saying to the administrator: "Since you were dependable in a small matter I will put you in charge of larger affairs" (cf. Mt 25:14–30; Lk 19:11–27).

These Gospel parables express the dynamic of fidelity required in the Lord's service; and through them it becomes clear that, as in a Council, the dynamic and fidelity must converge.

The hermeneutic of discontinuity is countered by the hermeneutic of reform, as it was presented first by Pope John XXIII in his Speech inaugurating the Council on 11 October 1962 and later by Pope Paul VI in his Discourse for the Council's conclusion on 7 December 1965.

Here I shall cite only John XXIII's well-known words, which unequivocally express this hermeneutic when he says that the Council wishes "to transmit the doctrine, pure and integral, without any attenuation or distortion." And he continues: "Our duty is not only to guard this precious treasure, as if we were concerned only with antiquity, but to dedicate ourselves with an earnest will and without fear to that work which our era demands of us. . . ." It is necessary that "adherence to all the teachings of the Church in its entirety and preciseness . . ." be presented in "faithful and perfect conformity to the authentic doctrine, which, however, should be studied and expounded through the methods of research and through the literary forms of modern thought. The substance of the ancient doctrine of the deposit of faith is one thing, and the way in which it is presented is another . . . ," retaining the same meaning and message.[2]

It is clear that this commitment to expressing a specific truth in a new way demands new thinking on this truth and a new and vital relationship with it; it is also clear that new words can only develop if they come from an informed understanding of the truth expressed, and on the other hand, that a reflection on faith also requires that this faith be lived. In this regard, the programme that Pope John XXIII proposed was extremely demanding, indeed, just as the synthesis of fidelity and dynamic is demanding.

However, wherever this interpretation guided the implementation of the Council, new life developed and new fruit ripened. Forty years after the Council, we can show that the positive is far greater and livelier than it appeared to be in the turbulent years around 1968. Today, we see that although the good seed developed slowly, it is nonetheless growing; and our deep gratitude for the work done by the Council is likewise growing.

In his Discourse closing the Council, Paul VI pointed out a further specific reason why a hermeneutic of discontinuity can seem convincing.

In the great dispute about man which marks the modern epoch, the Council had to focus in particular on the theme of anthropology. It had to question the relationship between the Church and her faith on the one hand, and man and the contemporary world on the other.[3] The question becomes even clearer if, instead of the generic term "contemporary world," we opt for another that is more precise: the Council had to determine in a new way the relationship between the Church and the modern era.

This relationship had a somewhat stormy beginning with the Galileo case. It was then totally interrupted when Kant described "religion within pure reason" and when, in the radical phase of the French Revolution, an image of the State and the human being that practically no longer wanted to allow the Church any room was disseminated.

In the 19th century under Pius IX, the clash between the Church's faith and a radical liberalism and the natural sciences, which also claimed to embrace with their knowledge the whole of reality to its limit, stubbornly proposing to make the "hypothesis of God" superfluous, had elicited from the Church a bitter and radical condemnation of this spirit of the modern age. Thus, it seemed that there was no longer any milieu open to a positive and fruitful understanding, and the rejection by those who felt they were the representatives of the modern era was also drastic.

In the meantime, however, the modern age had also experienced developments. People came to realize that the American Revolution was offering a model of a modern State that differed from the theoretical model with radical tendencies that had emerged during the second phase of the French Revolution.

The natural sciences were beginning to reflect more and more clearly their own limitations imposed by their own method, which, despite achieving great things, was nevertheless unable to grasp the global nature of reality.

So it was that both parties were gradually beginning to open up to each other. In the period between the two World Wars and especially after the Second World War, Catholic statesmen demonstrated that a modern secular State could exist that was not neutral regarding values but alive, drawing from the great ethical sources opened by Christianity.

Catholic social doctrine, as it gradually developed, became an important model between radical liberalism and the Marxist theory of the State. The natural sciences, which without reservation professed a method of their own to which God was barred access, realized ever more clearly that this method did not include the whole of reality. Hence, they once again opened their doors to God, knowing that reality is greater than the naturalistic method and all that it can encompass.

It might be said that three circles of questions had formed which then, at the time of the Second Vatican Council, were expecting an answer. First of all, the relationship between faith and modern science had to be redefined. Furthermore, this did not only concern the natural sciences but also historical science for, in a certain school, the historical-critical method claimed to have the last word on the interpretation of the Bible and, demanding total exclusivity for its interpretation of Sacred Scripture, was opposed to important points in the interpretation elaborated by the faith of the Church.

Secondly, it was necessary to give a new definition to the relationship between the Church and the modern State that would make room impartially for citizens of various religions and ideologies, merely assuming responsibility for an orderly and tolerant coexistence among them and for the freedom to practise their own religion.

Thirdly, linked more generally to this was the problem of religious tolerance—a question that required a new definition of the relationship between the Christian faith and the world religions. In particular, before the recent crimes of the Nazi regime and, in general, with a retrospective look at a long and difficult history, it was necessary to evaluate and define in a new way the relationship between the Church and the faith of Israel.

These are all subjects of great importance—they were the great themes of the second part of the Council—on which it is impossible to reflect more broadly in this context. It is clear that in all these sectors, which all together form a single problem, some kind of discontinuity might emerge. Indeed, a discontinuity had been revealed but in which, after the various distinctions between concrete historical situations and their requirements had been made, the continuity of principles proved not to have been abandoned. It is easy to miss this fact at a first glance.

It is precisely in this combination of continuity and discontinuity at different levels that the very nature of true reform consists. In this process of innovation in continuity we must learn to understand more practically than before that the Church's decisions on contingent matters—for example, certain practical forms of liberalism or a free interpretation of the Bible—should necessarily be contingent themselves, precisely because they refer to a specific reality that is changeable in itself. It was necessary to learn to recognize that in these decisions it is only the principles that express the permanent aspect, since they remain as an undercurrent, motivating decisions from within. On the other hand, not so permanent are the practical forms that depend on the historical situation and are therefore subject to change.

Basic decisions, therefore, continue to be well-grounded, whereas the way they are applied to new contexts can change. Thus, for example, if religious freedom were to be considered an expression of the human inability to discover the truth and thus become a canonization of relativism, then this social and historical necessity is raised inappropriately to the metaphysical level and thus stripped of its true meaning. Consequently, it cannot be accepted by those who believe that the human person is capable of knowing the truth about God and, on the basis of the inner dignity of the truth, is bound to this knowledge.

It is quite different, on the other hand, to perceive religious freedom as a need that derives from human coexistence, or indeed, as an intrinsic consequence of the truth that cannot be externally imposed but that the person must adopt only through the process of conviction.

The Second Vatican Council, recognizing and making its own an essential principle of the modern State with the Decree on Religious Freedom, has recovered the deepest patrimony of the Church. By so doing she can be conscious of being in full harmony with the teaching of Jesus himself (cf. Mt 22:21), as well as with the Church of the martyrs of all time. The ancient Church naturally prayed for the emperors and political leaders out of duty (cf. I Tm 2:2); but while she prayed for the emperors, she refused to worship them and thereby clearly rejected the religion of the State.

The martyrs of the early Church died for their faith in that God who was revealed in Jesus Christ, and for this very reason they also died for freedom of conscience and the freedom to profess one's own faith—a profession that no State can impose but which, instead, can only be claimed with God's grace in freedom of conscience. A missionary Church known for proclaiming her message to all peoples must necessarily work for the freedom of the faith. She desires to transmit the gift of the truth that exists for one and all.

At the same time, she assures peoples and their Governments that she does not wish to destroy their identity and culture by doing so, but to give them, on the contrary, a response which, in their innermost depths, they are waiting for—a response with which the multiplicity of cultures is not lost but instead unity between men and women increases and thus also peace between peoples.

The Second Vatican Council, with its new definition of the relationship between the faith of the Church and certain essential elements of modern thought, has reviewed or even corrected certain historical decisions, but in this apparent discontinuity it has actually preserved and deepened her inmost nature and true identity.

The Church, both before and after the Council, was and is the same Church, one, holy, catholic and apostolic, journeying on through time; she continues "her pilgrimage amid the persecutions of the world and the consolations of God," proclaiming the death of the Lord until he comes.[4]

Those who expected that with this fundamental "yes" to the modern era all tensions would be dispelled and that the "openness towards the world" accordingly achieved would transform everything into pure harmony, had underestimated the inner tensions as well as the contradictions inherent in the modern epoch.

They had underestimated the perilous frailty of human nature which has been a threat to human progress in all the periods of history and in every historical constellation. These dangers, with the new possibilities and new power of man over matter and over himself, did not disappear but instead acquired new dimensions: a look at the history of the present day shows this clearly.

In our time too, the Church remains a "sign that will be opposed" (Lk 2:34)—not without reason did Pope John Paul II, then still a Cardinal, give this title to the theme for the Spiritual Exercises he preached in 1976 to Pope Paul VI and the Roman Curia. The Council could not have intended to abolish the Gospel's opposition to human dangers and errors.

On the contrary, it was certainly the Council's intention to overcome erroneous or superfluous contradictions in order to present to our world the requirement of the Gospel in its full greatness and purity.

The steps the Council took toward the modern era which had rather vaguely been presented as "openness to the world," belong in short to the perennial problem of the relationship between faith and reason that is re-emerging in ever new forms. The situation that the Council had to face can certainly be compared to events of previous epochs.

In his First Letter, St. Peter urged Christians always to be ready to give an answer (*apologia*) to anyone who asked them for the *logos*, the reason for their faith (cf. 3:15). This meant that biblical faith had to be discussed and come into contact with Greek culture and learn to recognize through interpretation the separating line but also the convergence and the affinity between them in the one reason, given by God.

When, in the 13th century through the Jewish and Arab

philosophers, Aristotelian thought came into contact with Medieval Christianity formed in the Platonic tradition and faith and reason risked entering an irreconcilable contradiction, it was above all St. Thomas Aquinas who mediated the new encounter between faith and Aristotelian philosophy, thereby setting faith in a positive relationship with the form of reason prevalent in his time. There is no doubt that the wearing dispute between modern reason and the Christian faith, which had begun negatively with the Galileo case, went through many phases, but with the Second Vatican Council the time came when broad new thinking was required.

Its content was certainly only roughly traced in the conciliar texts, but this determined its essential direction, so that the dialogue between reason and faith, particularly important today, found its bearings on the basis of the Second Vatican Council.

This dialogue must now be developed with great open-mindedness but also with that clear discernment that the world rightly expects of us in this very moment. Thus, today we can look with gratitude at the Second Vatican Council: if we interpret and implement it guided by a right hermeneutic, it can be and can become increasingly powerful for the ever necessary renewal of the Church.

—Address to the Roman Curia
December 22, 2005

The Beginning of Change

JAMES CARROLL

They were old men (average age sixty), temperamentally conservative, culturally detached. Men of contradiction, they were schooled in anachronism in how they thought, spoke, dressed, and lived—yet they presided at a climax of modernity. They were princes in a democratic age. Gathered from all corners of the earth, yet they engaged in a quintessentially European task. They were holders of unlimited authority in their spheres on the periphery of power, but absolutely submissive in the power center, where they gathered. Rigidly orthodox, they took instruction from innovators they had silenced. Responsible for the governance of the last divine-right monarchy, they were summoned to begin, unawares, its dismantling. They were totally committed to its mission, which was to protect and promote a precious revelation, transcendent and immutable. Yet these men of tradition launched a revolution that transformed how that revelation is understood. The largest contradiction of all: it was *a revolution from the top*.

Having generated that tidal wave, many of them would spend the rest of their lives, like the mythic King Canute, futilely commanding it to roll back. Even fifty years later, what they did is as little understood by a broad public as it is still coming, despite the Canutes, to fulfillment. They were the fathers of the Second Vatican Council of the Roman Catholic Church.

There has been, on average, one Ecumenical Council every century across nearly two thousand years, convocations summoned for the purpose of Church administration, theological reckoning, or renewal of discipline. Popes had been more or less supreme in the magisterium, or teaching authority, of the Latin Church since Pope Gregory VII wrested control of the appointment of bishops from competing princes in the 11th century, but Councils had served to amplify papal authority, and at times to check it.

Vatican II met in the great nave of St. Peter's Basilica in Rome in four sessions in the autumns of the years 1962 to 1965, with committees doing extensive work between sessions. Made up of about 2,400 bishops, with about 500 periti, or experts, and something between 50 and 200 "observers" and "auditors" in attendance, the Council issued sixteen distinct statements (four "constitutions," nine "decrees," and three "declarations"), the most important of which are published here.

The previous Council had been Vatican I (1869–1870), which notably responded to the loss of the Papacy's temporal power to Italian nationalists by absolutizing its spiritual power over the whole Catholic Church with the doctrine of papal infallibility. Little notice was taken of the contradiction in the Council's promulgation of *Pastor Aeternus:* How do we know that the pope is the Church's sole and preeminent teacher? A Council says so.

It had been three centuries since the Council before that, the Council of Trent (1545–1563), which responded to the crisis of the Reformation by establishing the disciplines and norms that defined Catholic culture into the 20th century. Because Vatican I's declaration of papal infallibility was assumed to mean that Church teaching authority would in the future be exercised by the pope acting alone, few expected that there would be any further Councils after Vatican I. But neither did they imagine a figure like Angelo Giuseppe Roncalli ever being elevated to the Chair of St. Peter.

A man of peasant stock, not an aristocrat like his predecessors; a veteran of the Holy See's diplomatic service, spending most of his priesthood outside of the narrowly Catholic milieu of Rome; an elderly nonentity in the College of Cardinals, elected as a compromise by a deadlocked conclave to wear the beehive tiara only until the power brokers could agree on a fit candidate—the corpulent and jovial Roncalli replaced the stern and ascetic Pius XII in 1958. Among his first acts upon becoming pope were to take the name John XXIII, to declare that he would never speak infallibly, and, against all expectations, to summon an Ecumenical Council. That act alone defined his boldness—and lasting significance. That his initiative was historic is indicated by the fact that, upon his untimely death from cancer in 1963, between the first and second sessions, Pope John's spirit was essentially continued for the rest of the Council by the very different Giovanni Battista Montini, a longtime Vatican insider, who took the name Paul VI.

Upon his own election, Pope John immediately captured the imagination and affection of the world, even beyond the Church. He was a modest man, capable of good-humored self-deprecation. "Anybody can be pope," he declared. "The proof of this is that I have become one." Yet he was no lightweight. The pope's prophetic gift was to see below the surface of the apparent triumph of midcentury Roman Catholicism: seminaries and convents around the world were overflowing with recruits; missionary priests and nuns in Africa and Latin America were moving into the postcolonial vacuum; the Cold War struggle with Communism had validated Catholic politics, with Asian figures like the Diem family in Vietnam, European leaders like Konrad Adenauer in Germany and Charles de Gaulle in France, with even Protestant America having just elected John F. Kennedy as president.

Yet Pope John intuited that there was something profoundly out of sync in the inner life of the Church: intellectually sterile, liturgically lifeless, moral instruction depending more on imperatives than on invitations, fear emphasized over hope, a clergy cut off from the laity, the razor wire of the Reformation still dividing Christendom, the living Word of Scripture all but forgotten, Jesus himself on the margin of piety. And all of that was implicated both in the human dilemma just then reaching fever pitch and in the historic, still unreckoned-with Church failure of which Pope John had more reason than most to be aware.

The *texts* of the Council presented in this book cannot be fully appreciated apart from the *context* out of which they came. Two world historic events offer a shorthand definition of that context—Hiroshima and Auschwitz. The threat of nuclear annihilation was palpably felt by the Council fathers because, as it happened, that threat was more dangerously immediate at exactly that moment than it had been before or has been since. The Council opened on October 11, 1962. Three days later an American reconnaissance airplane established that the Soviet Union was building nuclear missile sites in Cuba, the beginning of the Cuban Missile Crisis. For the Council's first decisive weeks, the fathers made their choices knowing that the prospect of human self-extinction had never been more real. That awareness was one half of the unprecedented state of mind that propelled the urgency of deliberations.

As a result, one of the Council's most dramatic manifestations took place, in fact, not in Rome but in New York. In the midst of the fourth session, on October 4, 1965, Pope Paul VI addressed the United Nations. In effect, he was a passionate emissary from the Vatican Council, embodying its stunning transformation of a Church that had provided justifying rationale—the "Just War"—for countless wars across the centuries. No more! Indeed, that was precisely Pope Paul's message, as he cried out in the Assembly Hall, "No more war! War never again! It is peace, peace, that must guide the destiny of the peoples of the world and of all humanity." The medieval pope who had launched the Crusades with the cry "God wills it!" at last had his comeuppance, and so did those accustomed to the inevitability of violence. Vatican II, in numerous ways, and quite explicitly in *Gaudium et Spes*, "The Pastoral Constitution on the Church in the Modern World," made the once militant Catholic Church into a peace Church.

The other Council-shaping historic event was the Holocaust. In a second coincidence of timing, a broad cultural reckoning with the anti-Jewish Nazi genocide was just coming to a head in 1962. The Jerusalem trial of Adolf Eichmann had recently riveted the attention of the world; the *Diary of a Young Girl* by Anne Frank, a publishing, theater, and film phenomenon, had stricken the global conscience; and, in Berlin, only months before the Council's convening, the play *The*

Deputy by Rolf Hochhuth had brought sensational charges against Pope Pius XII for complicity with the Nazi crime.

Even more to the point, though, was Pope John's own experience as one of the few Catholic prelates to have actively resisted the Holocaust while it unfolded. As Papal Legate in Turkey from 1935 to 1944, he had provided forged baptismal certificates to fugitive Jews, enabling hundreds, perhaps thousands, to obtain visas to escape. From 1944 to 1953, he was Papal Legate to Paris, where his largest duty was to reckon with the French Catholic hierarchy's complicity in the crimes of the Nazi-friendly Vichy regime. Roncalli, that is, saw the Christian failure up close.

Pope John did not explicitly define the Holocaust as background for the Council, but his early and continuing insistence on the Council's taking up the legacy of Christian antisemitism suggests that, for him, that is just what it was. So, too, for many of that generation of Catholic bishops, who joined the broader culture in beginning to look directly at what had happened. This moral accounting would lead to what is arguably the Council's most momentous act—the renunciation in *Nostra Aetate,* "Declaration on the Church's Relation to Non-Christian Religions," of the "Christ-killer" slander against the Jewish people, and the affirmation of the ongoing validity of the Jewish religion.

Pope John declared that he would be not a museum keeper, but a gardener—an image that suggested his appreciation for the underlying principle of the created world, that life assumes change. Change or die. But, across centuries of being thrown on the defensive by Reformation, Enlightenment, and Revolution, the Catholic Church had survived by walling itself off from change. Indeed, the Church had come to understand change as its enemy, a mistake which itself had marked a change, and which had condemned modern Catholicism to a visceral negativity.

For all of Pope John's grasp of the Catholic Church's unseen problems, his response to what he saw drew on an apparently bottomless well of positive energy. Indeed, so thoroughly affirmative was his spirit that his opening remarks to the Council—aptly entitled from their first three words, *Gaudet Mater Ecclesia*, "Mother Church Rejoices"—were a denunciation of denunciation itself, a resounding critique of those to whom "the modern world is nothing but betrayal and ruin . . . prophets of doom who are forever forecasting calamity." Even Catholics could hear in that characterization a criticism of the Hell-threatening negativity that had marked the Church for centuries. John's vision, by contrast, summoned his Council to something very different: "Today, rather, Providence is guiding us toward a new order of human relationships, which, thanks to human effort and yet far surpassing human hopes, will bring us to the realization of still higher and undreamed of experiences." Pope John's positive élan infused the deliberations and conclusions of Vatican II, and that in itself defined the Council's truest revolution.

A prophet can act without foreseeing the consequences of his action, and surely that was true of Pope John. After all, he delivered his resoundingly fresh Council-opening statement in Latin, the Church's stoutest symbol of changelessness. Yet within weeks, the Council fathers moved away from Latin, having immediately joined the core question—Does the Church change?—by taking up as a first order of business the underlying issue of language.

One of the Council's organizing committees, centered in the Curia, or Vatican bureaucracy, presented to the fathers an already drafted document on the liturgy, affirming the permanence of Latin as the tongue of Church prayer. If even Jesus had said the Mass in Latin—so the thoroughly ahistorical reasoning went—by what authority could it be changed? Not incidentally, this was done on October 22, the day President Kennedy went on television to threaten Moscow with nuclear war. Instead of sheepishly voting to approve the document, thereby defining the Council as a rubber stamp for the Curia's well-prepared defense of the status quo, the bishops rebelled, and commissioned their own document on the liturgy. That was drawn up in short order to include approval of the use of the vernacular. Latin would quickly and almost completely disappear from Catholic life. When the Council Fathers voted on *Sacrosanctum Concilium*, "Constitution on Sacred Liturgy," they passed it by a margin of 1,922 to 11. Pope John said, "Now begins my Council."

In the ordinary life of the Catholic people, nothing defines the impact of Vatican II more than the intimate and literate experience of worship in their own language, the transformation of the laity from passive spectators to informed participants. Use of the vernacular had been a defining issue of the Reformation, and with this one change, the Catholic Church was signaling the end of the Counter-Reformation.

If, for all of the troubles racking the Catholic Church in the era of the clergy sex-abuse scandal, Catholic membership holds at surprisingly high levels, especially in America and in the global South, surely this one change is key. Masses everywhere in the Catholic world are vital and engaging enough to keep even otherwise disenchanted Catholics connected to their Church. But more than ritual is at stake. Questions of rational understanding, power, the meaning of revelation, sacred texts, the mystery of how words can be used to speak of what is literally unspeakable—all of this is embedded in the issue of language, and the Council fathers boldly took it on.

Change is human, and so is the Catholic Church—however its transcendent nature is to be understood. Against reactionaries who still insist that nothing of substance changed at Vatican II (and for whom the restoration of the Latin Mass is an iconic symbol), change was the Council's overriding motif. True, the at times contentious deliberations laid bare profound ambivalence about change, as members of the Church magisterium sought balance between perennial tensions of continuity and transformation. That ambivalence showed itself in the characteristic style of the Council documents—which is to make innovative, even revolutionary pronouncements as if they are nothing new, a tendency that has itself led Catholics and others to underappreciate just how innovative they are.

So what did change at Vatican II? At the most obvious level, the Church again and again affirmed what it had once condemned, from the all-trumping dignity of conscience, to separation of Church and State, to the idea that salvation is available outside the Catholic Church—and even to a definition of "Church" that allows it to apply to non-Catholic Christians. But Catholicism can be understood to have been transformed at even deeper levels, too.

The Church's worldview changed. When an overly abstract and leaden caricature of the thinking of Thomas Aquinas was removed from the center of Catholic theology, the insights of modernity were allowed. A static scholasticism opened to a dynamic philosophy that itself stood at the threshold of contemporary science, obliterating the old idea that religion and science are enemies. That a formerly censured Catholic theologian like the German Jesuit Karl Rahner depended on the existentialist Martin Heidegger was no longer a problem but a solution. This shift had implications for everything from evolution to the idea of "natural law," to the so-called development of doctrine, which now moved from the periphery of Catholic thought to its center.

The Church's politics changed. From the personal example of John XXIII to the definition of the Church as the "People of God" in *Lumen Gentium*, "Dogmatic Constitution on the Church," not only medieval monarchy was rejected as the model; so was Constantine's empire-church. In 1899 the Vatican had condemned the heresy of "Americanism," but now basic notions of the liberal democracy that had flourished in America were affirmed, especially in *Dignitatis Humanae*, "Declaration on Religious Freedom." The main author of that document was another formerly censured Jesuit, John Courtney Murray, whose own 1960 masterwork celebrating the relevance of American democracy for the Catholic Church was pointedly entitled *We Hold These Truths*. That the Catholic people took to heart the elevation of conscience in *Dignitatis Humanae* is reflected in their resounding rejection—even while remaining Catholics in good standing—of *Humanae Vitae*, the birth-control-condemning encyclical issued by Pope Paul VI in 1968.

The Church's exclusivity changed. Roman Catholicism no longer understands itself as the only way to God. That is the core meaning of *Nostra Aetate*'s affirmation of the Jewish covenant as permanent and unbreakable. That the Council included as "observers" dozens of leaders from Protestant and Orthodox religious bodies emphasized its hope for Christian Unity not by a "return" to the One True Church but by means of "dialogue" among partners. Indeed, the Council ushered in the era when Catholics made intimate alliances with other believers, in the streets, demanding peace and social justice, and in sanctuaries, praying for God's blessing on the living and the dead. The precondition of this holy mutuality was the theological humility embodied in the Council's new definition of the Church as a Pilgrim People—a decided move away, for example, from Pope Leo XIII's "Perfect Society" (the definition of the Church given in his 1885 encyclical *Immortale Dei*). The Church, that is, is a people on the way to the Truth, not yet in full possession of it.

Indeed, the Church's idea of Truth changed. In its affirmations of both contemporary philosophy and contemporary Biblical scholarship, the Council accepted that all truth involves interpretation (hermeneutics), and that all truth is perceived from a point of view. This is not relativism, of which reactionaries warn, but perspectivism. In fact, this understanding that each person is a perceiving center who perceives uniquely opens to a deeper regard for Tradition itself—a return to the idea that all religious language is necessarily elusive, and the best religious language is *allusive*. This is so because God can be grasped only indirectly. All that can be known of God with absolute certainty is that God is unknowable—and that is knowledge. What the tradition calls *via negativa* ("the negative way"). Thomas Aquinas affirmed this idea when he explained that, while the Truth is always absolute, the perceiver of truths never is. A due Catholic modesty was recovered.

The Church's relation to Scripture changed. Where before, Catholics were warned away from the Bible, now they were invited to live by it, to study it, to become Biblically literate. The Roman Missal was revised to center the sacraments in Scripture. Preachers returned to the Word of God, leaving behind the accumulated pieties of novenas, cults, and a plethora of saints. Revelation went from being mainly a matter of God's Law, to being an invitation into a relationship with the Holy One. As he hadn't been in centuries, Jesus was once more lifted up as the norm of Christian life, reclaiming a place of precedence over the Saints in Heaven, including even his Blessed Mother. And this Jesus, a man of peace, love, and forgiveness, replaced in the Catholic imagination the stern, condemning Judge who had so traumatized Catholics for generations. Standing with the renewed liturgy as the most powerful demonstration of the achievement of Vatican II is the astonishing rapidity with which the ruthless God of omnidirectional damnation disappeared from Catholic life, and with Him the acutely felt dread of Hell—"infinite pain, infinitely felt, forever." Evil and sin remain facts of the human condition, of course, and so does moral consequence, but the sadistic religious construct of Hell went the way of Latin.

As Pope John XXIII had so poignantly invited them to do, the Council fathers said the word "yes" again and again. Yes to the "world," with that aptly titled "Pastoral Constitution on the Church *in* the Modern World" (not "and," as if the Church is apart, much less "against," as if the world is the enemy). Yes to history, God's own workshop, with the affirmation that cultural context always matters, whether of Scripture, Tradition, or Doctrine. Yes to the impoverished, whose cause the Church has taken up freshly since the Council, and yes to the Earth, which, in its jeopardy, is more sacred than ever.

And the fathers of the Council said a resounding yes to people of other faiths, and to people of no faith, addressing, in the words that gave *Gaudium et Spes* its title, "the joys and the hopes, the griefs and the anxieties of the people of this age." Yes to conscience, to democracy, to the end of war, and to the urgent project of human survival.

All of that is why what began at Vatican II must continue, why its momentous changes must be acknowledged as such, and why attempts to roll them back must not be allowed to prevail. The documents presented in this volume are, therefore, a resource for nothing less than the human future. Essential texts, indeed.

The Catholic Church is a worldwide community of well over a billion people: North and South, rich and poor, intellectually sophisticated and illiterate. The Church of these legions is not going away. The only question is whether it will continue on the path toward positive, fully ecumenical renewal onto which Pope John XXIII, Pope Paul VI, and the Council fathers set it. As the human species flirts with its own extinction, whether through weapons of mass destruction or through environmental degradation, the world urgently needs this global institution to be rational, historically minded, pluralistically respectful, committed to peace, a tribune of justice, a source of hope, not fear. That Vatican II occurred at all is enough to validate belief in the Holy Spirit, who is sent forth, in the words of the old Catholic prayer, to fill the hearts of the faithful, to kindle in them the fire of love, and to renew the face of the Earth.

DOCUMENTS

PREFATORY MATERIAL
BY EDWARD P. HAHNENBERG

Constitution on Sacred Liturgy
(Sacrosanctum Concilium)

When the Second Vatican Council began, in October 1962, the very first text discussed was the document on the liturgy. This turned out to be a fortunate choice. Of the nearly seventy different documents drafted in preparation for the council, the document on the liturgy was the simplest and the strongest. More than any of the others, it reflected the theological and pastoral renewal that prepared the way for Vatican II.

Before the council, most Catholics experienced the Mass as a ritual that was both mysterious and mechanical. Prayers were in Latin. And for much of the service, the priest had his back to the congregation. Separated from the sanctuary by a communion rail and removed from the sacred action taking place at the altar, the laity "attended" Mass but did not actively participate in it. Pre-conciliar Catholicism was marked by a rich devotional life—Rosary groups and First Fridays, benedictions and novenas, a host of prayers and practices that fed the spiritual life of ordinary Catholics. But at Mass the laity were largely passive, watching a ritual done for them but not by them.

And yet, at the same time, a liturgical renewal was under way. It began in the monasteries of Europe and slowly spread to parishes. In 1833, the Benedictine monk Prosper Guéranger refounded the monastery of Solesmes in France. His goal was to offer an alternative to the encroaching evils of the "modern world" by modeling a true Christian community centered on the liturgy. The movement was at first fueled by a romanticism for all things medieval (thus the recovery of Gothic architecture and Gregorian chant). Historical research soon pushed back further to the patristic era of the fourth and fifth centuries, which became for scholars the Golden Age of liturgical life. Thus from the start, the liturgical renewal was cast in terms of return—a "return to the sources" (ressourcement) whose purpose was to bring into the present the richer traditions of the past.

At the start of the 20th century, the Belgian Dom Lambert Beauduin led the way in translating this renewal for the people in the pews. He and others lamented the passivity of Catholics at Mass, calling instead for the full and active participation of everyone in the Eucharistic liturgy. Popes joined in. Pius X (1903–1914) launched an extensive and astonishingly successful campaign to promote more frequent reception of communion. Some thirty years later, Pope Pius XII dedicated an entire encyclical to the liturgy. In Mediator Dei (1947) he confirmed the basic direction of the liturgical movement, particularly its call for the active participation of all the faithful in the liturgy. Later he reformed the rites for the Easter Vigil and Holy Week.

When the draft document on the liturgy was introduced to the full assembly of bishops at Vatican II, the newly appointed secretary of the Liturgical Commission, Ferdinando Antonelli, placed the text in continuity with this recent history of papal teaching. He identified five principles that had guided its preparation: The document intended to (1) protect the rich liturgical patrimony of the church, (2) offer general guidelines for reform, (3) base itself on church doctrine, (4) inspire the clergy with a deeper "liturgical spirit," and (5) promote a more active participation of the faithful in the liturgy.

As the bishops began to debate the draft, they found broad agreement on the document's call for greater participation, its emphasis on the paschal mystery of Christ, its attention to ritual simplicity and intelligibility, and its stress on spiritual nourishment and Christian holiness. Disagreements surfaced concerning two issues in particular: the use of vernacular languages and the role of national bishops' conferences in regulating the liturgy. Both issues revolved around the tension between unity and diversity. How much should the liturgy remain a uniform and universal reality? How much should it be allowed to adapt to the particularities of different social and cultural contexts? Influential members of the Vatican curia tended to favor greater unity—wanting to maintain Latin and limit the authority of episcopal conferences. Bishops from outside Rome tended to favor more room for local adaptation.

Debate dragged on for three weeks, from October 22 to November 13. Those bishops who expected the Second Vatican Council to wrap up its entire agenda before Christmas were dismayed as nearly half of the scheduled working sessions—fifteen days—were eaten up by discussion of the very first text! Although individual speeches were limited to ten minutes, the council rules had failed to provide a mechanism for closing debate on a topic. The proceedings seemed stuck. And so on November 6, Pope John XXIII intervened. He changed the rules to allow for a simplified vote to end debate on each chapter. This freed the council to move on more efficiently.

Still, it was unclear how deep the divisions were between those favorable to liturgical reform and those opposed to it. On October 30, Cardinal Alfredo Ottaviani gave a speech strongly criticizing the draft document. Ottaviani was the powerful head of the Holy Office (now called the Congregation for the Doctrine of the Faith), who would come to symbolize the opposition to the reforming impulses at the council. He attacked the document for proposing changes that would confuse and scandalize the faithful. "What, now, are we dealing here with a revolution regarding the whole

Mass?" he asked. Ottaviani had so many complaints that his speech ran over the allotted time. When he was cut off, the assembly broke out in applause. Here was a clear sign that most of the bishops did not agree with the tenor of his remarks. Perhaps resistance to the document was not as widespread as some of the speeches indicated. Two weeks later, on November 14, when the first vote was taken to determine if the document was an acceptable basis for further revision, the results shocked everyone. Out of 2,215 votes cast, only 46 opposed the text. This show of support was seen as an affirmation of the movement toward reform that was taking shape at the council. The following fall, on December 4, 1963, the council overwhelmingly approved (2,147 in favor, 4 against) Sacrosanctum Concilium, *Vatican II's Constitution on the Sacred Liturgy.*

The final text of Sacrosanctum Concilium was broad, and relatively brief. An opening chapter laid out general principles for reform—emphasizing lay participation, ritual diversity, and noble simplicity in liturgy. The six chapters that followed applied these principles to the Mass, the other sacraments, the liturgy of the hours, the liturgical calendar, sacred music, and art.

But the promulgation of Sacrosanctum Concilium was just the beginning. Even before the Second Vatican Council closed, a commission was established to implement the recommendations of the constitution. The respected liturgist Annibale Bugnini, who had served as adviser to Pius XII and as the first secretary of the council's preparatory commission on the liturgy, was named secretary of this new commission, called the Consilium. Through their work, and under the attentive eye of Pope Paul VI, the church set out on a systematic restructuring of its entire liturgical life—on a scale and to a degree unprecedented in its two-thousand-year history. Nowhere was the impact of Vatican II so immediately and deeply felt by the world's Catholics, who received these changes with a mixture of resistance, bewilderment, and genuine enthusiasm. Guiding it all were a few basic principles articulated in

Sacrosanctum Concilium, *principles that spilled out beyond the debate on the liturgy to influence the council as a whole: renewal rooted in ressourcement, the value of local churches and episcopal authority as a balance to papal centralization, and the active role demanded of all the faithful in the life and mission of the church.*

Sacrosanctum Concilium
Constitution on Sacred Liturgy

TRANSLATED BY PHILIP ENDEAN, S.J.

Constitution on the sacred liturgy

1. It is the intention of this holy council to improve the standard of daily christian living among Catholics; to adapt those structures which are subject to change so as better to meet the needs of our time; to encourage whatever can contribute to the union of all who believe in Christ; and to strengthen whatever serves to call all people into the embrace of the church. It therefore, and with quite special reason, sees the taking of steps towards the renewal and growth of the liturgy as something it can and should do.

2. This is because the liturgy, through which, especially in the divine sacrifice of the eucharist, "the act of our redemption is being carried out,"[1] becomes thereby the chief means through which believers are expressing in their lives and demonstrating to others the mystery which is Christ, and

the sort of entity the true church really is. For what marks
out the church is that it is at once human and divine, visible
and endowed with invisible realities, vigorously active and
yet making space in its life for contemplation, present in the
world and yet in pilgrimage beyond—all this, moreover, in
such a way that the human within it is ordered and subordinated to the divine, and likewise the visible to the invisible,
activity to contemplation, and the present to the city of the
future which we seek.[2] Thus, since the liturgy is each day
building up those who are within into a holy temple in the
Lord, into a dwelling place for God in the Spirit,[3] until they
reach the stature of the age of Christ's fullness,[4] it is, by the
same token, also strengthening remarkably their capacity to
preach Christ. Thus it is displaying the church to those who
are outside as an ensign raised for the nations,[5] under which
the scattered children of God can be brought together into
one[6] until there is one fold and one shepherd.[7]

3. It is in this context that this holy council has judged that
the following principles, dealing with the renewal and progress of the liturgy, should be recalled to mind, and practical
norms laid down.

   Among these principles and norms there are some which
can and should be applied both to the Roman rite and to all
the other rites; however, the practical norms which follow
are to be understood as referring only to the Roman rite,
unless it is a matter which, by the very nature of the topic,
affects also the other rites.

4. Finally, faithfully in accordance with the tradition, this
holy council declares that the church regards all duly recognised rites as having equal legal force and as to be held in
equal honour; it wishes to preserve them for the future and
encourage them in every way. Moreover, where necessary,

it wants them to be revised in the light of sound tradition, and to be given new vigour in order to meet today's circumstances and needs.

Chapter 1. General principles regarding the renewal and encouragement of the liturgy

I. The nature of the liturgy and its significance in the life of the church

5. God's desire is that "all human beings should be saved and come to the recognition of the truth" (1 Tm 2, 4), and he "spoke in many and various ways in the past to our ancestors through the prophets" (Heb 1, 1). When the fullness of time came, he sent his Son, the Word made flesh, anointed with the holy Spirit. He was to preach the good news to the poor, and bind up hearts that were broken[8]—a healer who was both flesh and spirit,[9] a mediator between God and human beings.[10] For the humanity of this very Son, in the unity of the person of the Word, was the means of our salvation. Thus, in Christ, "the perfect peace which is our reconciliation came into being, and it became possible for us fully to express our worshipful relationship with God."[11]

The great divine acts among the people of the old covenant foreshadowed this deed of human redemption and perfect glorification of God; Christ the lord brought it to its completion, above all through the paschal mystery, that is, his passion, his resurrection from the dead and his glorious ascension. Through this, "in dying he destroyed our death; in rising he restored our life."[12] For the tremendous sacrament which is the whole church arose from the side of Christ as he slept on the cross.[13]

6. Just as Christ was sent by the Father, he himself sent apostles, filled with the holy Spirit, and for the same purpose: that

they should preach the good news to every creature,[14] and thus announce that the Son of God, by his death and resurrection, had freed us from the power of Satan[15] and death, and carried us over into the Father's kingdom. Not only this, however: they were also to enact what they were announcing through sacrifice and sacraments, the things around which the whole of liturgical life revolves. This is how it is that people are implanted into the paschal mystery of Christ through baptism: how they die with him, are buried with him and rise with him;[16] how they receive the spirit of adoption as daughters and sons, the spirit "in whom we cry, Abba, Father" (Rm 8, 15), and thus become the true worshippers whom the Father seeks.[17] In a similar way, each time people eat the Lord's supper, they are proclaiming the death of the Lord until he comes.[18] This is the principle operative as, on the very day of Pentecost, when the church appeared in the world, those who received Peter's word "were baptized." And they were "steadfast in the apostles' teaching and the fellowship of breaking bread and the prayers . . . praising God together and winning the good opinions of all the people" (Ac 2, 41–42, 47). Since then, therefore, the church has never failed to meet together to celebrate the easter mystery, reading "in all the scriptures the things concerning himself" (Lk 24, 27), and celebrating the eucharist, in which "the victory and triumph of his death are represented."[19] At the same time it gives thanks to God in Christ Jesus "for his inexpressible gift" (2 Cor 9, 15) "in praise of his glory" (Eph 1, 12), through the power of the holy Spirit.

7. Christ is always present to his church, especially during the liturgy, so that this great task can be fully accomplished. He is present through the sacrifice which is the mass, at once in the person of the minister—"the same one who then offered himself on a cross is now making his offering through

the agency of priests"[20]—and also, most fully, under the eucharistic elements. He is present through his power in the sacraments; thus, when anyone baptises, Christ himself is baptising.[21] He is present through his word, in that he himself is speaking when scripture is read in church. Finally, he is present when the church is praying or singing hymns, he himself who promised, "where two or three are gathered in my name, there I am in the midst of them" (Mt 18, 20).

In fact, throughout this great process by which God is being perfectly glorified and human beings becoming holy, Christ is uniting the church, his dearly cherished wife, to himself, the church who calls upon her Lord, and worships the eternal Father through him.

It is therefore quite right to think of the liturgy as the enacting of the priestly role of Jesus Christ. In the liturgy, the sanctification of human beings is being expressed through signs accessible to the senses, and carried out in a way appropriate to each of them. Furthermore, the mystical body of Jesus Christ, that is the head and the members, is together giving complete and definitive public expression to its worship.

This is why every liturgical celebration, inasmuch as it is the act of Christ the priest and his body which is the church, is above all an activity of worship. No other activity of the church equals it in terms of its official recognition or its degree of effectiveness.

8. In the liturgy on earth, we are sharing by anticipation in the heavenly one, celebrated in the holy city, Jerusalem, the goal towards which we strive as pilgrims, where Christ is, seated at God's right hand, he who is the minister of the saints and of the true tabernacle.[22] We are singing the hymn of God's glory with all the troops of the heavenly army. In lovingly remembering the saints in our liturgy, we are hop-

ing in some way to share in what they now enjoy, and to become their companions. We are waiting for our Saviour, our lord Jesus Christ, until he, our life, appears, and until we appear with him in glory.[23]

9. Liturgy is not the only activity of the church. Before people can come to the liturgy, they must be called to faith and conversion. "How shall people call on him in whom they have not believed? Or how are they to believe in him of whom they have not heard? And how are they to hear without a preacher? How, indeed, will people preach unless they are sent?" (Rm 10, 14–15).

Thus the church is publicly proclaiming the message of salvation to those who do not believe, so that all people may know the only true God and Jesus Christ whom he has sent, and turn away from their self-centred ways, doing penance.[24] As for believers, of course the church must always preach faith and repentance; but, in addition, it must also prepare them for the sacraments, it must teach them to observe all that Christ has commanded,[25] and it must attract them to the whole range of activities involved in love, holiness and the apostolate. These activities will make it plain that those who believe in Christ, though indeed they are not of this world, are nevertheless the light of the world, and glorifying the Father among human beings.

10. The liturgy is, all the same, the high point towards which the activity of the church is directed, and, simultaneously, the source from which all its power flows out. For the point of apostolic work is that all those who have become children of God through faith and baptism can assemble together in order to praise God in the midst of the church, to share in sacrifice, and to eat the Lord's supper.

In turn, the liturgy itself inspires those who have eaten their fill of the "easter sacraments" to become "united in holiness and mutual love."[26] It prays that, "as they live their lives they may hold fast to what they have perceived through faith."[27] The renewal of the Lord's covenant with human beings in the eucharist really does have the effect of drawing believers into the overwhelming love of Christ, and fires them with it. From the liturgy, then, especially from the eucharist, grace comes flowing to us as if from a fountain; and in it the holiness of human beings and the glory of God in Christ, the purpose towards which everything else going on in the church is directed, is realised in a fully effective way.

11. If, however, this fully effective presence is to be appropriated, believers must approach the liturgy with the dispositions of a suitable heart and mind. What they think and feel must be at one with what they say; they must do their part in the working of the grace that comes from above if they are not to have received it in vain.[28] And so, those with responsibility for leadership in worship must take care, not only to see that the laws regarding valid and licit celebration are kept while the liturgy is being done; but also that the people are able to take part in it in such a way that they are active, that they know what is going on, and that they will receive benefit.

12. However, the spiritual life has more to it than sharing the liturgy. Christians, though called to prayer together, must nevertheless also go to their own room and pray to their Father in secret.[29] Indeed, according to Paul's teaching, they must pray without ceasing.[30] Again we are taught, also by Paul, always to carry round the dying of Jesus in our bodies, so that the life of Jesus also can be manifested in our mortal flesh.[31] It is on this account that, during the sacrifice of the mass, we pray the Lord, "to receive the offering of the spiritual victim," and then raise "our very selves" to their perfection in becoming "an eternal gift" for himself.[32]

13. Provided they conform to the laws and norms of the church, the devotions found among the christian people are strongly affirmed, especially when they have the authorisation of the apostolic see.

The devotions found in individual churches, celebrated with episcopal authorisation and following legitimately approved customs or books, are also especially valued.

However, these devotions need to be kept under control, in keeping with the liturgical seasons, so that they cohere with the liturgy, in some way derive from it, and lead the people to it, inasmuch as the liturgy, by its nature, is far more important than they are.

II. Fostering liturgical formation and active participation

14. The church very much wants all believers to be led to take a full, conscious and active part in liturgical celebration. This is demanded by the nature of the liturgy itself; and, by virtue of their baptism, it is the right and the duty of the christian people, "the chosen race, the royal priesthood, the holy nation, the people of whom God has taken possession" (1 Pt 2, 9; see 2, 4–5). This full and active sharing on the part of the whole people is of paramount concern in the process of renewing the liturgy and helping it to grow, because such sharing is the first, and necessary, source from which believers can imbibe the true christian spirit. Therefore, in all pastoral activity, those charged with responsibility must work strenuously towards this sharing by means of appropriate formation.

However, there is no clear prospect of this coming about unless those who are responsible for pastoral care first get thoroughly immersed in the spirit and power of the liturgy themselves, and become competent in it. Therefore it is especially necessary that priority be given to decisions on the liturgical formation of the clergy. All this leads this holy council to make the following stipulations.

15. Professors put in charge of teaching the subject of liturgy in seminaries, religious houses of study and faculties of theology, must be thoroughly trained for their posts in institutions specially designed for the purpose.

16. The subject of liturgy must be regarded in seminaries and in religious houses of study as a compulsory "core" subject; in theology faculties, it is to be regarded as one of the principal areas of enquiry. It must be taught both theologically and historically, and also with regard to its spiritual, pastoral and juridical aspects. Moreover, teachers of other branches of study, especially dogma, scripture, spirituality and pastoral theology, should see that they give due respect to the mystery which is Christ and the history of salvation, against the background of the intrinsic demands of the subject-matter dealt with specifically by each of them. In this way, the connection between these subjects and the liturgy, and the underlying unity of priestly formation, will become self-evidently clear.

17. Clerical students should get a spiritual formation in their seminaries and religious houses that is oriented towards the liturgy. This should come both through suitable guidance, enabling the students to understand the rites of worship and share them wholeheartedly, and also through the actual celebration of the mysteries of worship, together with other religious activities imbued by the spirit of the liturgy. Equally, they are also to learn the observance of liturgical laws, so that life in seminaries and in religious houses can be decisively shaped by the spirit of the liturgy.

18. Priests, whether secular or religious, who are already engaged in apostolic work, should be helped by every appropriate means to grow continually in their understanding of

what they are doing in their liturgical roles, to live the life of the liturgy, and to communicate this to the people in their care.

19. Those responsible for pastoral care should conscientiously and patiently work to impart a liturgical formation to the people and to foster their taking an active part in the liturgy, both inwardly and outwardly, in ways suited to their age, the circumstances they are in, the kind of life they lead, and their level of religious culture. In this they will be fulfilling one of the most important tasks of a faithful steward of God's mysteries. Their leadership of their people in this matter should be a matter not just of words, but also of example.

20. Broadcasts of liturgical events on radio or television— especially if it is a question of a mass—should be done tastefully and fittingly. They should be supervised and guaranteed by a suitable person designated for the purpose by the bishops.

III. The renewal of the liturgy

21. In order that the christian people can more surely obtain the abundance of graces in the liturgy, the church wishes to make strenuous efforts at a general reform of the liturgy itself. For the liturgy consists both of a part that cannot be changed, insofar as it has been divinely laid down, and also of parts that are subject to modification, parts which in the course of time can vary—indeed, which must do so if, by any chance, things have crept in which might be less appropriate to the innermost character of the liturgy as such, or which might have become less suitable than they once were.

Moreover, in the course of this renewal, the texts and rites must be organised so as to express more clearly the holy things which they represent, and so that thus the christian people, insofar as this is possible, will be able to understand these things easily, and to enter into them through a celebration that is expressive of their full meaning, is effective, involving, and the community's own.

Thus, this holy council has decided on these generalised norms.

A) General norms

22. §1. The regulation of the liturgy depends solely on the authority of the church, which resides with the apostolic see and, within the normal functioning of the law, with the bishop.

§2. As a result of the power that the law has devolved on them, the regulation of the sphere of liturgy within fixed boundaries belongs also to the competent local episcopal groupings of various kinds that have been legally set up.

§3. Thus, absolutely no one other than these, even a priest, should disruptively add, remove or change anything in the liturgy on his or her own.

23. In order that healthy tradition can be preserved while yet allowing room for legitimate development, thorough investigation—theological, historical and pastoral—of the individual parts of the liturgy up for revision is always to be the first step. The general laws regarding the structure and intention of the liturgy should also be taken into account, as well as the experience stemming from more recent liturgical renewal and from the special concessions that have, from time to time, been granted. Finally, changes should not be made unless a real and proven need of the church requires them, and care should be taken to see that new forms grow in some way organically out of the forms already existing.

As far as possible, moreover, marked differences between the rites found in neighbouring places should be avoided.

24. The importance of scripture in the celebration of the lit-

urgy is paramount. For it is texts from scripture that form the readings and are explained in the homily; it is scripture's psalms that are sung; from scripture's inspiration and influence flow the various kinds of prayers as well as the singing in the liturgy; from scripture the actions and signs derive their meaning. The ancient tradition of both the eastern and the western rites tells of a heartfelt and living love for scripture. This love must be allowed to grow if there is to be a renewal, development and adaptation of the liturgy.

25. As soon as possible, the books used in the liturgy are to be revised, with experts brought in, and bishops from various parts of the world consulted.

B) Norms which derive from the nature of the liturgy as an activity which is hierarchical and belonging to the community

26. Liturgical events are not private actions but celebrations of the church, which is "the sacrament of unity," the holy people drawn into an ordered whole under the bishops.[33]

Therefore these celebrations are for the whole body which is the church, making this whole body visible and having effects on it; in a different kind of way they touch the individual members of the church, a way related to the differences of ranks, of roles and of levels of participation.

27. Whenever the particular character of the rites suggests a community celebration, with a congregation present and actively taking part, it should be stressed that this sort of celebration is to be preferred, as far as possible, to a celebration of them by one person alone, as it were in private.

This applies especially to the celebration of mass and to the administration of the sacraments, although it remains true that any mass whatsoever is, by nature, public and communal.

28. During liturgical celebration, everyone, whether minister

or in the congregation, should, while carrying out their own role, do all that and only that which is their due—this being determined by the nature of the celebration and by liturgical norms.

29. Servers, readers, commentators and those who belong to the choir are also performing a genuine liturgical ministry. They should therefore play their part with the kind of real devotion and decorum that is appropriate in a ministry of such importance and that the people of God rightfully demand of them.

They must thus be thoroughly steeped in the spirit of the liturgy, each in their own way, and trained to play their parts properly and with decorum.

30. In order to encourage their taking an active share, acclamations for the people, together with responses, psalmody, antiphons and hymns, should be developed, as well as actions, movements and bodily self-expression. When it is appropriate, a worshipping silence should also be kept.

31. When the books used in the liturgy are being revised, great care is to be taken that the official instructions envisage parts for the people.

32. In the liturgy, no special preference should be given either to private individuals or to social classes, whether in ceremonies or exterior display—this apart from the distinctions grounded on liturgical functions or the sacrament of order, and the honour due to civil authority as set out in liturgical law.

C) Norms deriving from the educational and pastoral nature of the liturgy

33. Although the liturgy is primarily the worship of the divine majesty, it contains also a large element of instruction for the believers who form the congregation.[34] For, in the lit-

urgy, God is speaking to his people; Christ is still proclaiming his good news. The people are responding to God himself, both in their singing and in their prayers.

Moreover, the prayers addressed to God by the priest, who presides over the gathering in the role of Christ, are said in the name of the entire holy people, and of all who are present. Finally, the visible signs which the liturgy uses to symbolise invisible divine things have been chosen for this purpose either by Christ or by the church. And so, it is not just when the things which "are written for our instruction" (Rm 15, 4) are read out, but also while the church is singing, praying or performing, that the faith of those taking part is nourished and their minds raised to God, enabling them to give him free and conscious service and to receive his grace more abundantly.

In the light of this, the following generalised guidelines are to be observed in the process of renewal.

34. The rites should radiate a rich simplicity; they should be brief and lucid, avoiding pointless repetitions; they should be intelligible to the people, and should not in general require much explanation.

35. In order that the intimate connection between word and ritual in the liturgy can become clearly apparent:

1) In liturgical celebrations, a fuller, more varied and more appropriate approach to the reading of scripture is to be restored.

2) Because the sermon is part of the liturgical event, it also, to the extent that the rite allows, should be given a more suitable place in the official instructions; and the ministry of preaching should be carried out properly and very conscientiously. The first sources of this ministry should in fact be none other than scripture and the liturgy, in that these are the proclamation of the wonderful deeds of God in the

history of salvation, the mystery that is Christ, always present and at work in and among us, especially in liturgical celebrations.

3) In addition, every step should be taken to get across the meaning of the liturgy more explicitly. In the rites themselves, room should be made, if necessary, for short pieces of commentary. These should be done by the priest or by a competent minister, following more or less closely a formula laid down. They should happen only at more appropriate points.

4) The worshipping celebration of the Word of God is to be encouraged. This may take place through all-night vigils on the night before more special feasts, on some days of Advent or Lent, or on Sundays and feast days, especially in places where there is no priest. In this case, a deacon or some other person chosen by the bishop should lead the celebration.

36. §1. The use of the Latin language is to be maintained in the Latin rites, except where a particular law might indicate otherwise.

§2. However, in the mass, the administration of the sacraments, and in other parts of the liturgy, there cannot at all infrequently exist a practice of using the local language, a practice which is really helpful among the people. It should therefore become possible for more scope to be given for such practices, firstly in the readings and in instructions given to the people, in some prayers and in some of the singing, following the norms laid down on this point in the individual subsequent chapters.

§3. Beyond the observance of these norms, it is a matter for the competent local church authority (see article 22 §2), if necessary also in consultation with bishops from neighbouring areas which have the same language, to lay down regulations as to whether and how the local language should be used. These decisions should be examined or confirmed by the apostolic see.

§4. The translation of the Latin text into the local language, for use in the liturgy, must be approved by the competent local church authority mentioned above.

D) Norms aimed at bringing about adaption to the temperament and traditions of peoples

37. In matters that do not affect the faith or the well-being of the whole community, the church has no desire, not even in the liturgy, to impose a rigid monolithic structure. Rather, on the contrary, it cultivates and encourages the gifts and endowments of mind and heart possessed by various races and peoples. It examines sympathetically whatever elements among peoples' customs do not constitute an irretrievable connivance with superstitions or false beliefs, and, if it can, it preserves them safe and sound. Indeed, it sometimes allows them into the liturgy itself, provided they are consistent with the thinking behind the true and authentic spirit of the liturgy.

38. Provided that the fundamental unity of the Roman rite is preserved, room is to be left, even when the books used in the liturgy are revised, for legitimate variations and adaptations to meet the needs of different gatherings, areas and peoples, especially in mission territories. Due weight should be given to this consideration in drawing up ritual forms or official instructions.

39. Within limits to be laid down in the standard editions of the books used in the liturgy, it will be the job of the competent local church authority (see article 22 §2) to specify adaptations—especially regarding the administration of the sacraments, regarding sacramentals, processions, liturgical

language, and the art and music of worship. But they should follow the basic norms to be found in this constitution.

40. However, in some places or in some situations, there may arise a pressing need for a more radical adaption of the liturgy. This will turn out to be more difficult. In this case:

1) The competent local church authority (see article 22 §2) should carefully and conscientiously consider, in this regard, which elements from the traditions and particular talents of individual peoples can be brought into divine worship. Adaptations which are adjudged useful or necessary should be proposed to the apostolic see, and introduced with its consent.

2) That said, in order that the necessary careful consideration can go into the process of adaptation, the apostolic see will, if necessary, give to the above-mentioned church authority general permission to allow and direct the necessary prior experimentation for a limited period of time—this among certain gatherings suitable for this purpose.

3) Because liturgical laws tend to involve particular difficulties when it comes to adaptation, especially in the missions, there should be experts on this particular matter available while things are in their early stages.

IV. The encouragement of liturgical life in the diocese and the parish

41. The bishop should be thought of as the high priest of his flock; the life of his people in Christ in some way derives from him and depends on him.

Therefore, everyone should regard the liturgical life of the diocese centring on the bishop, above all in the cathedral church, as of the highest importance. They should be convinced that the church is displayed with special clarity when the holy people of God, all of them, are actively and fully sharing in the same liturgical celebrations—especially when it is the same eucharist—sharing one prayer at one altar, at which the bishop is presiding, surrounded by his presbyterate and his ministers.[35]

42. Since the bishop himself in his church cannot always or everywhere preside over the whole flock, he must of necessity set up assemblies of believers. Parishes, organised locally under a parish priest who acts in the bishop's place, are the most important of these, because in some way they exhibit the visible church set up throughout the nations of the world.

Therefore, the way in which clergy and people think and act must be more deeply marked by the liturgical life of the parish, and by the relationship which that has to the bishop. Special effort is to be made in order that there can be, within the parish, a flourishing sense of community, in the first place through what really is a communal celebration of Sunday mass.

V. The development of liturgically oriented pastoral activity

43. The current enthusiasm for the encouragement and renewal of the liturgy is rightly seen as a sign of God's providential designs with regard to our time, and as a movement of the holy Spirit within his church. This enthusiasm has left its own mark on the church's life, and indeed on the whole concept of religious awareness and action as it is found in our time.

Therefore, this holy council, in order further to facilitate the growth of this liturgically oriented pastoral activity, stipulates:

44. It would be desirable for the competent local church authority (see article 22 §2) to set up a liturgical commission,

helped by experts in liturgical theory, music, sacral art, and pastoral practice. This commission should, as far as possible, be helped by some kind of institute of pastoral liturgy, whose members should consist of people who are outstanding in this field—not excluding lay people if they are the ones who are the experts. Under the leadership of the competent local church authority mentioned above, the role of this commission will be to direct liturgically oriented pastoral activity within the area under its care, and, whenever there is a question of suggesting adaptations to the apostolic see, to set in motion studies and the necessary experimentation.

45. In the same way, there should be a commission to deal with the liturgy in each individual diocese in order to develop liturgical activity under the guidance of the bishop.

It may sometimes turn out to be convenient for a number of dioceses to set up one commission which can develop the area of liturgy by pooling ideas.

46. As well as a commission for the liturgy, there should also be in every diocese, as far as possible, commissions for the music and art of worship.

It is necessary that these commissions enhance their work by co-ordinating their efforts. Indeed, often it will be appropriate for them to come together into one commission.

Chapter 2. The holy mystery which is the eucharist

47. Our Saviour inaugurated the eucharist sacrifice of his body and blood at the last supper on the night he was betrayed, in order to make his sacrifice of the cross last throughout time until he should return; and indeed to entrust a token to the church, his beloved wife, by which to remember his death and resurrection. It is a sacrament of faithful relationships, a

sign of unity, a bond of divine love,[1] a special easter meal. In it, "Christ is received, the inner self is filled with grace, and a pledge of future glory is given to us."[2]

48. And so the church devotes careful efforts to prevent christian believers from attending this mystery of faith as though they were outsiders or silent onlookers: rather, having a good understanding of this mystery, through the ritual and the prayers, they should share in the worshipping event, aware of what is happening and devoutly involved. They should be formed by God's word, and refreshed at the table of the Lord's body; they should give thanks to God; they should learn to offer themselves as they offer the immaculate victim—not just through the hands of the priest, but also they themselves making the offering together with him; and, as each day goes by, they should be led towards their final goal of unity with God and among themselves through the mediation of Christ,[3] so that finally God may be all in all.

49. With these things in mind, this holy council has made the following stipulations, taking account of masses celebrated with the people present, particularly on Sundays and holy-days of obligation. The reason for this is so that the very design of the rites may make a contribution towards bringing about the full pastoral effect of the sacrifice of the mass.

50. There is to be a revision of the way the mass is structured, so that the specific ideas behind the individual parts and their connection with one another can be more clearly apparent, and so that it becomes easier for the people to take a proper and active part.

Therefore the rites, in a way that carefully preserves what really matters, should become simpler. Duplications which have come in over the course of time should be discontinued, as should the less useful accretions. Some elements which have degenerated or disappeared through the ill effects of the passage of time are to be restored to the ancient pattern of the fathers, insofar as seems appropriate or necessary.

51. In order that believers can be provided with a richer diet of God's word, the rich heritage of the Bible is to be opened more widely, in such a way that a fuller and more nourishing selection of the scriptures gets read to the people within a fixed period of years.

52. Through the homily, the hidden realities of faith and the guiding principles of christian life are explained over the course of the liturgical year from the text of scripture. It is strongly encouraged, as it forms a part of the liturgy itself. Indeed, in masses celebrated on Sundays and holydays of obligation with the people present, it is not to be left out unless there is a cogent reason for doing so.

53. The "common prayer" or "prayer of the faithful," which comes after the gospel and the homily, is to be restored, especially on Sundays and holydays of obligation. Thus there will be prayers, shared by the people, for the church, for those who have secular power over us, for those who are beset by needs of various kinds, and finally for all men and women, and the salvation and well-being of the whole world.[4]

54. There may well be a suitable place for the local language in masses celebrated with a congregation—especially in the readings, the "common prayer," and, if local circumstances warrant, in the parts which call for the people to join in, following article 36 of this constitution. But steps should be taken so that christian believers can at the same time also say or sing in Latin the parts of the mass which are appropriately theirs.

However, if a fuller use of the local language in the mass than this seems appropriate anywhere, the regulation in article 40 of this constitution is to be observed.

55. It is strongly encouraged that the people take part in the mass more fully by receiving the body of the Lord, after the priest's communion, from the same sacrifice as that from which he has received. Without in any way retracting the dogmatic principles laid down by the council of Trent,[5] communion under both kinds may be allowed at the discretion of bishops, both to clergy and religious, and to lay people, in cases to be determined by the apostolic see. Examples might be: people being ordained during the mass of their ordination, people being professed in the mass of their religious profession, and people who have been newly baptised in the mass following on their baptism.

56. The two parts which in some way go to make up the mass, namely the liturgy of the word and the liturgy of the eucharist, are so closely bound up with each other that they amount to one single act of worship. Therefore the synod strongly encourages those with pastoral responsibility to instil in their people, when they pass on instruction, the need to share in the whole mass, especially on Sundays and holy-days of obligation.

57. §1. Concelebration, which is a good way of demonstrating the unity of the priesthood, has remained in use within the church, both east and west, until now. The council has therefore decided to extend permission for concelebration so that it covers the following occasions:

    1. *a*) Holy Thursday, at both the chrism mass and the evening mass;

      b) masses during councils, conferences of bishops and synods;

      c) mass for the blessing of an abbot.

    2. In addition, with the agreement of the ordinary, who has the role of deciding whether or not concelebration is appropriate:

a) conventual mass and the principal mass in a church, when the needs of christian believers do not require each of the priests available to celebrate individually;

b) masses at every kind of meeting of priests, either secular or religious.

§2. 1. However, it is for the bishop to superintend the practice of concelebration within his diocese.

3. Without prejudice to the fact that every priest may always celebrate an individual mass, this should not happen at the same time in the same church, nor on Holy Thursday.

58. A new rite of concelebration is to be composed, and put into the pontifical and the Roman missal.

Chapter 3. The other sacraments, and sacramentals

59. The purpose of the sacraments is to make people holy, to build up the body of Christ, and finally, to express a relationship of worship to God; because they are signs, they certainly also belong under the heading of teaching. They not only presuppose faith; they also nourish it, strengthen it and express it, both through words and through objects. This is why they are called sacraments of faith. It is true that they confer grace; but, while they are being celebrated, they also are very powerful in opening people up to receive this same grace fruitfully, so that they can express properly their relationship to God, and enact divine love.

Thus it is most important that the people can easily understand the symbolism of the sacraments, and attend these sacraments, whose purpose is the nourishment of the christian life, frequently and eagerly.

60. The church has also set up sacramentals. These are sacred signs through which, rather like with the sacraments, effects brought about primarily on the spiritual level are

symbolised, and obtained through the prayer of the church. Through them people are opened up to absorb the action of the sacraments, action of such crucial importance; and various features of life are sanctified.

61. Thus, for believers who are suitably open, the liturgy of sacraments and sacramentals brings it about that practically everything which happens in life is sanctified with the grace that flows from the easter mystery of Christ's passion, death and resurrection: the source from which all sacraments and sacramentals draw their power. And there is hardly any reputable use of material things that cannot be pointed towards the sanctification of humanity and the praise of God.

62. However, in the course of time, certain things have crept into the rites of the sacraments and of the sacramentals which have the effect of making their nature and purpose less clear in our time, so much so that there is great need to adapt certain things in them to the needs of our age. With this in mind, this holy council makes the following stipulations concerning their review.

63. It is not at all uncommon for the use of the local language to be really helpful among the people in the administration of the sacraments and sacramentals. More room is to be made for this, in line with the following norms:

a) In the administration of the sacraments and the sacramentals, the local language may be introduced, following what is laid down in article 36;

b) There is to be a new edition of the Roman book of rites, and, following this as a model, each competent local church authority (see article 22 §2) should prepare its own, adapted to the needs of individual areas, including those to do with language, as soon as possible. Once these have been reviewed by the apostolic see, they should be introduced in the appropriate areas. However, when these books or local collections of rites are being drawn up, the instructions put in the Roman ritual before each individual rite are not to be left out, whether these be instructions of a pastoral and practical kind, or instructions which have some special social concern.

64. The catechumenate for adults is to be renewed and broken up into more stages, a reform to be introduced at the discretion of the local ordinary. In this way, the time of the catechumenate, which is set aside for appropriate initiation, can be sanctified through liturgical rites to be celebrated at a series of points.

65. In mission countries, in addition to what is given in the christian tradition, it should also be permitted to incorporate whatever means of initiation are found to be the custom among each individual people, insofar as these can be sensitively integrated with the christian ritual, following articles 37–40 of this constitution.

66. Both rites of adult baptism are to be revised, the simpler one and the more elaborate one, the latter with reference to the renewed catechumenate. A special mass is to be put into the Roman missal entitled "For the conferring of baptism."

67. The rite of infant baptism is to be revised, and adapted to the reality of the situation with babies. Moreover, the roles of the parents and godparents, together with their duties, should become clearer in the actual rite.

68. Within the rite of baptism, there should be ways of adapting it for the baptism of a large number of candidates, to be introduced at the discretion of the local ordinary. There should be a shorter way of doing it, which catechists, especially in mission lands, can use in the absence of a priest or deacon—as well as believers at large when there is danger of death.

69. In place of the rite called, "How to make up for what

has been left out during the baptism of a baby," a new one should be composed. This is to signify more clearly and more appropriately that the baby who was baptised according to a short rite has now been received into the church. Likewise a new rite should be drawn up for converts to the catholic church who have already been validly baptised; this should signify that they are being admitted to the communion of the church.

70. Apart from during the season of Easter, the water of baptism may be blessed during the actual rite of baptism, using an approved fairly short formula.

71. The rite of confirmation is also to be revised. The point of this revision is that the very close connection of this sacrament with the whole process of christian initiation may become more clearly visible. For this reason, it will be a good idea for people to make a renewal of baptismal promises prior to receiving this sacrament.

If the occasion allows, confirmation can be administered during mass; as for the rite when mass is not celebrated, a formula for use as a kind of introduction should be drawn up.

72. The rites and formulas of penance are to be revised in such a way that they express more clearly what the sacrament is and what it brings about.

73. "Final anointing," which can also and better be called "anointing of the sick," is not a sacrament exclusively for those who are involved in the final crisis of life and death. There can therefore be no doubt that the point when a Christian begins to be in danger of death, either through illness or old age, is already a suitable time to receive it.

74. To supplement the separate rites of the anointing of the sick and communion for the dying, a continuous rite is to be drawn up, in which a sick person will be anointed after making a confession and before receiving communion.

75. The number of anointings should be whatever suits the occasion, and the prayers which belong to the rite of anointing the sick should be revised in such a way as to meet the differing circumstances of the sick people who receive the sacrament.

76. The rites for different kinds of ordination are to be revised—both the ceremonies and the texts. Addresses by the bishop at the beginning of any ordination or consecration can be made in the local language.

During the consecration of a bishop, it is permissible for the laying on of hands to be carried out by all the bishops present.

77. The rite of celebrating marriage in the Roman book of rites is to be revised, and made richer, in such a way that it will express the grace of the sacrament more clearly, and emphasise the duties of wife and husband.

"If any parts of the world . . . use other praiseworthy customs and ceremonies" while celebrating the sacrament of matrimony, "the synod is very concerned that they be preserved in their entirety."[1]

Moreover, in accordance with article 63, the competent local church authority (see article 22 §2 of this constitution) has been delegated the power to compose its own rite, one that is matched to the customs of the places and of the peoples that come under it. However, the law which requires the priest witnessing the marriage to ask for and obtain the consent of the parties contracting it should remain.

78. Marriage should normally be celebrated during mass, after the reading of the gospel and the homily, and before the "prayer of the faithful." The prayer over the bride, duly corrected so as to emphasise the equal duty of both husband and wife to remain faithful to each other, may be said in the local language.

If in fact the marriage is celebrated without there being mass, the epistle and the gospel of the nuptial mass should be read at the beginning of the ceremony, and the blessing should always be given to the couple.

79. The sacramentals should be revised, bearing in mind the fundamental principle that people should be able to take part actively, easily and with awareness of what is happening; the revision should also pay attention to the needs of our time. When, in accordance with article 63, the books of rites are being revised, new sacramentals can also be added as need dictates.

Reserved blessings should be very few; they should be only for bishops or ordinaries.

Provision should be made so that some sacramentals, at least in special circumstances and at the discretion of the ordinary, can be administered by suitably qualified lay people.

80. The rite of consecration of virgins found in the Roman pontifical is to be subjected to review.

Moreover, a rite of religious profession and renewal of vows is to be drawn up, which should make it a more integrated, restrained and dignified occasion. Except where there is some particular law to the contrary, it is to be adopted by those who make their profession or renewal of vows during mass.

It is a very good idea for religious profession to take place during mass.

81. The funeral rites should express more clearly the paschal character of christian death, and should correspond more closely to the circumstances and traditions of individual parts of the world. This also applies to the question of liturgical colour.

82. The rite for burying little children should be revised, and a special mass provided.

Chapter 4. The divine office

83. When he assumed human nature, the high priest of the new and eternal covenant, Christ Jesus, introduced into this exile here on earth the hymn which is sung in the realms above throughout every age. He joins the whole human community to himself, and makes it his partner in this divine singing together of a song of praise.

For he is carrying on that priestly role through none other than his church, which is continually praising the Lord and interceding for the salvation and well-being of the whole world, not only by celebrating the eucharist, but also in other ways, above all by carrying out the divine office.

84. Following ancient christian tradition, the divine office is arranged in such a way that the whole cycle of day and night can be consecrated through the praise of God. When priests and others assigned to this task by a decision of the church perform this wonderful hymn of praise properly—or when it is done by christian believers at large together with a priest, praying it according to an approved form—then it is really the voice of the bride herself, speaking to her husband: and, what is even more, it is the prayer of Christ to the Father, which he makes in union with his whole body.

85. Thus all those who have this responsibility are at once carrying out an office of the church, and are sharing in the highest honour of Christ's bride, because while they perform their acts of praising God, they are standing in front of God's throne explicitly as the church.

86. To the extent that they become more clearly aware of their need to follow the advice of Paul when he said, "pray constantly" (1 Th 5, 17), priests assigned to pastoral ministry will be all the more assiduous in carrying out the liturgy of the hours. For only the Lord can give effectiveness and

growth to the task at which they are working—the Lord who said, "apart from me you can do nothing" (Jn 15, 5). It is this which led the apostles, when they were instituting deacons, to say, "Our really pressing occupations will be prayer and the ministry of the word" (Ac 6, 4).

87. But so that, given present circumstances, the divine office can be carried out better and more adequately, whether by priests or by other members of the church, the holy council has decided to make the following stipulations regarding the office used in the Roman rite, carrying on further a renewal which fortunately has been begun by the apostolic see.

88. The purpose of the office is to sanctify the day. Therefore the traditional sequence of the hours should be restored in such a way that, as far as possible, each hour of the office should once again match a time in the day. At the same time, the circumstances of life today should be kept in mind—circumstances which particularly affect those who devote their energies to apostolic tasks.

89. The following norms are therefore to be kept in the process of the renewal of the office:

a) It is a hallowed tradition of the whole church that lauds, as morning prayers, and vespers, as evening prayers, are regarded as the twofold hinge of the daily office. They are thus to be considered the principal hours, and celebrated as such.

b) Compline is to be organised in such a way as to be well suited to the end of the day.

c) The hour which is called "matins" is to be adapted so that it can be said at any hour of the day, although in choir it is to retain the character of nocturnal praise. It should consist of fewer psalms and longer readings.

d) The hour of prime is to be suppressed.

e) In choir, the minor hours of terce, sext and none should be kept. Outside choir, one of the three may be chosen, the one more suited to the time of the day.

90. The divine office is also a source of holiness and of nourishment for personal prayer, insofar as it is the public prayer of the church. Priests, and everyone else who shares in the divine office, are therefore urged very strongly to carry it out inwardly as well as vocally. In order better to achieve this, they should deepen their training in liturgy and in the Bible, especially the psalms.

Moreover, in the process of renewal, the ancient and hallowed heritage of the Roman office is to be modified in such a way that all to whom it is handed on will be able to enjoy it more easily and more fully.

91. In order for it to be possible in practice to keep the scheme of hours put forward in article 89, the psalms should no longer be distributed over one week, but rather over a more extended period of time.

The job of revising the psalter, which fortunately has already begun, should be completed as soon as possible. The revision should bear in mind church conventions of Latin usage, and the liturgical use of the psalms, including their sung use—not forgetting the whole tradition of the Latin church.

92. As for readings, the following stipulations are to be kept:

a) The reading of scripture is to be organised in such a way that the richnesses of the divine word become freely and more fully accessible;

b) The readings taken from works written by the fathers, the doctors and the writers of the church are to be better chosen;

c) The accounts of martyrdoms or lives of the saints are to be restored to historical credibility.

93. To the extent that seems fitting, the hymns are to be re-

stored to their original form. Things which smack of my thology or which are less suited to christian holiness are to be removed or changed. Other hymns from the tradition may, if it seems appropriate, be brought in.

94. It is important that the time of day given over to carrying out the hours is the one closest to the time implicit in each individual hour—both in order genuinely to sanctify the day, and so that spiritual benefit can be derived from saying them.

95. Communities with choral obligations must celebrate the divine office daily in choir, as well as their conventual mass. More specifically:

   a) orders of canons, monks and nuns, as well as of others under rule, who have choral obligations under law or their constitutions, are bound to the whole office;

   b) cathedral or collegiate chapters are bound to those parts of the office imposed on them by general or particular law;

   c) all members of those communities who are in major orders or who have been solemnly professed must recite on their own the canonical hours which they have not performed in choir. This does not apply to lay sisters or brothers.

96. Clerics who do not have choral obligations are under obligation, if they are in major orders, to carry out the whole office each day, either in a group or on their own. This is to be understood in terms of article 89.

97. There should be official instructions setting out when it is permissible to replace the divine office with a liturgical event.

   In individual cases, and for a good reason, ordinaries can excuse those under them from their obligation of reciting the office, either completely or partially; or they can replace it with another obligation.

98. Members of any organisation of religious life who, under their constitutions, carry out some parts of the divine office, are carrying out the public prayer of the church.

They are likewise carrying out the public prayer of the church if they recite any little office under their constitutions, provided it is drawn up on lines similar to those of the divine office and is properly approved.

99. The divine office is the voice of the church, of the whole mystical body, praising God in public. It is therefore recommended that clerics who do not have choral obligations—especially priests who live together or who are meeting together—carry out at least some part of the divine office as a group.

All who carry out the office either in choir or in a group should play the part entrusted to them as fully as possible, both in their inward devotion of mind and heart and in their visible style of conduct.

Moreover, it is preferable for the office in choir and in common to be sung, as circumstances allow.

100. Those responsible for pastoral care should see that the principal hours, especially vespers, be celebrated together by a group in the church on Sundays and on more special feasts. It is recommended that lay people also recite the divine office—either with priests, or gathered among themselves, or even each person alone.

101. §1) Following the age-old tradition of the Latin rite, Latin is to be kept in the divine office for clerics. However, power is given to ordinaries to allow in individual cases the use of a version in the local language, drawn up in accordance with the guidelines found in article 36, for those clerics for whom the use of Latin is a major obstacle to fulfilling the office properly.

§2) The competent superior can allow nuns and members of religious institutes—either men who are not clerics or women—to use the local language in the divine office, even when it is celebrated in choir, provided that the version has been approved.

§3) Any cleric who is bound to say the divine office, fulfils his obligation if he says office in the local language together with a group of Christians or with those mentioned under §2, provided that the text of the version has been approved.

Chapter 5. The liturgical year

102. The church considers it her role to celebrate the salvific action of her divine husband by recalling it to mind in worship on fixed days throughout the course of the year. In each week, on the day it has called "the Lord's day" (Sunday), the church has a commemoration of the resurrection of the Lord, which, in union with his passion, it also celebrates once a year in the greatest of festivals, Easter.

Moreover, the church unfolds the whole mystery of Christ over the cycle of the year, from his incarnation and birth to his return to heaven, to the day of Pentecost, and to our waiting for our hope of bliss and the return of the Lord.

By renewing in this way the mysteries of our redemption, the church opens to believers the riches of the greatness and achievements of its Lord, so much so that these can, in some way, be made present to every period of time. Thus believers can come into contact with them, and be filled with the grace of salvation.

103. While it celebrates this annual round of the events of Christ's sacramental life and work, the church gives honour to Mary, the mother of God, with a quite special love. She is inseparably linked to the saving activity of her son; in her, the church admires and holds up the outstanding result

of the redemption, and joyfully contemplates what is, as it were, a totally undistorted picture of its desires and hopes for itself as a whole.

104. The church has also put commemorations of martyrs and of other saints into the cycle of the year. These people were brought to their full potential through the grace of God active in many different ways: and they already possess eternal salvation. They are singing perfect praise to God in heaven, and are interceding for us. By celebrating the days on which the saints died, the church proclaims the easter mystery as found in the holy ones who have suffered with Christ and been glorified with him, puts the example of these people before believers as models who attract all women and men to the Father through Christ, and begs God for favours through what they have gained.

105. Finally, at various times in the year, the church uses traditional means to complete the formation of its members: religious activities for mind, heart and body; instruction; prayer; penance; helping others. In regard to these matters, this holy council has decided to make the following stipulations.

106. Every seventh day, the church celebrates the easter mystery. This is a tradition going back to the apostles, taking its origin from the actual day of Christ's resurrection—a day thus appropriately designated "the Lord's day." For on this day, christian believers should come together, in order to commemorate the suffering, resurrection and glory of the lord Jesus, by hearing God's word and sharing the eucharist; and to give thanks to God who has made them, "born anew to a living hope through the resurrection of Jesus Christ from the dead" (1 Pt 1, 3). Thus Sunday is the fundamental feast day; it should be presented as such for the religious observance of believers, and the point driven home, so that it also

becomes a day of rejoicing and of rest from work. Other celebrations, unless they really are of the highest importance, should not take precedence over it, in that the Sunday is the basis and centre of the whole liturgical year.

107. The liturgical year is to be revised. The traditional customs and practices of the liturgical seasons are to be preserved or restored, in line with the circumstances of our time. Their basic thrust is to be retained, so that they nourish as they should people's religious observance in celebrating the mysteries of christian redemption—above all the easter mystery. If adaptations turn out to be necessary, given the situations in different places, they should be made in accordance with articles 39 and 40.

108. The first loyalty of believers should be directed towards the feast days of the Lord, on which the sacramental events of salvation are celebrated over the course of the year. Therefore the liturgy of the season should be given its proper place above the feasts of the saints, so that the whole cycle of the mysteries of salvation can be appropriately recalled.

109. The twofold character of the season of Lent—for Lent, through reminding believers of baptism or preparing them for it, and through penance, makes them ready to celebrate the easter mystery, as they listen more attentively to the word of God and set aside time for prayer—should be brought out more clearly, both in the liturgy and in teaching based on the liturgy. Accordingly:

a) the baptismal features particular to the liturgy of Lent are to be brought into it more fully; indeed, insofar as circumstances allow, certain elements from earlier tradition are to be restored;

b) the same goes for the penitential elements. Moreover, in teaching, the distinctive character of penance as a repudiation of sin, inasmuch as it constitutes an offence against God, is to be impressed on the minds and hearts of believers. This should go together with a sense of the consequences of sin in society. Also, the roles of the church in penitential activity should not be omitted, and the need to pray for sinners should be emphasised.

110. Penance during the lenten season should not only be inward and individual, but also public and collective. Moreover, penitential activity, in ways suited to our time, to different parts of the world, and to the situations in which believers find themselves, must really be encouraged and recommended by the authorities mentioned in article 22.

However, the paschal fast must be kept sacrosanct. It is to be observed everywhere on Good Friday, and, if circumstances allow, it should be carried over to Holy Saturday. This is so that people can thus come through to the joys of Easter Sunday with minds and hearts concentrated and receptive.

111. It is traditional to honour the saints in the church, and to hold their authentic relics and pictures in veneration. The feasts of the saints proclaim what are in fact the wonders of Christ in those who serve him, and they provide for believers models that can properly be imitated.

In order to avoid the feasts of saints being given more weight than the feasts renewing the actual mysteries of salvation, more of them should be left to be celebrated by an individual church, country or religious family. Only those feasts commemorating saints whose importance really is universal should be extended over the whole church.

Chapter 6. The music of worship

112. The musical tradition of the universal church constitutes a priceless treasure, more so than other artistic expressions,

especially insofar as the sacral chant which is superimposed onto words makes a necessary and integral contribution to solemn liturgy.

The use of worshipping music has obviously been strongly affirmed, both in scripture[1] and by the fathers and popes. More recently, these last, beginning with St. Pius X, have brought out more clearly the ministerial role of sacral music in the service of the Lord.

And so, the closer the music of worship is linked to liturgical activity, the holier it will be—whether it is expressing prayer more eloquently, or building unity of heart and mind, or enriching the rites of worship with greater solemnity. The church approves of all forms of true art if they have the necessary qualities, and receives them into divine worship.

In this light, this holy council, continuing the norms and rules of church tradition and discipline, and keeping in mind the purpose of music in worship, that is, the glory of God and the growth in holiness of believers, has made the following stipulations.

113. When singing is used to heighten the celebration of religious services, with ministers of worship taking part and the people actively joining in, the liturgical activity takes on a richer character.

As for the language to be used, the instructions of article 36 should be followed; for mass, see article 54; for sacraments, see article 63; for the divine office, see article 101.

114. Very great efforts should be made to preserve and develop the rich heritage of music in churches. The growth of choirs should be energetically fostered, especially in cathedral churches. At the same time, bishops and others in positions of pastoral responsibility should make strenuous efforts to see that the whole gathering of believers are able

to take the active part which is proper to them in any event of worship meant to be conducted through song, in keeping with articles 28 and 30.

115. A lot should be made of musical education and of musical activity in seminaries, in noviceships and houses of studies for religious of both sexes, and in other catholic schools and institutions. Thus, in order for this education to become a reality, professors put in charge of teaching the music of worship should be thoroughly trained.

In addition, it is recommended that higher institutes of the music of worship be set up as circumstances allow.

Also, it is important that specialist musicians and singers, especially children, be given a genuine liturgical training.

116. The church recognises Gregorian chant as something special to the Roman liturgy, which should thus, other things being equal, be given a place of primacy in liturgical activity. Other sorts of sacral music, especially of course polyphony, are in no way excluded from the celebration of religious services, provided that they fit in with the spirit of the liturgical event, in keeping with article 30.

117. The standard edition of the books of Gregorian chant is to be completed; moreover, a more critical edition should be prepared of the books that have already been edited following the reform of St. Pius X.

It would also be good if an edition comprising simpler melodies could be prepared, for use in smaller churches.

118. Religious singing by the people is to be resourcefully encouraged, so as to enable the voices of believers to ring out in their religious devotions and worship—and indeed in liturgical events—following the norms and provisions officially laid down.

119. In some parts of the world, especially mission areas, peoples are found who have a musical tradition of their own,

a tradition which has great importance for their religious and cultural way of life. This music must be taken with due seriousness; suitable scope is to be given for it to contribute both to their development of their sense of the religious, and to the adaptation of religious worship to their particular temperament, in keeping with articles 39 and 40.

For this reason, special care should be taken in the musical training of missionaries, so that, as far as possible, they will be able to encourage the traditional music of these peoples in schools, in choirs, and in acts of worship.

120. The pipe organ should be held in great honour in the Latin church, in that it is the traditional musical instrument, whose sounds can add a remarkable dignity to the ceremonies of the church, and powerfully raise minds and hearts to God and to things above.

At the same time, other instruments may be brought into the worship of God, at the discretion of the competent local church authority and with its agreement—following articles 22 §2, 37 and 40—insofar as they are suitable for purposes of worship or can be made so, insofar as they cohere with the dignity of the temple, and insofar as they really contribute to the building up of believers.

121. Those who work with music, and who have absorbed the spirit of Christianity, should feel themselves called to cultivate the music of worship, and to contribute to its rich tradition.

They should bring together compositions which exhibit the characteristics of true worshipping music, and which can be sung not only by major choirs, but which are also suitable for more modest ones, and encourage the whole gathering of believers actively to take part.

The texts which are chosen for the music of worship should be in conformity with catholic teaching: indeed, they should draw principally on scripture and on sources from within the liturgy.

Chapter 7. The art and furnishings of worship

122. The fine arts are very rightly reckoned among the most noble expressions of human creativity—and especially religious art, together with its highest form, namely the art of worship. By their nature, they are oriented to the infinite divine beauty, which is in some way to be expressed through works done by human beings. Insofar as their only purpose is to do as much as possible to turn human minds and hearts towards a right relationship with God, they are thought of as God's, and as praising him, extending his glory.

Thus the church has always been a friend of the fine arts. It has never ceased to seek after the noble service they provide and to train artists and craftspeople. The chief purpose for this has been so that the things which form part of liturgical worship can be suitable, dignified and beautiful—signs and symbols of things above. Moreover, the church has always, with good reason, thought of itself as a kind of judge, separating out works of art that are religiously consistent with its traditions of faith, holiness and law, and that are to be regarded as suitable for use in worship.

In permitting the alterations in material, design or decoration which have come as a result of the advance of artistic technique through the course of time, the church has been especially careful to see that sacral furnishings contribute to the decorum of worship by being dignified and beautiful.

These considerations have led the council in its decision to make the following stipulations on these matters.

123. The church has not regarded any style of art as its own: rather, it has taken in what has been current in every age,

in the light of the temperaments of peoples, their circumstances, and the needs of the various rites. In doing this through the course of centuries, it has brought into being a rich heritage, and every care is to be taken to preserve it. The art of our time also, and the art of every race and part of the world, should be allowed to function freely in the church, provided it is of service to the buildings of worship and the rites of worship, exhibiting due reverence and honour. Thus it will be able to join its voice to the wonderful chorus of glory in which great masters have sung throughout past ages of catholic faith.

124. Ordinaries should see to it, in their encouragement and support of authentic worshipping art, that their aim is noble beauty rather than mere sumptuousness. This should also apply to the vestments and decoration of worship. Bishops should see that works done by artists which clash with faith, with the requirements of morality, and with the religious attitude appropriate to Christianity, and which are offensive to a true religious sense, be kept well and truly out of the house of God and out of other places of worship—whether this is because of the decadence of the forms, or because the art is below standard, mediocre and pretentious.

Moreover, when churches are being built, care should be taken to see that they are suitable for the conducting of liturgical events, and for bringing it about that believers actively share in them.

125. The practice of putting worshipful symbols in churches for people to venerate should be uncompromisingly maintained. However, the number put out should be kept under control, and they should be arranged in a suitable pattern, in case they excite sensationalism among the christian people or pander to a devotion that is not quite right.

126. Local ordinaries should take advice from the diocesan

commission for sacral art when they are taking decisions on works of art, and, if appropriate, from other really expert people; also from the commissions mentioned in articles 44, 45 and 46.

Ordinaries should be very careful not to lose ownership of sacral furnishings or works of value, nor to destroy them, for they are the ornaments of God's house.

127. Bishops, either personally or through suitable priests gifted with expertise and love of art, should look after artists and craftspeople, so as to instil in them the spirit of the liturgy and of worshipping art.

It is also recommended that schools or academies of worshipping art be set up to form artists and craftspeople in those parts of the world where it seems appropriate.

All artists and craftspeople, who, led by their creativity, want to give service to God's glory in the church, should always remember that they are dealing with a kind of worshipping imitation of God the Creator, as well as with works of art set aside for catholic worship, for the spiritual growth of believers, and for their devotion and religious formation.

128. The ecclesiastical canons and statutes which deal with the provision of visible things for worship are to be revised as soon as possible, in conjunction with the revision of the books used in the liturgy as laid down in article 25. This applies especially to the following: how churches should be built in a way that is dignified and suitable; the design and construction of altars; the need for the eucharistic tabernacle to be dignified, well positioned and secure; the practicability of having a suitable place for baptism, and how it should be respected; a suitable set of principles for regulating worshipful symbols, decoration and ornamentation. What seems to be less in keeping with the renewed liturgy should be cor-

rected or abolished; what in fact suits it should be kept or introduced.

In this matter, especially regarding the material and design of the furnishings and vestments of worship, local groupings of bishops have been given the power to adapt things to the needs and customs of their areas, in keeping with article 22 of this constitution.

129. While they are doing their studies in philosophy and theology, clerics should also be trained in the history of the art of worship and its development, together with the sound principles on which works of art for worship should be based. They will thus appreciate and preserve the hallowed monuments of the church, and be able to give suitable advice to artists and craftspeople as they bring their works into being.

130. It is appropriate for the use of pontifical insignia to be reserved to those ecclesiastics who either are bishops or hold some special jurisdiction.

—December 4, 1963

Appendix

Declaration by the second holy ecumenical council held at the Vatican concerning the revision of the calendar

The second holy ecumenical council held at the Vatican regards the wishes of many people to assign the feast of Easter to a fixed Sunday and to stabilise the calendar as a matter of considerable importance. It has taken great trouble to assess all the consequences that might come from bringing in a new calendar, and declares the following:

1. This holy council has no difficulty with assigning the feast of Easter to a fixed Sunday within the Gregorian calendar if

other interested parties agree, especially sisters and brothers who are separated from communion with the apostolic see.

2. Likewise, this holy council declares that it is not opposed to initiatives aimed at introducing a permanent stabilisation of the calendar into civil society.

However, from among the various systems aimed at fixing a permanent calendar and introducing it into civil society, the church is prepared to accept only those systems which preserve a week of seven days with a Sunday, and guarantee it, without throwing in any days outside the week, thus leaving the succession of weeks intact. This applies unless very serious factors intervene, in which case the apostolic see is to make a decision.

Dogmatic Constitution on Divine Revelation
(Dei Verbum)

On November 14, 1962, the draft document on revelation was introduced to the council assembly for debate. Unlike the document on liturgy, which earlier that day had received an almost unanimous vote of support, the document on revelation met quick and sharp criticism. As soon as Cardinal Alfredo Ottaviani and his deputy had finished introducing the text, Cardinal Achille Liénart of Lille took the microphone to declare the text "unacceptable" (non placet). Cardinal Josef Frings of Cologne rose to second the motion. Then, as one observer noted in his diary, "The dam broke." A flood of criticism poured out, causing a crisis not only for the document on revelation but also for the council as a whole.

Opposition to the text on revelation had been building even before the opening of the first session. Influential theologians like Karl Rahner, Edward Schillebeeckx, and Joseph Ratzinger (who would later become Pope Benedict XVI) had published critical analyses of the draft text. These periti ("experts" and official advisers) had earned the respect of bishops who would become leaders at the council. Their collaboration brought to light the deficiencies of the draft presented by Cardinal Ottaviani's Doctrinal Commission. Many saw it as still too caught up in Counter-Reformation polemics and the theological jargon of Neo-Scholastic seminary textbooks. It was defensive in tone, anti-ecumenical in outlook, and suspicious about the work of biblical scholars.

The text that met such widespread criticism laid out the relationship between scripture, tradition, and the church's teaching authority in five chapters. Chapter 1 treated "the two sources of revelation": scripture and tradition. The relationship between these two had been controversial since the Reformation. When Martin Luther emphasized "scripture alone," Catholic theologians responded by defending church tradition. Their goal was to protect developments in Catholic doctrine, sacramental practice, and church structure against the Reformers' claim that these were unbiblical. Such a defense gave rise to a theory that described "tradition" as a separate, and almost independent, source of revelation standing alongside the Bible—a theory repeated in the preparatory draft. Chapter 2 of the draft argued that belief in biblical inspiration meant believing that the Bible was without error in all things "religious and profane" (in qualibet re religiosa vel profana). Chapter 3, "On the Old Testament," described the Hebrew scriptures as wholly oriented toward the Christian New Testament. Chapter 4, "On the New Testament," condemned modern biblical research, arguing for the complete historical accuracy of the Gospels. Finally, Chapter 5 called attention to the preeminence of the Latin Vulgate version of the Bible. While acknowledging the benefit of studying scripture in modern translations, the draft warned of the danger of reading the Bible apart from the authoritative interpretation of the magisterium.

During a week of debate, the draft was attacked on both substance and style. Liénart's opening salvo argued that the "two-source" theory of revelation was a fairly recent innovation that misrepresented the teaching of the Council of Trent and overlooked the deeper truth that there is only one source of revelation—the Word of God. He was joined by many others who found the tone to be too negative, too rigid, too quick to condemn. Cardinal Augustin

Bea, the progressive head of the Secretariat for Promoting Christian Unity, reminded everyone of Pope John XXIII's opening speech to the council. Vatican II was meant to be a pastoral council; it was meant to reach out to other Christians and to the whole world; it was meant to revitalize the church. But the draft on revelation did none of these things. Bea concluded that it must be redone—made shorter, more pastoral, and more open.

Beneath this debate, and the seemingly technical issues treated in this document, lay deeper concerns about the overall direction and purpose of the council. Thus the draft on revelation quickly came to symbolize larger questions about what kind of assembly Vatican II would be. Those who criticized the text wanted a new start. They wanted to free the council from the antimodern mentality that had come over church teaching in recent decades. And they saw, paradoxically, that the key to moving forward was to recover the deeper wisdom of the past. Those who defended the draft felt quite at home in its antimodern approach. They questioned the authority of the assembly to reject a preparatory text in its entirety. They expressed fears that the doctrinal purity of the faith was being clouded by calls for adaptation, ecumenical openness, and the incorporation of modern methods of historical research. The fault lines first revealed in the debate on liturgy became even more pronounced. It was unclear how the council would move forward given this growing divide between those in favor of reform and those opposed to it.

On November 20, the Council of Presidents announced a vote on whether discussion of the draft should be ended. Ending debate would, in effect, kill the draft, sending it back for a complete rewrite. But the wording of the vote—"Should the discussion be interrupted?"—caused confusion. The bishops were being asked to vote "yes" in order to reject the text. Beyond the initial confusion this caused was an important procedural oversight. According to the council rules, a two-thirds majority was needed to approve a text—meaning that only one-third of the vote was sufficient to reject it. With the unfortunate wording of this particular vote, those opposed to the draft now had to gather a full two-thirds. When the ballots were counted, 1,368 were for ending debate, 822 for continuing—a clear majority, and a clear victory for those opposed to the document. But they fell just 105 votes short of the two-thirds needed to officially reject the text. The council was stuck with a document that the majority found unacceptable.

The very next day Pope John XXIII intervened. He overruled the council regulations and ordered that the document be withdrawn. Instead of sending it back to the Doctrinal Commission, however, the pope decided that it would be revised by a newly created "mixed commission," with Cardinals Ottaviani and Bea as joint presidents.

The pope's action was a turning point for the council. For the majority, it sparked a new spirit of hope, encouraging progressives that real renewal was possible. For the minority, it caused consternation and a recalibration as the balance of power in the assembly shifted before their eyes. For everyone involved, it was clear something significant was happening.

But the story of the document on revelation was not over. Months of debate and redrafting lay ahead. The question of the relationship between scripture and tradition remained a touch point for the conservative minority, who wanted to see the council clearly affirm that tradition contains truths of revelation not found in scripture. Questions about biblical inerrancy and the historical accuracy of the Gospels sparked sharp disagreement. At work were two different visions of church. Is the church an eternal authority, constantly vigilant, defending doctrinal purity against errors lurking everywhere? Or is the church a community passing through history, handing on the Good News through its life, worship, and teaching?

When the Dogmatic Constitution on Divine Revelation (Dei

Verbum) *was formally approved and promulgated on November 18, 1965, it placed the church's teaching authority not over and above the Word of God, but as its servant. Instead of portraying revelation as a series of discrete propositions, it envisioned revelation first and foremost as God's desire to communicate with people, to bring salvation through Christ, to be in relationship with all of humanity. Scripture and tradition are not "two sources" but two streams that flow from one divine source, streams that merge and flow toward the same goal. After two chapters that discuss this vision of revelation and its transmission,* Dei Verbum *goes on in chapter 3 to offer a nuanced treatment of biblical inspiration and a positive appraisal of the methods of contemporary biblical scholarship. Chapters 4 and 5 treat the Old and New Testaments respectively. And a final chapter concludes that sacred scripture ought to be made more widely available to all of the faithful.*

In the end, the document's legacy lies not in settling some theological debate but in inspiring a new generation of biblical scholars, helping to imbue Catholic worship with the scriptures, and encouraging countless Catholics to pick up the Bible and read for themselves the Word of God.

Dei Verbum
Dogmatic Constitution on Divine Revelation
TRANSLATED BY ROBERT MURRAY, S.J.

Introduction

1. The Word of God calls for reverent attention and confident proclamation. In response this council does as St. John says: "We proclaim to you the eternal life which was with the Father and was made manifest to us—that which we have seen and heard we proclaim also to you, so that you may have fellowship with us, and that our fellowship may be with the Father and with his Son Jesus Christ" (1 Jn 1, 2–3). This council aims, then, following in the steps of the councils of Trent and Vatican I, to set forth authentic teaching on God's revelation and how it is communicated, desiring that the whole world may hear the message of salvation, and thus grow from hearing to faith, from faith to hope, and from hope to love.[1]

Chapter 1. Revelation in itself

2. It has pleased God, in his goodness and wisdom, to reveal himself and to make known the secret purpose of his will (see Eph 1, 9). This brings it about that through Christ, God's Word made flesh, and in his holy Spirit, human beings can draw near to the Father and become sharers in the divine nature (see Eph 2, 18; 2 Pt 1, 4). By thus revealing himself God, who is invisible (see Col 1, 15; 1 Tm 1, 17), in his great love speaks to humankind as friends (see Ex 33, 11; Jn 15, 14–15) and enters into their life (see Bar 3, 38), so as to invite and receive them into relationship with himself. The pattern of this revelation unfolds through deeds and words bound together by an inner dynamism, in such a way that God's works, effected during the course of the history of salvation, show forth and confirm the doctrine and the realities signified by the words, while the words in turn proclaim the works and throw light on the meaning hidden in them. By this revelation the truth, both about God and about the salvation of humankind, inwardly dawns on us in Christ, who is in himself both the mediator and the fullness of all revelation.[2]

3. God creates and conserves all things through his Word (see Jn 1, 3). In the created order he offers to humankind a lasting testimony to himself (see Rm 1, 19–20). Further, in his plan to open up the way of heavenly salvation, he made himself known to our first parents from the beginning. After their fall he aroused them to hope for salvation by the promise of redemption (see Gn 3, 15), and he has constantly kept the human race in his care, so as to grant eternal life to all those who persevere in doing good in search of salvation (see Rm 2, 6–7). In his good time he called Abraham, in order to make of him a great nation (see Gn 12, 2–3). After the era of the patriarchs, he taught this nation, through Moses and the prophets, to acknowledge himself as the only living and

true God, the all-caring Father and just judge, and to wait for the promised Saviour. In this way, down the centuries, he prepared the way for the gospel.

4. After God had spoken in many and various ways by the prophets, "in these last days he has spoken to us by a Son" (Heb 1, 1–2). He sent his Son, the eternal Word who enlightens all humankind, to live among them and to tell them about the inner life of God (see Jn 1, 1–18). Thus it is that Jesus Christ, the Word made flesh, sent as a human being among humans,[3] "speaks the words of God" (Jn 3, 34) and accomplishes the work of salvation which the Father gave him to do (see Jn 5, 36; 17, 4). To see Jesus is to see his Father also (see Jn 14, 9). This is why Jesus completes the work of revelation and confirms it by divine testimony. He did this by the total reality of his presence and self-manifestation—by his words and works, his symbolic acts and miracles, but above all by his death and his glorious resurrection from the dead, crowned by his sending the Spirit of truth. His message is that God is with us, to deliver us from the darkness of sin and death, and to raise us up to eternal life.

5. In response to God's revelation our duty is "the obedience of faith" (see Rm 16, 26; compare Rm 1, 5; 2 Cor 10, 5–6). By this, a human being makes a total and free self-commitment to God, offering "the full submission of intellect and will to God as he reveals,"[4] and willingly assenting to the revelation he gives. For this faith to be accorded we have need of God's grace, both anticipating and then accompanying our act, together with the inward assistance of the holy Spirit, who works to stir the heart and turn it towards God, to open the eyes of the mind, and to give "to all facility in accepting and believing the truth."[5] The same holy Spirit constantly perfects faith by his gifts, to bring about an ever deeper understanding of revelation.

6. By divine revelation God has chosen to manifest and communicate both himself and the eternal decrees of his will for the salvation of humankind, "so as to share those divine treasures which totally surpass human understanding."[6]

This council reaffirms that "God, the first principle and last end of all things, can be known with certainty from the created order by the natural light of human reason" (See Rm 1, 20). Further, this teaching is to be held about revelation: "in the present condition of the human race, even those truths about God which are not beyond the reach of human reason, require revelation for them to be known by all without great effort, with firm certainty and without error entering in."[7]

Chapter 2. The transmission of divine revelation

7. God in his goodness arranged that whatever he had revealed for the salvation of all nations should last for ever in its integrity and be handed on to all generations. Accordingly Christ our lord, in whom the whole revelation of God is summed up (see 2 Cor 1, 20 and 3, 16—4, 6), entrusted the apostles with his gospel. This had been promised through the prophets; he revealed its fullness and published it by his own lips, to be a universal source of saving truth and moral teaching.[1] This gospel the apostles were to preach to all peoples, sharing God's gifts with them. This has in fact been faithfully carried out. The apostles handed on, by their own preaching and examples and by their dispositions, whatever they had received from Christ's lips, his way or life or his works, or had learned by the prompting of the holy Spirit; secondly, some apostles, with others of the apostolic age, under the interior guidance of the same Spirit, committed the message of salvation to writing.[2]

In order that the gospel should be preserved in the church

for ever living and integral, the apostles left as their successors the bishops, "handing on their own teaching function"
to them.[3] By this link, this sacred tradition and the sacred
scripture of the two testaments are like a mirror in which the
church, during its pilgrimage of earth, contemplates God,
the source of all that it has received, until it is brought home
to see him face to face as he is (see 1 Jn 3, 2).

8. Thus the apostolic preaching, which is expressed in a
special way in the inspired books, was to be preserved by
a continuous succession until the end of time. This is why
the apostles, handing on what they had received, warn the
faithful to hold fast to the traditions which they had learned,
either by word of mouth or by letter (see 2 Th 2, 15), and to
fight for the faith that had been delivered to them once for
all (see Ju 3).[4] The expression "what has been handed down
from the apostles" includes everything that helps the people
of God to live a holy life and to grow in faith. In this way the
church, in its teaching, life and worship, perpetuates and hands
on to every generation all that it is and all that it believes.

This tradition which comes from the apostles progresses
in the church under the assistance of the holy Spirit.[5] There
is growth in understanding of what is handed on, both
the words and the realities they signify. This comes about
through contemplation and study by believers, who "ponder
these things in their hearts" (see Lk 2, 19 and 51); through the
intimate understanding of spiritual things which they experience; and through the preaching of those who, on succeed-
ing to the office of bishop, receive the sure charism of truth.
Thus, as the centuries advance, the church constantly holds
its course towards the fullness of God's truth, until the day
when the words of God reach their fulfilment in the church.

The fathers of the church bear witness to the enlivening
presence of this tradition, and show how its riches flow into

the practice and life of the believing and praying church. By this tradition comes the church's knowledge of the full canon of biblical books; by this too, the scripture itself comes to be more profoundly understood and to realise its power in the church. In this way the God who spoke of old still maintains an uninterrupted conversation with the bride of his beloved Son. The holy Spirit, too, is active, making the living voice of the gospel ring out in the church, and through it in the world, leading those who believe into the whole truth, and making the message of Christ dwell in them in all its richness (see Col 3, 16).

9. Hence sacred tradition and scripture are bound together in a close and reciprocal relationship. They both flow from the same divine wellspring, merge together to some extent, and are on course towards the same end. Scripture is the utterance of God as it is set down in writing under the guidance of God's Spirit; tradition preserves the word of God as it was entrusted to the apostles by Christ our lord and the holy Spirit, and transmits it to their successors, so that these in turn, enlightened by the Spirit of truth, may faithfully preserve, expound and disseminate the word by their preaching. Consequently, the church's certainty about all that is revealed is not drawn from holy scripture alone; both scripture and tradition are to be accepted and honoured with like devotion and reverence.[6]

10. Tradition and scripture together form a single sacred deposit of the word of God, entrusted to the church. Holding fast to this, the entire holy people, united with its pastors, perseveres always faithful to the apostles' teaching and shared life, to the breaking of bread and prayer (see Ac 2, 42 Greek text). Thus, as they hold, practise and witness to the heritage of the faith, bishops and faithful display a unique harmony.[7]

The task of authentically interpreting the word of God, whether in its written form or in that of tradition,[8] has been entrusted only to those charged with the church's ongoing teaching function,[9] whose authority is exercised in the name of Jesus Christ. This teaching function is not above the word of God but stands at its service, teaching nothing but what is handed down, according as it devotedly listens, reverently preserves and faithfully transmits the word of God, by divine command and with the help of the holy Spirit. All that it proposes for belief, as being divinely revealed, is drawn from the one deposit of faith.

Thus it is clear that, by God's wise design, tradition, scripture and the church's teaching function are so connected and associated that one does not stand without the others, but all together, and each in its own way, subject to the action of the one holy Spirit, contribute effectively to the salvation of souls.

Chapter 3. The divine inspiration of holy scripture and its interpretation

11. Those things revealed by God which are contained and presented in the text of holy scripture were written under the influence of the holy Spirit. By the faith handed down from the apostles, holy mother church accepts as sacred and canonical all the books of both the old Testament and the new, in their entirety and with all their parts, in the conviction that they were written under the inspiration of the holy Spirit (see Jn 20, 31; 2 Tm 3, 16; 2 Pt 1, 19–21; 3, 15–16) and therefore have God as their originator: on this basis they were handed on to the church.[1] In the process of composition of the sacred books God chose and employed human agents, using their own powers and faculties,[2] in such a way

that they wrote as authors in the true sense, and yet God acted in and through them,[3] directing the content entirely and solely as he willed.[4] It follows that we should hold that whatever the inspired authors or "sacred writers" affirm, is affirmed by the holy Spirit; we must acknowledge that the books of scripture teach firmly, faithfully and without error such truth as God, for the sake of our salvation, wished the biblical text to contain.[5] Therefore "all scripture is inspired by God and profitable for teaching, for reproof, for correction, and for training in righteousness, that the man of God may be complete, equipped for every good work" (2 Tm 3, 16–17 Greek text).

12. Now since in the Bible God has spoken through human agents to humans,[6] if the interpreter of holy scripture is to understand what God has wished to communicate to us, he must carefully investigate what meaning the biblical writers actually had in mind; that will also be what God chose to manifest through their words.

In order to get at what the biblical writers intended, attention should be paid (among other things) to *literary genres*.

This is because truth is presented and expressed differently in historical, prophetic or poetic texts, or in other styles of speech. The interpreter has to look for that meaning which a biblical writer intended and expressed in his particular circumstances, and in his historical and cultural context, by means of such literary genres as were in use at his time.[7] To understand correctly what a biblical writer intended to assert, due attention is needed both to the customary and characteristic ways of feeling, speaking and storytelling which were current in his time, and to the social conventions of the period.[8]

Further, holy scripture must be read and interpreted in the light of the same Spirit through whom it was written.[9]

Consequently a right understanding of the sacred texts demands attention, no less than that mentioned above, to the content and coherence of scripture as a whole, taking into account the whole church's living tradition and the sense of perspective given by faith. It is the function of exegetes to work, in accord with these rules, towards a more perceptive understanding and exposition of the meaning of holy scripture, so that through their study the church's judgment may mature. All that concerns the way to interpret scripture is ultimately subject to the judgment of the church, to which God has entrusted the commission and ministry of preserving and interpreting the word of God.[10]

13. In holy scripture, together with the manifestation of God's truth and holiness, we see the eternal wisdom stoop down, as it were, "to teach us God's inexpressible kindness, and how thoughtfully he has accommodated his way of speaking to our nature."[11] Indeed, God's words, expressed through human language, have taken on the likeness of human speech, just as the Word of the eternal Father, when he assumed the flesh of human weakness, took on the likeness of human beings.

Chapter 4. The old Testament

14. God in his supreme love and concern intended the salvation of the entire human race. In preparation for this, by a special plan, he chose a people for himself, to entrust with his promises. By making his covenant with Abraham (see Gn 15, 18) and with the people of Israel through Moses (see Ex 24, 8) he "acquired" a people for himself, and by words and acts revealed himself to it as the only God, true and living. His purpose was that Israel might learn by experience how God acts towards human beings; that, as he spoke through

the prophets, his people might understand his ways ever more deeply and clearly, and demonstrate them more widely to the nations (see Ps 21, 28–29; 95, 1–3; Is 2, 1–4; Jer 3, 17). This plan and pattern of salvation—foretold, recounted and explained by the biblical writers—is there to read, as the true word of God, in the books of the old Testament. These books, therefore, written as they are under divine inspiration, retain lasting value: "Whatever was written in former days was written for our instruction, that by steadfastness and by the encouragement of the scriptures we might have hope" (Rm 15, 4).

15. The plan and pattern of the old Testament was directed above all towards the coming of Christ, the universal Redeemer, and of the messianic kingdom: to prepare for this, to announce it prophetically (see Lk 24, 44; Jn 5, 39; 1 Pt 1, 10) and to point towards it by various foreshadowing symbols (see 1 Cor 10, 11). The old Testament books manifest to all readers the knowledge of God and of humankind, and how God in his justice and mercy acts towards them, in the context of human history before the era of salvation brought by Christ. These books, though they also contain things that are imperfect and of merely temporary value, still demonstrate God's ways of teaching.[1] They ought therefore to be accepted by Christians, because they express a vivid sense of God, because they enshrine sublime teaching about God, salutary wisdom for human life and wonderful treasures of prayer, and finally because in the old Testament books our salvation in Christ is hinted at under signs and symbols.

16. Thus God, the inspirer and originator of the books of both testaments, has brought it about in his wisdom that the new Testament should be hidden in the old, and the old Testament should be made manifest in the new.[2] Though Christ established the new covenant in his blood (see Lk 22, 20; 1

Cor 11, 25), nevertheless the old Testament books, all and entire, were retained in the preaching of the gospel;[3] in the new Testament they acquire and display their full meaning (see Mt 5, 17; Lk 24, 27; Rm 16, 25–26; 2 Cor 3, 14–16), and in their turn they shed light on it and explain it.

Chapter 5. The new Testament

17. The Word of God, which is the power of God for salvation to everyone who has faith (see Rm 1, 16), is presented and shows its force supremely in the writings of the new Testament. When the fullness of time came (see Gal 4, 4), the Word became flesh and dwelt among us, full of grace and truth (see Jn 1, 14). Christ inaugurated the reign of God on earth, manifested his Father and himself by deeds and words, and completed his work by his death, resurrection and glorious ascension, and by sending the holy Spirit. Lifted up from the earth, he draws all to himself (see Jn 12, 32 Greek text)—he who alone has the words of eternal life (see Jn 6, 68). This is a mystery which was not made known to other generations as it has now been revealed to his holy apostles and prophets through the holy Spirit (see Eph 3, 4–6 Greek text), so that they might preach the gospel, stir up faith in Jesus as Christ and lord, and bring together the church. The writings of the new Testament stand as a perpetual and divine testimony to all this.

18. It is evident that among all the inspired writings, even those of the new Testament, the gospels rightly have the supreme place, because they form the primary testimony to the life and teaching of the incarnate Word, our Saviour.

The four gospels originate from the apostles, as the church has held always and everywhere and still holds. The apostles preached as Christ had charged them to do. Then, under the guidance of the Spirit of God, they and others of the apostolic age delivered to us the same preaching in writing, as the foundation of our faith, the fourfold gospel, according to Matthew, Mark, Luke and John.[1]

19. Holy mother church has firmly and constantly held, and continues to hold and unhesitatingly assert, that the four gospels just named are historical documents and faithfully communicate what Jesus, the Son of God, during his life among men and women, actually did and taught for their eternal salvation, until the day when he was taken up (see Ac 1, 1–2). First the apostles, after the Lord's ascension, passed on to their hearers what he had said and done, but—having learned by experiencing the glorious events of Christ and by enlightenment from the Spirit of truth[2]—with the fuller insight which they now possessed.[3] Next, inspired writers composed the four gospels, by various processes. They selected some things from the abundant material already handed down, orally or in writing. Other things they synthesised, or explained with a view to the needs of the churches. They preserved the preaching style, but worked throughout so as to communicate to us a true and sincere account of Jesus;[4] for whether they wrote from their own memory and recollections, or from the evidence of "those who from the beginning were eyewitnesses and ministers of the word," their intention was that we might know "the truth" concerning the things of which we have been informed (see Lk 1, 2–4).

20. Besides the four gospels, the new Testament canon also contains the letters of St. Paul and other apostolic writings, which were also composed under the inspiration of the holy Spirit. By God's wise plan, these writings contain confirmation of what is told about Christ, give further explanation of his authentic teaching, preach about how Christ's divine work has the power to save, tell the story of the church's

beginnings and wonderful expansion, and foretell its glorious consummation.

For the lord Jesus was with the apostles as he had promised (see Mt 28, 20), and he sent them the Spirit, the counsellor, to lead them into the fullness of truth (see Jn 16, 13).

Chapter 6. Holy scripture in the life of the church

21. The church has always held the divine scriptures in reverence no less than it accords to the Lord's body itself, never ceasing—especially in the sacred liturgy—to receive the bread of life from the one table of God's word and Christ's body, and to offer it to the faithful. The church has kept and keeps the scriptures, together with tradition, as the supreme rule of its faith, since the Bible, being inspired by God and committed to writing once for all, communicates the word of God in an unalterable form, makes the voice of the holy Spirit sound through the words of the prophets and the apostles. Accordingly all the church's preaching, no less than the whole christian religion, ought to be nourished and ruled by holy scripture. In the sacred books the Father who is in heaven comes lovingly to meet his children and talks with them. There is such force and power in the word of God that it stands as the church's support and strength, affording her children sturdiness in faith, food for the soul and a pure and unfailing fount of spiritual life. It is supremely true of holy scripture that "the word of God is living and active" (Heb 4, 12), "which is able to build you up and to give you the inheritance among all those who are sanctified" (Ac 20, 32; see 1 Th 2, 13).

22. Easy access to holy scripture should be available to all the christian faithful. This is why, from the very beginning, the church took as its own the ancient translation of the old

Testament called the Septuagint; it also keeps in honour the other versions, in oriental languages and in Latin, especially that known as the Vulgate. Further, since the word of God ought to be available at all times, the church, with motherly care, sees to it that appropriate and correct translations are made into different languages, especially from the original texts of the sacred books. If the opportunity arises, and church authority approves, such versions may be prepared in collaboration with Christians of other denominations; all Christians will then be able to use them.

23. The church, the "spouse of the incarnate Word," taught by the holy Spirit, strives to attain, day by day, an ever deeper understanding of holy scripture, so that she may never fail to nourish her children with God's utterances. With this in view the church appropriately encourages the study also of the fathers of the church, both eastern and western, and of the sacred liturgies. Catholic exegetes and other theologians should work together, under the eye of the church's teaching authority, taking all suitable means to study and expound the Bible, so that ministers of the word may be able, as widely as possible, to nourish God's people with the food of the scriptures, and so produce the effect of enlightening minds, strengthening wills and firing hearts with the love of God.[1] The synod encourages those members of the church who are engaged in biblical studies to renew their efforts and forge ahead, thinking with the church, in the work they have so happily undertaken.[2]

24. Sacred theology takes its stand on the written word of God, together with tradition, as its permanent foundation. By this word it is made firm and strong, and constantly renews its youth, as it investigates, by the light of faith, all the truth that is stored up in the mystery of Christ. The holy scriptures contain the word of God and, since they are

inspired, really *are* the word of God; therefore the study of the "sacred page" ought to be the very soul of theology.[3] The same word of scripture is the source of healthy nourishment and holy vitality for the ministry of the word—pastoral preaching, catechetics and all forms of christian instruction, among which the liturgical homily should have the highest place.

25. For these reasons it is essential that all the clergy, especially priests of Christ and others who as deacons or catechists are officially engaged in the ministry of the word, should stick to their spiritual reading and to serious bible study. It must not happen that any of them becomes "an empty preacher of the word of God outwardly, who is not a listener inwardly,"[4] when it is their duty to be sharing the abundant riches of the divine word with the faithful entrusted to their care, especially in the sacred liturgy. Likewise the synod strongly and specially urges all the faithful, particularly religious, to learn by frequent study of the scriptures "the surpassing worth of knowing Jesus Christ" (Ph 3, 8), for "ignorance of the scriptures is ignorance of Christ."[5] They should approach the sacred text with joy—when it is expounded during the liturgy, or in private spiritual reading, or by means of bible courses or other aids to study, such as, with the approval and involvement of the church's pastors, we are glad to see are widely available today. Let it never be forgotten that prayer should accompany the reading of holy scripture, so that it becomes a dialogue between God and the human reader; for "when we pray, we talk to him: when we read the divine word, we listen to him."[6]

It is the duty of bishops, "who have the apostolic ministry of teaching,"[7] duly to instruct the faithful entrusted to them in the right use of the biblical books, especially of the new Testament and above all of the gospels. Biblical translations should be published, equipped with such explanatory notes as are necessary and really meet all needs, so that members of the church can become familiar with holy scripture to their profit and without danger of misunderstanding, and can become soaked in its spirit.

Further, editions of holy scripture should be prepared with suitable notes which are adapted to the conditions of non-Christians also, and both pastors and Christians of whatever walk of life should take all means to distribute these imaginatively.

26. Thus, in conclusion, by reading and study of the sacred books "may the word of the Lord speed on and triumph" (2 Th 3, 1), and the treasure of revelation, entrusted to the church, fill human hearts ever more and more. Just as faithful and frequent reception of the eucharistic mystery makes the church's life grow, so we may hope that its spiritual life will receive a new impulse from increased devotion to the word of God, which "abides for ever" (Is 40, 8; 1 Pt 1, 23–25).

—November 18, 1965

Dogmatic Constitution on the Church
(Lumen Gentium)

The Constitution on the Church was the most anticipated document of the Second Vatican Council. The bishops all knew that the last ecumenical council, Vatican I (1869–1870), had proposed a comprehensive statement on the nature of the church. But because of the outbreak of the Franco-Prussian War, Vatican I was forced to adjourn before it had completed the text. It promulgated only the chapters on papal primacy and papal infallibility. Thus as the Second Vatican Council began, many saw it as taking up Vatican I's unfinished agenda. It would treat not just the pope, but all bishops, priests, and the whole community of believers.

Vatican I's definitions of primacy and infallibility belong to the longer story of the Catholic Church's response to modernity. Following the Protestant Reformation of the sixteenth century, Roman Catholicism was increasingly driven into a posture of defensiveness vis-à-vis the intellectual and political currents of Europe. Whether it was the Reformers' critique of papacy, priesthood, and the sacramental structures of the church, or the Enlightenment's challenge to church authority and tradition, or the French Revolution's outright assault on clergy and church property—in wave after wave, the church was under attack. This confrontation between the church and "the modern world" culminated in the battle for the Papal States, that large swath of central Italy ruled by the pope until the late 1800s, territory that was finally seized from the church by the forces of Italian unification.

Popes of the nineteenth and early twentieth centuries responded to these enormous shifts largely by condemning all things modern. They were encouraged by a movement known as Ultramontanism, which was led by European Catholics who looked "over the mountains" of northern Italy to the pope in Rome. In the person of the pope, these Catholics found a bulwark of truth and stability in a rapidly changing world. The ecclesiology (study of the church) taught in seminaries at the time was conditioned by this fortress mentality. What was stressed in these textbooks was precisely what was under attack: the primacy of the pope, the hierarchical structures of the church, the authority of the magisterium. So much attention was devoted to the juridical and institutional structures of the church that its spiritual and communal dimensions were almost forgotten.

When the bishops at Vatican II took up the document on the church in the closing days of the first session, they found a draft shaped largely by the defensive language and questionable presuppositions of these seminary textbooks. The draft had been prepared by Cardinal Alfredo Ottaviani's Doctrinal Commission. And to its credit, the commission had incorporated several of the positive developments in ecclesiology then current: Pope Pius XII's notion of the church as "the mystical body of Christ," a generous treatment of the laity, an initial opening to ecumenism. Still, the draft remained largely reactive, dominated by concerns about the hierarchical structures of the church. A number of speakers criticized the text, with the sharpest critique coming from Bishop Josef De Smedt of Bruges, who denounced the draft for its triumphalism (a romantic vision of the church that overlooks its flaws), clericalism *(seeing the church as a pyramid with the pope on top and laypeople on the bottom), and juridicalism (an obsession with rules and the letter of the law). By the end of a week of debate, it was clear the document would have to be significantly revised.*

In fact, a whole new draft was produced. In the months between the first and second council sessions, the decision was made to work off an alternative text composed by the Belgian theologian Gérard Philips. Thus when the bishops reconvened in the fall of 1963, they had before them a text that was simpler in structure but more expansive in its biblical imagery and patristic references. Gone were the technical chapters on the magisterium and "authority and obedience" in the church. Sections on ecumenism, church-state relations, and evangelization were moved to other documents. The original draft's eleven chapters had been replaced by four: (1) the mystery of the church; (2) the hierarchy, especially bishops; (3) the people of God, especially laity; and (4) the call to holiness. Before the new draft was circulated, however, Cardinal Léon-Joseph Suenens of Belgium had made the recommendation that the third chapter be divided. Some of the material should be used to form a new chapter on "the people of God," which would then be followed by chapters on the hierarchy and the laity. This proposal, ultimately approved by the council, symbolized a significant ecclesiological transformation: The church is not first and foremost the clergy; it is first of all the whole people of God.

Given the profound impact this notion of the "people of God" would have on the broader Catholic consciousness following the council, we might be surprised at how little debate it generated at the council. The same could be said for other equally transformative ideas in this new text: the primacy of baptism, the importance of the laity, and the universal call to holiness. Indeed, no previous church document had ever given the laity such an extensive and positive treatment. The laity are called leaven in the world, active participants in the priestly, prophetic, and kingly work of Christ. They share a common dignity with the ordained and are to collaborate with the clergy in serving the community. They are even duty bound to express their opinion on matters that concern the good of the church.

None of this was particularly controversial at the time. Instead, it was the chapter on the hierarchy that generated the most heated debates. Three issues, in particular, were contested: (1) the call to reinstate the diaconate as a permanent office in the church, and open it to married men; (2) the recognition of the sacramental nature of episcopal consecration; and (3) the affirmation of episcopal collegiality. The first issue was controversial not only because it suggested a fairly significant reconfiguration of ministerial structures but also because it broached a topic never adequately addressed by the council: clerical celibacy. The second and third issues, though distinct theologically, often ran together in the council debates. Both had to do with the relationship of local bishops to the bishop of Rome, the pope.

This relationship proved to be one of the most contentious issues of the whole council. It was not only debated theoretically but also experienced practically as Pope Paul VI increasingly interjected his authority as pope into the debates and proceedings of the council assembly. "Collegiality" refers to the idea that the pope shares authority with his brother bishops. Those in support of the idea argued that collegiality belonged to the ancient tradition of the church. All of the bishops—together with and under the pope—constitute a "college," which exercises supreme authority in the governance of the church. Those opposed to the notion argued that collegiality was a novelty. They saw it contradicting Vatican I's definition of papal primacy. If the pope shared authority, they claimed, his authority would be weakened. He would lose his ability to lead the universal church effectively.

During a week and a half of debate, speeches seemed evenly divided. In order to find a way forward, the moderators decided to hold a series of "orienting votes" on the issue of collegiality (and on the permanent diaconate). After some delay the straw vote was taken on October 30, 1963. The results showed overwhelming support for the principle of collegiality (and strong support for deacons). While a minority of conservative bishops continued to question the binding nature of this straw vote, it marked a breakthrough for the document.

By the third session of the council, a third version of the Constitution on the Church was ready. The text was divided into eight chapters, which would ultimately structure the final document: (1) the mystery of the church, (2) the people of God, (3) the hierarchy, (4) the laity, (5) the universal call to holiness, (6) religious life, (7) the eschatological nature of the pilgrim church, and (8) Mary. (The last two chapters offer a biblical and balanced treatment of the communion of saints, fulfilling John XXIII's wish that the council address this topic.) The chapters were in turn divided into fifty-five smaller sections that were voted on individually. The individual sections—and the document as a whole—passed with large majorities. Part of this result was thanks to Pope Paul VI, who sought as broad a consensus as possible and so did all he could to address the concerns of the conservative minority. This effort often took the form of recommending minor changes that nuanced the document's treatment of controversial issues. To this end, a footnote explaining the meaning of collegiality (Nota Explicativa Praevia) was inserted after the final text had been approved—a move that frustrated many of the council participants for its obvious attempt to placate the minority.

The Dogmatic Constitution on the Church (Lumen Gentium) was approved and solemnly promulgated on November 21, 1964— receiving only five negative votes. From the initial drafting to the final document, the history of Lumen Gentium marks a profound *ecclesiological evolution: from tight Neo-Scholastic definitions to expansive biblical images, from papal maximalism to episcopal collegiality, from reflexive clericalism to affirmation of the laity, from the triumphalism of eternal structures to the dynamism of a pilgrim people on the way to the reign of God.*

Lumen Gentium
Dogmatic Constitution on the Church
TRANSLATED BY CLARENCE GALLAGHER, S.J.

Chapter 1. The mystery of the church

1. Since Christ is the light of the nations, this holy synod, called together in the holy Spirit, strongly desires to enlighten all people with his brightness, which gleams over the face of the church, by preaching the gospel to every creature (see Mk 16, 15). And since the church is in Christ as a sacrament or instrumental sign of intimate union with God and of the unity of all humanity, the council, continuing the teaching of previous councils, intends to declare with greater clarity to the faithful and the entire human race the nature of the church and its universal mission. This duty of the church is made more urgent by the particular circumstances of our day so that all people, more closely bound together as they are by social, technological and cultural bonds, may also attain full unity in Christ.

2. The eternal Father, by a completely free and mysterious

design of his wisdom, created the whole world. He decided to raise human beings to share in the divine life; and when in Adam they fell, he did not abandon them but provided them always with the means of salvation, having in view Christ the Redeemer, "who is the image of the invisible God, the first-born of all creation" (Col 1, 15). All those chosen before time began the Father "foreknew and predestined to be conformed to the image of his Son, in order that he might be the first-born among many brethren" (Rm 8, 29). All those who believe in Christ he decided to call together within the holy church, which right from the beginning of the world had been foreshadowed, wonderfully prepared in the history of the people of Israel and in the ancient covenant,[1] established in these last times and made manifest through the outpouring of the Spirit; it will reach its glorious completion at the end of time. Then, as we read in the holy fathers, all the just from Adam onward, "from Abel the just right to the last of the elect,"[2] will be gathered together in the universal church in the Father's presence.

3. The Son came, therefore, sent by the Father, who chose us in him before the foundation of the world and predestined our adoption as sons and daughters, because he had decided to restore all things in him (see Eph 1, 4–5 and 10). Consequently, Christ, to carry out the will of the Father, has inaugurated the kingdom of heaven on earth and has revealed the mystery to us, and through his obedience has brought about the redemption. The church, as the kingdom of Christ already present in mystery, grows visibly in the world through the power of God. This beginning and this growth were symbolized by the blood and water that issued from the open side of Jesus crucified (see Jn 19, 34), and were predicted by the words of the Lord concerning his death on the cross: "And I, when I am lifted up from the earth, will

draw all people to myself" (Jn 12, 32 Greek text). As often as the sacrifice of the cross, by which "Christ our paschal lamb has been sacrificed" (1 Cor 5, 7), is celebrated on the altar, there is effected the work of our redemption. At the same time, through the sacrament of the eucharistic bread, there is represented and produced the unity of the faithful, who make up one body in Christ (see 1 Cor 10, 17). All people are called to this union with Christ, who is the light of the world; from him we come, through him we live and towards him we direct our lives.

4. When the task that the Father had entrusted to the Son on earth had been completed (see Jn 17, 4), on the day of Pentecost the holy Spirit was sent to sanctify the church continually so that believers would have through Christ access to the Father in one Spirit (see Eph 2, 18). This is the Spirit of life or the fountain of water bubbling up for eternal life (see Jn 4, 14; 7, 38–39), through whom the Father restores life to human beings who were dead through sin, until he raises up their mortal bodies in Christ (see Rm 8, 10–11). The Spirit dwells in the church and in the hearts of the faithful as in a temple (see 1 Cor 3, 16; 6, 19), and he prays in them and bears witness to their adoption as children (see Gal 4, 6; Rm 8, 15–16 and 26). He leads the church into all truth (see Jn 16, 13), and he makes it one in fellowship and ministry, instructing and directing it through a diversity of gifts both hierarchical and charismatic, and he adorns it with his fruits (see Eph 4, 11–12; 1 Cor 12, 4; Gal 5, 22). Through the power of the gospel he rejuvenates the church, continually renewing it and leading it to perfect union with its spouse.[3] For the Spirit and the bride say to the lord Jesus: Come! (see Ap 22, 17). In this way the universal church appears as "a people made one by the unity of the Father and the Son and the holy Spirit."[4]

5. The mystery of the holy church is clearly visible in its foun-

dation. For the lord Jesus inaugurated the church when he preached the happy news of the coming of the kingdom of God that had been promised in the scriptures for centuries: "The time is fulfilled and the kingdom of God is at hand" (Mk 1, 15; see Mt 4, 17). And this kingdom shines forth for humanity in the words, works and presence of Christ. The word of the Lord is compared to seed sown in a field (see Mk 4, 14): those who hear this word with faith and belong to the little flock of Christ (see Lk 12, 32) have accepted the kingdom itself; the seed then through its own power germinates and grows until the harvest time (see Mk 4, 26–29). The miracles of Jesus provide further evidence that the kingdom has come on earth: "If it is by the finger of God that I cast out demons, then the kingdom of God has come upon you" (Lk 11, 20; see Mt 12, 28). Above all, however, the kingdom is made manifest in the very person of Christ, Son of God and Son of man, who came "to serve and to give his life as a ransom for many" (Mk 10, 45).

Then when Christ, having undergone the death of the cross for humanity rose from the dead, he appeared as lord and Christ and priest set up forever (see Ac 2, 36; Heb 5, 6; 7, 17–21), and poured on his disciples the Spirit that had been promised by the Father (Ac 2, 33). When, therefore, the church, equipped with the gifts of its founder and faithfully keeping his precepts of love, humility and penance, receives the mission of announcing the kingdom of Christ and of God and of inaugurating it among all peoples, it has formed the seed and the beginning of the kingdom on earth. Meanwhile as it gradually grows, it aspires after the completion of the kingdom, and hopes and desires with all its strength to be joined with its king in glory.

6. As in the old Testament the revelation of the kingdom is often proposed figuratively, so also now the inner nature

of the church is revealed to us through a variety of images. These have been taken from the life of a shepherd, from agriculture, from the construction of buildings, and even from the family and betrothal; all of which are prepared in the books of the prophets. So the church is the *sheepfold*, whose single necessary door is Christ (see Jn 10, 1–10). It is also the flock, of which God himself foretold that he would be the shepherd (see Is 40, 11; Ez 34, 11 ff.), and whose sheep, even though governed by human shepherds, are continuously led and nourished by Christ himself, the good shepherd and prince of shepherds (see Jn 10, 11; 1 Pt 5, 4), who laid down his life for the sheep (see Jn 10, 11–15).

The church is the *estate* or field of God (see 1 Cor 3, 9). In this field the ancient olive grows whose holy root was constituted by the patriarchs, and in which was and will be effected the reconciliation of Jews and gentiles (see Rm 11, 13–16). The church has been planted by the heavenly vinedresser as a chosen vineyard (see Mt 21, 33–43 and parallels; Is 5, 1 ff.). Christ is the true vine who gives life and fruitfulness to us the branches; through the church we abide in him and without him we can do nothing (see Jn 15, 1–5).

More often the church is called God's *building* (see 1 Cor 3, 9). The Lord compared himself to the stone which the builders rejected but which was made the corner-stone (see Mt 21, 42 and parallels; Ac 4, 11; 1 Pt 2, 7; Ps 117, 22). On this foundation the church is built by the apostles (see 1 Cor 3, 11), and from this it receives cohesion and stability. This building is called various names: God's household (see 1 Tm 3, 15), in which his *family* lives, the dwelling-place of God in the Spirit (see 1 Eph 2, 19–22), "God's dwelling with human beings" (Ap 21, 3), and above all the church is the holy *temple* which is praised by the fathers of the church when they find it represented in sanctuaries made of stone, and in the liturgy it is rightly likened to the holy city, the new Jerusalem.[5] For in it we are built up as living stones here on earth (see 1 Pt 2, 5). John contemplates this holy city coming down out of heaven from God at the renewal of the world, "prepared as a bride adorned for her husband" (Ap 21, 1 f.).

Moreover the church, "which is the Jerusalem above" and is called "our mother" (Gal 4, 26; see Ap 12, 17), is described as the immaculate *spouse* of the immaculate lamb (see Ap 19, 7; 21, 2 and 9; 22, 17), whom Christ "loved . . . and for whom he delivered himself up that he might make her holy" (Eph 5, 25–26). He has bound the church to himself by an indissoluble covenant and continuously "nourishes and cherishes" it (Eph 5, 29), wanting it cleansed and joined to himself and subject to himself in love and fidelity (see Eph 5, 24); which finally he has enriched with heavenly goods for ever, so that we may understand the love of God and of Christ towards us which surpasses all knowledge (see Eph 3, 19). While, however, here on earth the church is on a pilgrimage from the Lord (see 2 Cor 5, 6), it is like an exile who seeks and savours the things that are above, where Christ is seated at the right hand of God, where the life of the church is hidden with Christ in God until it appears in glory with its spouse (see Col 3, 1–4). 7. The Son of God, in the human nature he had united to himself, overcame death by his own death and resurrection and in this way redeemed humanity and made it into a new creation (see Gal 6, 15; 2 Cor 5, 17). And by the communication of his Spirit he constituted his sisters and brothers, gathered from all nations, as his own mystical body.

In this body the life of Christ is communicated to believers, who by means of the sacraments in a mysterious but real way are united to Christ who suffered and has been glorified.[6] By baptism we are made into the likeness of Christ: "For by one Spirit we were all baptised into one body" (1 Cor

12, 13). Through this sacred rite the union with the death and resurrection of Christ is both symbolized and effected: "We were buried with him by baptism into death," but if "we have been united with him in a death like his, we shall certainly be united with him in a resurrection like his" (Rm 6, 4–5). When we really participate in the body of the Lord through the breaking of the eucharistic bread, we are raised up to communion with him and among ourselves. "Because there is one bread, we who are many are one body, for we all partake of the one bread" (1 Cor 10, 17). In this way all of us are made members of this body (see 1 Cor 12, 27), "individually members one of another" (Rm 12, 5).

Just as all the members of the human body, although they are many, nevertheless make up one body, in the same way the faithful are one in Christ (see 1 Cor 12, 12). In the structure of the body of Christ, too, there is a diversity of members and of functions. There is one Spirit who distributes his various gifts for the good of the church according to his own riches and the needs of the ministries (see 1 Cor 12, 1–11). Among these gifts the grace of the apostles holds first place, and the Spirit himself makes even the charismatics subject to their authority (see 1 Cor 14). The same Spirit makes the body one through himself and by his power and by the inner cohesion of the members, and he produces and urges charity among the faithful. Therefore, if one member suffers in any way, all the members suffer along with that member, and if one member is honoured then all the members rejoice together (see 1 Cor 12, 26).

Christ is the head of this body. He is the image of the invisible God and in him all things have their foundation. He is before all things and all things are held together in him. He is the head of the body which is the church. He is the beginning, the first-born from the dead, so that he may hold the primacy among all things (see Col 1, 15–18). By the might of his power he dominates all creatures both in heaven and on earth, and through his supereminent perfection and activity he fills the whole body with the riches of his glory (see Eph 1, 18–23).[7]

All the members must be made into his likeness until Christ is formed in them (see Gal 4, 19). Therefore we are taken up into the mysteries of his life, we are made like to him, we die and are raised to life with him, until we reign together with him (see Ph 3, 21; 2 Tm 2, 11; Eph 2, 6; Col 2, 12; etc.). While we are still making our pilgrimage on earth and follow in his footsteps in tribulation and persecution, we are associated with his sufferings as a body with its head, sharing his suffering that we may also share his glory (see Rm 8, 17).

From him "the whole body, nourished and knit together through its joints and ligaments, grows with a growth that is from God" (Col 2, 19). He perpetually distributes the gift of ministries in his body which is the church; and with these gifts, through his power, we provide each other with helps towards salvation, so that doing the truth in love, we grow up in all things into him who is our head (see Eph 4, 11–16 Greek text).

In order that we may be continually renewed in him (see Eph 4, 23), he gave us a share in his Spirit, who is one and the same in head and members. This Spirit gives life, unity and movement to the whole body, so that the fathers of the church could compare his task to that which is exercised by the life-principle, the soul, in the human body.[8]

Christ loves the church as his bride and has made himself the model of the husband loving his wife as his own body (see Eph 5, 25–28); and the church is submissive to its head (ibid. 23–24). "For in him the whole fullness of deity dwells bodily" (Col 2, 9); and he fills with his divine gifts the church, which is his body and his fullness (see Eph 1, 22–23), so that it may aspire towards and arrive at the whole fullness of God (see Eph 3, 19).

8. Christ, the one mediator, set up his holy church here on earth as a visible structure, a community of faith, hope and love; and he sustains it unceasingly[9] and through it he pours out grace and truth on everyone. This society, however, equipped with hierarchial structures, and the mystical body of Christ, a visible assembly and a spiritual community, an earthly church and a church enriched with heavenly gifts, must not be considered as two things, but as forming one complex reality comprising a human and a divine element.[10] It is therefore by no mean analogy that it is likened to the mystery of the incarnate Word. For just as the assumed nature serves the divine Word as a living instrument of salvation inseparably joined with him, in a similar way the social structure of the church serves the Spirit of Christ who vivifies the church towards the growth of the body (see Eph 4, 16).[11]

This is the unique church of Christ, which in the creed we profess to be one, holy, catholic and apostolic.[12] After his resurrection our Saviour gave the church to Peter to feed (see Jn 21, 17), and to him and the other apostles he committed the church to be governed and spread (see Mt 28, 18 ff.); and he set it up for all time as the pillar and foundation of the truth (1 Tm 3, 15). This church, set up and organised in this world as a society, subsists in the catholic church, governed by the successor of Peter and the bishops in communion with him,[13] although outside its structure many elements of sanctification and of truth are to be found which, as proper gifts to the church of Christ, impel towards catholic unity.

Just as Christ carried out the work of redemption in poverty and persecution, so the church is called to follow along the same way in order that it may communicate to humanity the fruits of salvation. "Though he was in the form of God," Christ Jesus "emptied himself, taking the form of a servant" (Ph 2, 6–7); and for our sake "though he was rich, he became poor" (2 Cor 8, 9). So also the church, though it needs human resources to carry out its mission, is not set up to seek earthly glory, but to spread humility and self-denial also through its own example. Christ was sent by the Father "to preach good news to the poor . . . to restore the broken-hearted" (Lk 4, 18), "to seek and to save the lost" (Lk 19, 10): in the same way the church surrounds with love all who are afflicted with human infirmity, indeed in the poor and the suffering it recognises the face of its poor and suffering founder, it endeavours to relieve their need and in them it strives to serve Christ. While Christ "holy, blameless, unstained" (Heb 7, 26) knew no sin (see 2 Cor 5, 21), and came only to expiate the sins of the people (see Heb 2, 17), the church, containing sinners in its own bosom, is at one and the same time holy and always in need of purification and it pursues unceasingly penance and renewal.

The church "proceeds on its pilgrim way amidst the persecutions of the world and the consolations of God,"[14] proclaiming the cross and the death of the Lord until he comes (see 1 Cor 11, 26). But it draws strength from the power of the risen Lord, to overcome with patience and charity its afflictions and difficulties, from within and from without; and reveals his mystery faithfully in the world—albeit amid shadows—until in the end it will be made manifest in the fullness of light.

Chapter 2. The people of God

9. At all times and in every nation whoever fears God and does what is right is acceptable to God (see Ac 10, 35). It has pleased God, however, to sanctify and save men and women not individually and without regard for what binds them together, but to set them up as a people who would acknowledge him in truth and serve him in holiness. Therefore he chose the people of Israel as a people for himself, and he made a covenant with them and instructed them step by step, making himself and his intention known to them in their history and sanctifying them for himself. All this took place, however, as a preparation and a figure of that new and perfect covenant which was to be struck with Christ, and of the more complete revelation that was to be made through the Word of God himself made flesh. "Behold, the days are coming, says the Lord, when I will make a new covenant with the house of Israel and the house of Juda . . . I will put my law within them, and I will write it in their hearts; and I will be their God, and they shall be my people . . . for they shall all know me, from the least of them to the greatest, says the Lord" (Jer 31, 31–34). This is the new covenant that Christ instituted, the new testament in his blood (see 1 Cor 11, 25), calling together from Jews and gentiles a people which would be bound together in unity not according to the flesh but in the Spirit, and which would be the new people of God. Believers in Christ have been born again not from a perishable but from an imperishable seed through the word of the living God (see 1 Pt 1, 23), not of flesh but of water and the holy Spirit (see Jn 3, 5–6); and they have been finally set up as "a chosen race, a royal priesthood, a holy nation, God's own people . . . once no people but now God's people" (1 Pt 2, 9–10).

This messianic people has for its head Christ, "who was

put to death for our trespasses and raised for our justification" (Rm 4, 25); and now having gained possession of that name which is above all names, he reigns gloriously in heaven. This people has been given the dignity and the freedom of sons and daughters of God, in whose hearts the holy Spirit dwells as in a temple. For its law it has the new commandment of love just as Christ has loved us (see Jn 13, 34). And finally for its goal it has the kingdom of God: inaugurated on earth by God himself and to be further extended until, at the end of time, it will be brought to its completion by the Lord when Christ will appear, our life (see Col 3, 4), and "creation itself will be set free from its bondage to decay and obtain the glorious liberty of the children of God" (Rm 8, 21). Consequently this messianic people, although in fact it does not include everybody, and more than once may appear as a tiny flock, nevertheless it constitutes for the whole human race a most firm seed of unity, hope and salvation. It has been set up by Christ as a communion of life, love and truth; by him too it is taken up as the instrument of salvation for all, and sent as a mission to the whole world as the light of the world and the salt of the earth (see Mt 5, 13–16).

Just as Israel according to the flesh, who wandered in the desert, is already called the church of God (see 2 Es 13, 1; Nm 20, 4; Dt 23, 1 ff.), so the new Israel, while journeying through this present world in search of a permanent city which lies in the future (see Heb 13, 14), is also called the church of Christ (see Mt 16, 18), since he has acquired it by his own blood (see Ac 20, 28), has filled it with his Spirit and set it up with means suitable for visible and social unity. God has called together the assembly of those who look to Jesus in faith as the author of salvation and the principle of unity and peace, and he has constituted the church that it may be for one and all the visible sacrament of this saving unity.[1] In order to spread to all regions, it enters into the history of humanity while at the same time transcending both times and the boundaries of nations. As the church journeys through temptations and tribulations, it is strengthened by the power of the grace of God that was promised it by the Lord, so that it does not fall away from perfect fidelity through the weakness of the flesh, but remains the worthy spouse of its Lord, and so that, under the action of the holy Spirit, it does not cease from renewing itself until, through the cross, it arrives at the light which knows no setting.

10. Christ the Lord, the high priest chosen from among human beings (see Heb 5, 1–5), has made the new people "a kingdom, priests to his God and Father" (Ap 1, 6; see 5, 9–10). For by the regeneration and anointing of the holy Spirit the baptised are consecrated as a spiritual dwelling and a holy priesthood, so that through all the activity of christian living they may offer spiritual sacrifices, and declare the powers of him who called them out of darkness into his marvellous light (see 1 Pt 2, 4–10). Therefore, all the disciples of Christ, persevering in prayer and praising God together (see Ac 2, 42–47), are to present themselves as a living sacrifice, holy and pleasing to God (see Rm 12, 1), witnessing to Christ throughout the world, and explaining to those who ask the hope they possess of eternal life (see 1 Pt 3, 15).

The common priesthood of the faithful and the ministerial or hierarchical priesthood, though they differ in essence and not simply in degree, are nevertheless interrelated: each in its own particular way shares in the one priesthood of Christ.[2] On the one hand, the ministerial priest, through the sacred power that he enjoys, forms and governs the priestly people; in the person of Christ he brings about the eucharistic sacrifice and offers this to God in the name of the whole people. The faithful, on the other hand, by virtue of their royal priesthood, join in the offering of the eucharist,[3] and they exercise their priesthood in receiving the sacraments, in prayer and thanksgiving, through the witness of a holy life, by self-denial and by active charity.

11. The sacred character and the organic structure of the priestly community are brought into effect by means of the sacraments and the virtues. Incorporated into the church through baptism, the faithful are by the baptismal character given a place in the worship of the christian religion; and reborn as children of God, they have an obligation to profess publicly the faith they have received from God through the church.[4] With the sacrament of confirmation they are bound more completely to the church; they are enriched by a special strength of the holy Spirit, and in this way are under more pressing obligation to spread the faith by word and deed as true witnesses of Christ.[5] When they take part in the eucharistic sacrifice, the source and the culmination of all christian life, they offer to God the divine victim and themselves along with him;[6] and so both in this offering and in holy communion all fulfil their own part in the liturgical action, not in a confused manner but one in one way and one in another. Indeed, refreshed as they are by the body of Christ in the sacred gathering, they show forth in a concrete way the unity of the people of God, which in this most noble sacrament is both suitably symbolized and wonderfully brought about.

Those who approach the sacrament of penance, through the mercy of God obtain pardon for any offence committed against him, and at the same time are reconciled with the church which they wounded by their sin and which strives for their conversion through charity, example and prayers. Through the sacred anointing of the sick and the prayer of the priests, the whole church commends the sick to the suffering and glorified Lord that he might relieve them and restore them to health (see Jas 5, 14–16), and indeed it exhorts them freely to associate themselves with the passion and death of Christ (see Rm 8, 17; Col 1, 24; 2 Tm 2, 11–12; 1 Pt 4, 13), and so contribute to the good of the people of God. Those of the faithful who are marked by holy order are appointed in the name of Christ to feed the church with the word and the grace of God. Finally, by virtue of the sacrament of matrimony, by which they both share in and symbolize the unity and the fertile love between Christ and the church (see Eph 5, 32), married Christians help each other towards holiness in their married life and in the acceptance and education of children. And so in their state and way of life, they have their own particular gift within the people of God.[7] From this married life comes the family, in which are born new citizens of human society who, by the grace of the holy Spirit, are raised by baptism to the status of heirs of God to carry on his people through the centuries. This is, as it were, the domestic church in which the parents must be for their children, by word and by example, the first preachers of the faith, encouraging each in her or his vocation and paying special attention to a sacred vocation.

Protected by such great and wonderful means of salvation, all the faithful of every state and condition are called by the Lord, each in their own way, to that perfect holiness whereby the Father is perfect.

12. The holy people of God has a share, too, in the prophetic role of Christ, when it renders him a living witness, especially through a life of faith and charity, and when it offers to God a sacrifice of praise, the tribute of lips that honour his name (see Heb 13, 15). The universal body of the faithful who have received the anointing of the holy one (see 1 Jn 2, 20 and 27), cannot be mistaken in belief. It displays this particular quality

through a supernatural sense of the faith in the whole people when "from the bishops to the last of the faithful laity,"[8] it expresses the consent of all in matters of faith and morals. Through this sense of faith which is aroused and sustained by the Spirit of truth, the people of God, under the guidance of the sacred magisterium to which it is faithfully obedient, receives no longer the words of human beings but truly the word of God (see 1 Th 2, 13); it adheres indefectibly to "the faith which was once for all delivered to the saints" (Ju 3); it penetrates more deeply into that same faith through right judgment and applies it more fully to life.

Moreover, the same holy Spirit not only sanctifies and guides the people of God by means of the sacraments and the ministries and adorns it with virtues, he also apportions his gifts "to each individually as he wills" (1 Cor 12, 11), and among the faithful of every rank he distributes special graces by which he renders them fit and ready to undertake the various tasks and offices which help the renewal and the building up of the church, according to that word: "To each is given the manifestation of the Spirit for the common good" (1 Cor 12, 7). These charismatic gifts, whether they be very outstanding or simpler and more widely diffused, are to be accepted with thanksgiving and consolation, since they are primarily suited to and useful for the needs of the church. Extraordinary gifts should not, however, be sought rashly nor should the fruits of apostolic works be presumptuously expected from them. The judgment about their genuineness and their ordered use belongs to those who preside over the church, to whom it belongs especially not to extinguish the Spirit but to test everything and hold fast to what is good (see 1 Th 5, 12 and 19–21).

13. All human beings are called to the new people of God. Therefore this people, while remaining one and unique, is to

be spread throughout the whole world and through every age to fulfil the design of the will of God, who in the beginning made one human nature and decreed that his children who had been scattered should at last be gathered together into one (see Jn 11, 52). For this God sent his Son, whom he appointed heir of all things (see Heb 1, 2), that he might be master, king and priest of all, head of the new and universal people of the children of God. For this finally God sent the Spirit of his Son, the Lord and giver of life, who is for the whole church and for each and every one of the faithful the principle of union and of unity in the teaching of the apostles, in communion, in the breaking of bread and in prayers (see Ac 2, 42 Greek text).

For all the nations of the earth, therefore, there is one people of God since it draws its citizens from all nations, but the kingdom is not earthly in character, but heavenly. For all the faithful scattered throughout the world are in communion with the rest in the holy Spirit, and so "the person who lives in Rome knows that Indians are his members."[9] Since, however, the reign of Christ is not of this world (see Jn 18, 36), therefore the church as the people of God, in bringing this kingdom into being, takes nothing away from the temporal well-being of any people. On the contrary, it takes up and encourages the riches, resources and customs of peoples in so far as they are good; and in taking them up it purifies, strengthens and raises them up. The church is mindful of the fact that it must gather in along with that king to whom the nations have been given for an inheritance (see Ps 2, 8), and into whose city they bring gifts and offerings (see Ps 71 [72], 10; Is 60, 4–7; Ap 21, 24). This note of universality, which adorns the people of God, is a gift of the Lord himself by which the catholic church effectively and continually tries to recapitulate the whole of humanity, with all its riches, under Christ the head in the unity of his Spirit.[10] By virtue of this catholicity, the individual parts bring their own gifts to the other parts and to the whole church, in such a way that the whole and individual parts grow greater through the mutual communication of all and their united efforts towards fullness in unity. It follows from this that the people of God is not only gathered together from diverse peoples, but within itself is made up out of the union of different orders. In fact among its members there is a diversity either because of duties, since some are engaged in the sacred ministry for the good of their sisters and brothers, or because of the conditions and arrangements of their lives, since many in the religious state, striving towards holiness by a stricter path, are a stimulus to their fellow Christians by their example. So also, within the ecclesiastical communion, there are lawfully particular churches which enjoy their own proper traditions, while the primacy of the see of Peter remains intact, which presides over the universal communion of charity[11] and safeguards legitimate differences while taking care that what is particular not only does no harm to unity but rather is conducive to it. Finally, between the different parts of the church there are bonds of intimate communion with regard to spiritual riches, apostolic workers and temporal assistance. For the members of the people of God are called to share their goods, and the words of the apostle are applicable also to the individual churches: "As each has received a gift, employ it for one another, as good stewards of God's varied grace" (1 Pt 4, 10).

Therefore to this catholic unity of the people of God, which prefigures and promotes universal peace, all are called, and they belong to it or are ordered to it in various ways, whether they be catholic faithful or others who believe in Christ or finally all people everywhere who by the grace of God are called to salvation.

14. The holy synod turns its attention first of all to the catholic faithful. Relying on sacred scripture and tradition, it teaches that this pilgrim church is necessary for salvation. For Christ alone, who is present to us in his body, which is the church, is the mediator and the way of salvation; and he, while expressly insisting on the need for faith and baptism (see Mk 16, 16; Jn 3, 5), at the same time confirmed the need for the church, into which people enter through baptism as through a door. Therefore, those cannot be saved who refuse to enter the church or to remain in it, if they are aware that the catholic church was founded by God through Jesus Christ as a necessity for salvation.

They are fully incorporated into the society of the church who, possessing the Spirit of Christ, accept its whole structure and all the means of salvation that have been established within it, and within its visible framework are united with Christ, who governs it through the supreme pontiff and the bishops, by the bonds of profession of faith, the sacraments, ecclesiastical government and communion. That person is not saved, however, even though he might be incorporated into the church, who does not persevere in charity; he does indeed remain in the bosom of the church "bodily," but not "in his heart."[12] But all sons and daughters of the church must be mindful that they owe their distinguished status not to their own merits but to Christ's special grace; and if they fail to respond to this grace in thought, word and deed, not only will they not be saved, they will be judged more severely.[13]

Catechumens who, under the impulse of the holy Spirit, expressly ask to be incorporated into the church are by this very desire joined to it, and mother church already embraces them with love and care as its own.

15. For several reasons the church recognises that it is joined to those who, though baptised and so honoured with the christian name, do not profess the faith in its entirety or do not preserve the unity of communion under the successor of Peter.[14] For there are many who hold the sacred scripture in honour as the norm for believing and living, and display a sincere religious zeal. They lovingly believe in God the almighty Father and in Christ, the Son of God and Saviour.[15] They are marked by baptism, by which they are joined to Christ; and indeed there are other sacraments that they recognise and accept in their own churches or ecclesiastical communities. Several among them possess the episcopate, celebrate the sacred eucharist and foster devotion to the virgin mother of God.[16] In addition to this, there is a communion in prayers and other spiritual benefits. Indeed there is a true bond in the holy Spirit, since it is he who is also at work in these persons with his sanctifying power through gifts and graces, and he has strengthened some of them to the point of the shedding of their blood. In this way the Spirit arouses in all of Christ's disciples desire and action so that all may be peacefully united, in the way established by Christ, in one flock under one shepherd.[17] To obtain this the church does not cease to pray, to hope and to work, and it exhorts its children to purification and renewal so that the sign of Christ may shine more clearly over the face of the church.

16. Finally, those who have not yet accepted the gospel are related to the people of God in various ways.[18] In the first place, there is that people to whom the testaments and promises were given and from whom Christ was born according to the flesh (see Rm 9, 4–5), a people according to their election most dear because of their ancestors: for God never goes

back on his gifts and his calling (see Rm 11, 28–29). But the plan of salvation also embraces those who acknowledge the Creator, and among these the Moslems are first; they profess to hold the faith of Abraham and along with us they worship the one merciful God who will judge humanity on the last day. There are others who search for the unknown God in shadows and images; God is not far from people of this kind since he gives to all life and breath and everything (see Ac 17, 25–28), and the Saviour wishes all to be saved (see 1 Tm 2, 4). There are those who without any fault do not know anything about Christ or his church, yet who search for God with a sincere heart and, under the influence of grace, try to put into effect the will of God as known to them through the dictate of conscience: these too can obtain eternal salvation.[19] Nor does divine Providence deny the helps that are necessary for salvation to those who, through no fault of their own, have not yet attained the express recognition of God yet who strive, not without divine grace, to lead an upright life. For whatever goodness and truth is found in them is considered by the church as a preparation for the gospel[20] and bestowed by him who enlightens everyone that they may in the end have life. More often, however, deceived by the evil one, people have gone astray in their thinking and exchanged the truth about God for a lie and served the creature rather than the Creator (see Rm 1, 21 and 25), or living and dying in this world without God they are exposed to the extreme of despair. For this reason, to promote the glory of God and the salvation of all these people, the church is mindful of the Lord's command when he said: "Preach the gospel to the whole creation" (Mk 16, 15), and so it sedulously encourages the missions.

17. Just as the Son was sent by the Father, he too sent the apostles (see Jn 20, 21), saying: "Go therefore and make dis-

ciples of all nations, baptising them in the name of the Father and of the Son and of the holy Spirit, teaching them to observe all that I have commanded you; and look, I am with you always, to the close of the age" (Mt 28, 19–20). This solemn command of Christ, to announce the saving truth, the church has received from the apostles to fulfil right to the ends of the earth (see Ac 1, 8). Therefore it makes its own the words of the apostle: "Woe . . . to me if I do not preach the gospel" (1 Cor 9, 16), and so it continues without ceasing to send out preachers until new churches are fully established and they themselves continue the work of evangelising. For it is compelled by the holy Spirit to cooperate in bringing to actual completion the design of God, who constituted Christ as the principle of salvation for the whole world. By preaching the gospel the church draws its hearers to faith and the profession of faith; it disposes them for baptism, draws them out of servitude to error and incorporates them into Christ, so that through charity they may grow to fullness in him. The result of its activity is that the good seed that is found in people's hearts and minds, or in their particular rites and cultures, is not only saved from destruction but is made whole, raised up and brought to completion to the glory of God, the confusion of the devil and the happiness of humanity. The duty of spreading the faith is incumbent on every disciple of Christ in so far as he or she can.[21] However, though anyone can baptise those who believe, it is the task of the priest to complete the building up of the body through the eucharistic sacrifice, fulfilling the words of God spoken through the prophets: "From the rising of the sun to its setting my name is great among the nations, and in every place sacrifice is offered to my name, and a pure offering" (Ml 1, 11).[22] So the church prays and works at the same time so that the fullness of the whole world may move into the people of God, the body of the Lord and the temple of the holy Spirit, and that all honour and glory be rendered in Christ, the head of all, to the Creator and Father of all.

Chapter 3. The hierarchical constitution of the church and in particular the episcopate

18. For the nourishment and continual growth of the people of God, Christ the lord instituted a variety of ministries which are directed towards the good of the whole body. Ministers who are endowed with sacred power are at the service of their brothers and sisters, so that all who belong to the people of God, and therefore enjoy real christian dignity, by cooperating with each other freely and in an orderly manner in pursuit of the same goal, may attain salvation.

This holy synod, following in the footsteps of the first Vatican council, teaches along with that council and declares that Jesus Christ, the eternal shepherd, built the holy church by sending apostles just as he himself had been sent by the Father (see Jn 20, 21); it was his will that their successors, namely the bishops, should be shepherds in his church right to the end of the world. So that the episcopate itself, however, should be one and undivided, he placed blessed Peter over the rest of the apostles, and in him he instituted a perpetual and visible principle and foundation for the unity of faith and communion.[1] This doctrine of the institution, the perpetuity, the force and the nature of the sacred primacy of the Roman pontiff and of his infallible magisterium, the synod once more sets out to be firmly believed by all the faithful. Continuing this same undertaking, it has decided to profess before all and to declare the teaching concerning the bishops, the successors of the apostles, who along with the successors of Peter, the vicar of Christ[7] and visible head of the whole church, govern the house of the living God.

19. The lord Jesus, after he had poured forth prayers to the Father, called to himself those whom he wished, and he appointed twelve to be with him whom he would send out to preach the kingdom of God (see Mk 3, 13–19; Mt 10, 1–42). These apostles (see Lk 6, 13) he established as a college or a permanent group over which he placed Peter, chosen from among them (see Jn 21, 15–17). He sent them first to the children of Israel and then to all nations (see Rm 1, 16), so that, sharing in his power, they might make all peoples his disciples, sanctify and govern them (see Mt 28, 16–20; Mk 16, 15; Lk 24, 45–48; Jn 20, 21–23), and in this way spread the church and by their ministry, under the guidance of the Lord, they would nourish it all days to the end of the world (see Mt 28, 20). In this mission they were fully confirmed on the day of Pentecost (see Ac 2, 1–36), in accordance with the Lord's promise: "You shall receive power when the holy Spirit has come upon you; and you shall be my witnesses in Jerusalem and in all Judaea and in Samaria and to the end of the earth" (Ac 1, 8). By preaching the gospel everywhere (see Mk 16, 20), which was accepted by their hearers through the work of the holy Spirit, the apostles gather together the universal church which the Lord founded on the apostles and built over their leader, blessed Peter, while the chief corner-stone is Christ Jesus himself (see Ap 21, 14; Mt 16, 18; Eph 2, 20).[3]

20. This divine mission, entrusted by Christ to the apostles, will continue to the end of the world (see Mt 28, 20), since the gospel which is to be handed on by them is for all time the principle of all life for the church. For this reason the apostles, within this hierarchically structured society, took care to arrange for the appointment of successors. For not

only did they have various helpers in the ministry,[4] but also, so that the mission entrusted to them might go on after their death, they handed on to their immediate fellow-workers, as a kind of testament, the task of perfecting and consolidating the work that had been begun by themselves,[5] commending to their attention the whole flock in which the holy Spirit had placed them to nourish the church of God (see Ac 20, 28). They therefore appointed such men and then ordered them that when they died other approved men would take on their ministry.[6] Among the different ministries that have been carried on in the church right from the earliest times, as tradition witnesses, the chief place belongs to the task of those who, having been appointed to the episcopate through a succession that goes back to the beginning,[7] possess the shoots that have grown from the apostolic seed.[8] So, as St. Irenaeus testifies, through those who were appointed bishops by the apostles and through their successors right down to us, the apostolic tradition is manifested[9] and safeguarded[10] all over the world.

The bishops, therefore, have undertaken along with their fellow-workers, the priests and deacons, the service of the community,[11] presiding in the place of God over the flock,[12] whose shepherds they are, as teachers of doctrine, priests of sacred worship and ministers of government.[13] Just as the office that was given individually by the Lord to Peter, the first of the apostles, is permanent and meant to be handed on to his successors, so also the office of the apostles of nourishing the church is a permanent one that is to be carried out without interruption by the sacred order of bishops.[14] Therefore the synod teaches that by divine institution the bishops have succeeded to the place of the apostles[15] as shepherds of the church: and the one who hears them hears Christ but whoever rejects them rejects Christ and him who send Christ (see Lk 10, 16).[16]

21. In the bishops, therefore, assisted by the priests, there is present in the midst of believers the lord Jesus Christ, the supreme high priest. Seated at the right hand of God the Father, he is not absent from the community of his pontiffs,[17] but primarily through their distinguished ministry he preaches the word of God to all nations and administers without ceasing the sacraments of faith to believers; by their fatherly office (see 1 Cor 4, 15) he incorporates new members into his body by a regeneration from above; and finally it is by their wisdom and prudence that he directs and governs the people of the new testament in its pilgrimage towards eternal happiness. These shepherds, chosen to nourish the Lord's flock, are the ministers of Christ and the dispensers of the mysteries of God (see 1 Cor 4, 1), to whom has been entrusted the bearing of witness to the gospel of God's grace (see Rm 15, 16; Ac 20, 24), and the service of the Spirit and of justice in glory (see 2 Cor 3, 8–9).

For the fulfilment of such great duties, the apostles were enriched by Christ with a special outpouring of the holy Spirit who came down upon them (see Ac 1, 8; 2, 4; Jn 20, 22–23), and they by the imposition of hands handed on the spiritual gift to their helpers (see 1 Tm 4, 14; 2 Tm 1, 6–7); and this has been handed down to us in episcopal consecration.[18] The synod teaches that the fullness of the sacrament of order is conferred by episcopal consecration; and this, both by the liturgical custom of the church and the voice of the holy fathers, is undoubtedly called the supreme priesthood, the highest point of the ministry.[19] Episcopal consecration, along with the office of sanctifying, confers also the offices of teaching and governing; these however by their very nature can only be exercised in hierarchical communion with the head of the college and its members. For it is clear from tradition—a tradition expressed especially in the liturgical rites and in the usage of the church both eastern and western—that through the imposition of hands and the words of consecration the grace of the holy Spirit is so conferred,[20] and the sacred character so imprinted,[21] that bishops in an eminent and visible way take on the functions of Christ the teacher, shepherd and pontiff and act in his person.[22] It is the task of bishops, by means of the sacrament of order, to admit those who have been newly elected into the episcopal order.

22. Just as, by the Lord's decree, St. Peter and the other apostles constitute one apostolic college, so in a similar way the Roman pontiff, Peter's successor, and the bishops, successors of the apostles, are joined together. The collegial character and nature of the episcopal order is shown in the very ancient practice by which bishops appointed throughout the world maintained communion with each other and with the bishop of Rome in the bonds of unity, charity and peace;[23] this is also shown in the councils that were convened,[24] by which all the most important matters were settled in common[25] and a decision carefully arrived at through the counsel of many.[26] This is clearly confirmed by the ecumenical councils that have been celebrated down the centuries. The same thing is already to be seen in that custom, going back to antiquity, of calling together several bishops to take part in raising a newly-elected person to the ministry of the high priesthood. A person is constituted a member of the episcopal body by virtue of sacramental consecration and by hierarchical communion with the head and members of the college.

However, the college or body of bishops does not have

authority unless this is understood in terms of union with the Roman pontiff, Peter's successor, as its head, and the power of this primacy is maintained intact over all, whether they be shepherds or faithful. For the Roman pontiff has, by virtue of his office as vicar of Christ and shepherd of the whole church, full, supreme and universal power over the church, a power he is always able to exercise freely. However, the order of bishops, which succeeds the college of apostles in teaching authority and pastoral government, and indeed in which the apostolic body continues to exist without interruption, is also the subject of supreme and full power over the universal church, provided it remains united with its head, the Roman pontiff, and never without its head;[27] and this power can be exercised only with the consent of the Roman pontiff. The Lord made Simon alone the rock and key-bearer of the church (see Mt 16, 18–19), and constituted him shepherd of his whole flock (see Jn 21, 15 ff.). It is clear, however, that this office of binding and loosing which was given to Peter (see Mt 16, 19), was also granted to the college of apostles in union with its head (see Mt 18, 18; 28, 16–20).[28] This college, in so far as it is composed of many, expresses the variety and the universality of the people of God, but in so far as it is gathered under one head it expresses the unity of the flock of Christ. In it the bishops, while faithfully maintaining the primacy and pre-eminence of its head, exercise their own proper power for the good of their faithful and indeed of the whole church, while the holy Spirit is constantly strengthening its organic structure and its harmony. The supreme power over the whole church which this college enjoys is solemnly exercised in an ecumenical council. There is never an ecumenical council which is not confirmed as such or at least accepted as such by the successor of Peter. It is the prerogative of the Roman pontiff to convoke these councils, to preside over them and to confirm them.[29] The same collegial power can be exercised by the bishops throughout the world in conjunction with the pope, provided that the head of the college calls them to collegial action or at least approves of, or willingly accepts, the united action of the dispersed bishops in such a way that the result is a truly collegial act.

23. Collegial unity can be seen also in the mutual relations of individual bishops with particular churches and with the universal church. The Roman pontiff, as the successor of Peter, is the perpetual and visible principle and foundation of unity both of the bishops and of the multitude of the faithful.[30] The individual bishops, however, are the visible principle and foundation of unity in their own particular churches,[31] formed in the likeness of the universal church; in and from these particular churches there exists the one unique catholic church.[32] For this reason individual bishops represent their own church, while all of them together with the pope represent the whole church in the bond of peace, love and unity. The individual bishops who are placed over particular churches exercise their pastoral government over the portion of the people of God that has been entrusted to their care, but not over other churches nor over the universal church. But as members of the episcopal college and legitimate successors of the apostles, the individual bishops, through the institution and command of Christ, are bound to be concerned about the whole church,[33] and even though this solicitude is not exercised by any act of jurisdiction, nevertheless it makes a very great contribution to the well-being of the universal church. All the bishops, in fact, have a duty to promote and defend the unity of faith and discipline common to the whole church, to instruct the faithful in the love of the whole mystical body of Christ—especially those members who are poor and suffering and those who are un-

dergoing persecution for righteousness' sake (see Mt 5, 10) and finally, to promote every activity that is common to the whole church, especially that which is aimed at the spread of the faith and the rising of the light of full truth over all people. For the rest, it is a holy reality that by governing well their own church as a portion of the universal church, they themselves make an effective contribution to the whole mystical body, which is also a body of churches.[34]

The charge of announcing the gospel throughout the world belongs to the body of shepherds, to all of whom in common Christ gave the command and imposed a common office, as Pope Celestine once commended to the fathers of the council of Ephesus.[35] Therefore the individual bishops, as far as the carrying out of their own particular task allows, are bound to collaborate among themselves and along with the successor of Peter, to whom the exalted task of spreading the christian name has been entrusted in a special way.[36] With all their strength, therefore, they ought to supply the missions not only with labourers for the harvest, but also with the spiritual and material helps both directly by themselves and also by arousing the ardent cooperation of the faithful. Finally, in the universal communion of charity, let the bishops willingly offer paternal aid to other churches, especially to neighbouring churches and to those that are in greater need, following the venerable example of antiquity. By divine providence it has come about that various churches, founded in various places by the apostles and by their successors, have in the course of time become joined together into several groups, organically united, which, while maintaining the unity of faith and the unique divine constitution of the universal church, enjoy their own discipline, their own liturgical usage and their own theological and spiritual patrimony. Among these there are some, especially the ancient patriarchal churches, like matrices of the faith, which have given birth to others as daughters; and right down to our own times they are more closely bound to these churches by the bond of charity in sacramental life and in mutual respect for rights and duties.[37] This variety of local churches, in harmony among themselves, demonstrates with greater clarity the catholicity of the undivided church. In a similar way episcopal conferences can today make a manifold and fruitful contribution to the concrete application of the spirit of collegiality.

24. The bishops, as successors of the apostles, receive from the Lord, to whom all power in heaven and on earth has been given, the mission to teach all nations and to preach the gospel to every creature, so that all may gain salvation through faith, baptism and the keeping of the commandments (see Mt 28, 18, 20; Mk 16, 15–16; Ac 26, 17 f.). To carry out this mission Christ the lord promised the apostles the holy Spirit and on the day of Pentecost he sent him from heaven, that by his strength they might be witnesses to him to the ends of the earth before nations and peoples and kings (see Ac 1, 8; 2, 1 ff.; 9, 15). This office which the Lord entrusted to the shepherds of his people is a true service, and in holy scripture it is significantly called "diaconia" or ministry (see Ac 1, 17 and 25; 21, 19; Rm 11, 13; 1 Tm 1, 12).

The canonical mission of bishops can come into being by means of lawful customs which have not been revoked by the supreme and universal power of the church, or by means of laws made by that same authority or recognised by it, or directly by the successor of Peter himself; and if the latter opposes the appointment or refuses apostolic communion, the bishop cannot be admitted to office.[38]

25. Among the principal tasks of bishops the preaching of

the gospel is pre-eminent.[39] For the bishops are the heralds of
the faith who bring new disciples to Christ. They are the authentic teachers, that is, teachers endowed with the authority of Christ, who preach to the people entrusted to them
the faith to be believed and put into practice; they illustrate
this faith in the light of the holy Spirit, drawing out of the
treasury of revelation things new and old (see Mt 13, 52),
they make it bear fruit and they vigilantly ward off errors
that are threatening their flock (see 2 Tm 4, 1–4). The bishops, when they are teaching in communion with the Roman
pontiff, are to be respected by all as witnesses to the divine
and catholic truth; and the faithful ought to concur with
their bishop's judgment concerning faith and morals which
he delivers in the name of Christ, and they are to adhere to
this with a religious assent of the mind. The religious assent
of will and intellect is to be given in a special way to the authentic teaching authority of the Roman pontiff even when
he is not speaking *ex cathedra;* in such a way, that is, that his
supreme teaching authority is respectfully acknowledged,
and sincere adherence given to decisions he has delivered,
in accordance with his manifest mind and will which is communicated chiefly by the nature of the documents, by the
frequent repetition of the same doctrine or by the style of
verbal expression.

Although individual bishops do not enjoy the prerogative
of infallibility, nevertheless, even though dispersed throughout the world, but maintaining the bond of communion
among themselves and with the successor of Peter, when in
teaching authentically matters concerning faith and morals
they agree about a judgment as one that has to be defini-
tively held, they infallibly proclaim the teaching of Christ.[40]
This takes place even more clearly when they are gathered

together in an ecumenical council and are the teachers and judges of faith and morals for the whole church. Their definitions must be adhered to with the obedience of faith.[41]

This infallibility, however, with which the divine Redeemer willed his church to be endowed in defining doctrine concerning faith or morals, extends just as far as the deposit of divine revelation that is to be guarded as sacred and faithfully expounded. The Roman pontiff, head of the college of bishops, by virtue of his office, enjoys this infallibility when, as supreme shepherd and teacher of all Christ's faithful, who confirms his brethren in the faith (see Lk 22, 32), he proclaims in a definitive act a doctrine on faith or morals.[42] Therefore his definitions are rightly said to be irreformable of themselves, and not from the consent of the church, for they are delivered with the assistance of the holy Spirit which was promised to him in blessed Peter; and therefore they have no need of approval from others nor do they admit any appeal to any other judgment. For then the Roman pontiff is not delivering a judgment as a private person, but as the supreme teacher of the universal church, in whom the church's own charism of infallibility individually exists, he expounds or defends a doctrine of the catholic faith.[43] The infallibility promised to the church exists also in the body of bishops when, along with the successor of Peter, it exercises the supreme teaching office. The assent of the church, however, can never fail to be given to these definitions on account of the activity of the same holy Spirit, by which the whole flock of Christ is preserved in the unity of faith and makes progress.[44]

But when the Roman pontiff or the body of bishops together with him define a decision, they do so in accordance with revelation itself, by which all are obliged to abide and to which all must conform. This revelation, as written or as handed down in tradition, is transmitted in its entirety through the lawful succession of the bishops and in the first place through the care of the Roman pontiff himself; and in the light of the Spirit of truth, this revelation is sacredly preserved in the church and faithfully expounded.[45] The Roman pontiff and the bishops, in virtue of their office and the seriousness of the matter, work sedulously through the appropriate means duly to investigate this revelation and give it suitable expression.[46] However, they do not accept any new public revelation as belonging to the divine deposit of faith.[47]

26. The bishop, marked with the fullness of the sacrament of order, is "the steward of the grace of the supreme priesthood,"[48] especially in the eucharist which he offers or which he ensures is offered,[49] and by which the church continuously lives and grows. This church of Christ is truly present in all the lawful local congregations of the faithful which, united to their shepherds, are themselves called churches in the new Testament.[50] For in their own locality, these are the new people called by God in the holy Spirit and with full conviction (see 1 Th 1, 5). In these the faithful are gathered together by the preaching of the gospel of Christ and the mystery of the Lord's supper is celebrated, "so that the whole fellowship is joined together through the flesh and blood of the Lord's body."[51] In any community of the altar, under the sacred ministry of the bishop,[52] there is made manifest the symbol of that charity and "unity of the mystical body without which there can be no salvation."[53] In these communities, although frequently small and poor, or dispersed, Christ is present by whose power the one, holy catholic and apostolic church is gathered together.[54] For "participation in the body and blood of Christ has no other effect than to make us pass over into what we are consuming."[55]

Every lawful celebration of the eucharist is directed by the bishop, to whom has been entrusted the duty of presenting the worship of the christian religion to the divine majesty, and of regulating it according to the commands of the Lord and the church's laws, which are further determined for the diocese by his particular judgment.

In this way the bishops, in their prayer and work for the people, pour forth abundantly and in many ways from the fullness of the holiness of Christ. By the ministry of the word they communicate to the faithful the power of God for their salvation (see Rm 1, 16), and through the sacraments, the regular and fruitful distribution of which they direct by their authority,[56] they sanctify the faithful. They direct the conferring of baptism, through which participation in the royal priesthood of Christ is granted. They are the original ministers of confirmation, the dispensers of sacred orders and the directors of penitential discipline. With solicitude they exhort and instruct their people so that in the liturgy, especially in the holy sacrifice of the mass, they fulfil their part with faith and devotion. Finally, they have a duty to help those over whom they are placed by the example of their manner of life, keeping their behaviour free from all evil and, as far as they can with the help of God, turning evil to good, so that, together with the flock entrusted to them, they may attain eternal life.[57]

27. The bishops govern the churches entrusted to them as vicars and legates of Christ,[58] by counsel, persuasion and example and indeed also by authority and sacred power which they make use of only to build up their flock in truth and holiness, remembering that the greater must become as the younger and the leader as one who serves (see Lk 22, 26–27). This power which they exercise personally in the name of Christ is proper, ordinary and immediate, although its exercise is ultimately controlled by the supreme authority of the church and can be circumscribed within certain limits for the

good of the church or the faithful. By virtue of this power, bishops have the sacred right and duty before the Lord of making laws for their subjects, of passing judgment on them and of directing everything that concerns the ordering of worship and the apostolate. The pastoral office, that is to say the habitual and daily care of their sheep, is completely entrusted to the bishops and they are not to be considered vicars of the Roman pontiffs, because they exercise a power that is proper to themselves and most truly are said to be presidents of the peoples they govern.[59] Therefore their power is not destroyed by the supreme and universal power, but on the contrary it is affirmed, strengthened and vindicated by it,[60] since the holy Spirit unfailingly preserves the form of government established in his church by Christ the lord.

Sent by the head of the household to govern his family, the bishop must keep before his eyes the example of the good shepherd, who came not to be served but to serve (Mt 20, 28; Mk 10, 45) and to lay down his life for his sheep (see Jn 10, 11). Taken from among human beings and subject to weakness himself, the bishop can sympathise with those who are ignorant and who go astray (see Heb 5, 1–2). Let him not refuse to listen to his subjects whom he looks after as truly his daughters and sons and whom he exhorts cheerfully to cooperate with him. As one who will have to give an account to God for their souls (see Heb 13, 7), by prayer, preaching and every work of charity let him look after both them and also those who are not yet members of the one flock but whom he must consider as commended to him in the Lord. Since like the apostle Paul he is debtor to all, let him be ready to preach the gospel to all (see Rm 1, 14–15), and exhort his faithful to apostolic and missionary activity. The faithful must adhere to the bishop as the church does to Jesus Christ, and as Jesus Christ does to the Father, so that all things may agree together through unity[61] and abound to the glory of God (see 2 Cor 4, 15).

28. Christ, whom the Father sanctified and sent into the world (see Jn 10, 36), has through his apostles made their successors, the bishops, share in his consecration and his mission;[62] and these have legitimately handed on the office of their ministry in varying degrees to various subjects in the church. In this way the divinely instituted ecclesiastical ministry is exercised in different orders by those who right from ancient times are called bishops, priests and deacons.[63] Although they do not possess the highest honour of the pontificate and depend on the bishops for the exercise of their power, priests nevertheless are united with them in priestly honour,[64] and by virtue of the sacrament of order[65] they are consecrated in the image of Christ, the high and eternal priest (see Heb 5, 1–10; 7, 24; 9, 11–28), as true priests of the new testament,[66] to preach the gospel and nourish the faithful and celebrate divine worship. In their own degree of ministry they share in the office of Christ the one mediator (see 1 Tm 2, 5), and proclaim the divine word to all people. But it is above all in the eucharistic worship or synaxis that they exercise their sacred function, when, acting in the person of Christ[67] and proclaiming his mystery, they unite the prayers of the faithful to the sacrifice of their head, and in the sacrifice of the mass make present and apply, until the coming of the Lord (see 1 Cor 11, 26), the one sacrifice of the new testament, that is, the sacrifice of Christ who once and for all offers himself as an unblemished victim to the Father (see Heb 9, 11–28).[68] For the faithful who are penitent or who are sick they exercise fully the ministry of reconciliation and comfort, and they convey to God the Father the needs and prayers of the faithful (see Heb 5, 1–3). According to their share of authority they exercise the office of Christ

the shepherd and head,[69] they gather together the family of God as a fellowship inspired by the spirit of unity[70] and lead them through Christ in the Spirit to God the Father. In the midst of the flock they adore him in spirit and in truth (see Jn 4, 24). Finally, they labour in preaching and teaching (see 1 Tm 5, 17), believing what they have read and meditated in the law of the Lord, teaching what they have believed and putting into practice what they have taught.[71]

As prudent cooperators of the episcopal order[72] and its instrument and help, priests are called to the service of the people of God and constitute along with their bishop one presbyterium[73] though destined to different duties. In the individual local congregations of the faithful in a certain sense they make the bishop present and they are united with him in a spirit of trust and generosity; and in accordance with their position they undertake his duties and his concern and carry these out with daily dedication. Under the authority of the bishop, priests sanctify and govern the portion of the Lord's flock entrusted to them, in their own locality they make visible the universal church and they provide powerful help towards the building up of the whole body of Christ (see Eph 4, 12). However, attentive always to the welfare of the children of God, they are to take pains that their work contributes to the pastoral work of the whole diocese, and indeed of the whole church. Because of this sharing in the priesthood and mission, priests are to recognise the bishop as truly their father and reverently obey him. The bishop, for his part, is to consider the priests his cooperators as sons and friends, just as Christ calls his disciples no longer servants but friends (see Jn 15, 15). By reason, therefore, of order and ministry, all priests both diocesan and religious, are associated with the body of bishops and according to their grace and vocation they work for the good of the whole church.

In virtue of sacred ordination and the mission they have in common, all priests are bound together in a close fraternity, which should be seen spontaneously and freely in mutual help both spiritual and material, both pastoral and personal, in reunions and in the fellowship of life, work and charity.

Like fathers in Christ, they are to look after the faithful whom they have spiritually brought to birth by baptism and by their teaching (see 1 Cor 4, 15; 1 Pt 1, 23). Having become examples to the flock (see 1 Pt 5, 3), they are to preside over their local community and serve it in such a way that it may deserve to be called by that name by which the one and entire people of God is distinguished, namely the church of God (see 1 Cor 1, 2; 2 Cor 1, 1; and passim). In their daily conduct and care they are to remember to present to the faithful and to unbelievers, to Catholics and non-Catholics, the face of a ministry that is truly priestly and pastoral, and that to all people they have a duty to bear witness to truth and life; and that, as good shepherds, they are to go in search of those (see Lk 15, 4–7) who, although baptised in the catholic church, have fallen away from the practice of the sacraments or even from the faith.

Since today the human race is moving together more and more towards civil, economic and social unity, it is that much more necessary that priests by their united care and resources, under the leadership of the bishops and the supreme pontiff, wipe out every cause of division so that the whole human race may be brought into the unity of God's family.

29. At a lower degree of the hierarchy stand the deacons, on whom hands are imposed "not for the priesthood, but for the ministry."[74] For strengthened by sacramental grace, they are at the service of the people of God in the ministry

of the liturgy, the word and charity, in communion with the bishop and his presbyterium. To the extent that he has been authorised by competent authority, he is to administer baptism solemnly, to reserve and distribute the eucharist, to assist at and bless marriages in the name of the church, to take viaticum to the dying, to read sacred scripture to the faithful, to instruct and exhort the people, to preside at the worship and prayer of the faithful, to administer sacramentals, and to preside at funeral services and burials. Dedicated to duties of charity and administration, deacons should bear in mind the admonition given by blessed Polycarp: "Merciful, sedulous, and walking in accordance with the truth of the Lord, who became the servant of all."[75]

Since these tasks, which are supremely necessary for the life of the church, can only with difficulty be carried out in many regions, according to the current discipline of the Latin church, the diaconate can for the future be restored as a proper and permanent grade of the hierarchy. It is, however, the responsibility of the competent territorial conferences of bishops, which are of different kinds, to decide with the approval of the supreme pontiff himself whether and where it is opportune for such deacons to be appointed for the care of souls. With the consent of the Roman pontiff it will be possible to confer this diaconate on men of more mature age, even upon those living in the married state, and also on suitable young men for whom, however, the law of celibacy must remain in force.

Chapter 4. The laity

30. Having set forth the functions of the hierarchy, the synod gladly turns its attention to the status of those members of the faithful who are called the laity. Although everything that

was said about the people of God applies equally to the laity, religious and clerics, nevertheless there are certain points which have special reference to the laity because of their situation and their mission. Because of the special circumstances of our time, these points call for a deeper examination. The sacred pastors are well aware of how much the laity contribute to the well-being of the whole church. They know that they were not instituted by Christ to undertake by themselves alone the church's whole mission of salvation to the world; but that it is their noble task to tend the faithful in such a way, and to acknowledge their ministries and their charisms, so that all may cooperate unanimously, each in her or his own way, in the common task. For it is necessary that all of us "doing . . . the truth in love, are to grow up in every way in him who is the head, Christ, from whom the whole body, joined and knit together by every joint with which it is supplied, when each part is working properly, makes bodily growth and upbuilds itself in love" (Eph 4, 15–16).

31. Under the title of laity are here understood all Christ's faithful, except those who are in sacred orders or are members of a religious state that is recognised by the church; that is to say, the faithful who, since they have been incorporated into Christ by baptism, constitute the people of God and, in their own way made sharers in Christ's priestly, prophetic and royal office, play their own part in the mission of the whole christian people in the church and in the world.

The laity have their own special character which is secular. For, although those in sacred orders can be engaged in secular activities, even practising a secular profession, they are by reason of their particular vocation principally and professedly ordained for the sacred ministry, while religious by their state give noble and outstanding witness to the fact that the world cannot be transformed and offered to God without the spirit of the beatitudes. It is the special vocation of the laity to seek the kingdom of God by engaging in temporal affairs and ordering these in accordance with the will of God. They live in the world, that is to say, in each and all of the world's occupations and affairs, and in the ordinary circumstances of family and social life; these are the things that form the context of their life. And it is here that God calls them to work for the sanctification of the world as it were from the inside, like leaven, through carrying out their own task in the spirit of the gospel, and in this way revealing Christ to others principally through the witness of their lives, resplendent in faith, hope and charity. It is, therefore, their special task to shed light upon and order all temporal matters, in which they are closely involved, in such a way that these are always carried out and developed in Christ's way and to the praise of the Creator and Redeemer.

32. Holy church, by divine institution, is ordered and directed with wonderful variety. "As in one body we have many members, and all the members do not have the same function, so we, though many, are one body in Christ, and individually members one of another" (Rm 12, 4–5).

Therefore the chosen people of God is one: "one Lord, one faith, one baptism" (Eph 4, 5). There is the common dignity of the members from their regeneration in Christ; they share in common the grace of being heirs, the call to perfection, one salvation, one hope and one undivided charity. There is, therefore, no inequality in Christ and in the church, with regard to race or nation, social condition or sex, because "there is neither Jew nor Greek, there is neither slave nor free, there is neither male nor female; for you are all *one* in Christ Jesus" (Gal 3, 28 Greek text; see Col 3, 11).

If, therefore, in the church all do not walk along the same path, nevertheless all are called to holiness and have received an equal faith in the righteousness of God (see 2 Pt 1, 1). And if some are appointed, by the will of Christ, as teachers, dispensers of the mysteries and pastors for the others, yet there is a true equality of all with regard to the dignity and action common to all the faithful concerning the building up of the body of Christ. For the distinction which the Lord made between sacred ministers and the rest of the people of God brings with it a connection between them, since pastors and the other faithful are bound together by a common bond. The church's pastors, following the Lord's example, are to minister to each other and to the rest of the faithful, and the faithful are to cooperate gladly with the pastors and teachers. So, in their variety, all bear witness to the wonderful unity in the body of Christ: for this very diversity of graces, ministries and works gathers the children of God into one, because "all are inspired by one and the same Spirit" (1 Cor 12, 11).

The laity, therefore, just as they have by divine condescension Christ as their brother who, although lord of all, came not to be served but to serve (see Mt 20, 28), so also they have as brothers those who have been appointed to the sacred ministry and who by Christ's authority—through teaching, sanctifying and governing—so look after the family of God that the new commandment of love is fulfilled by all. Concerning which St. Augustine has this very fine statement: "When what I am for you frightens me, what I am with you consoles me. For you I am a bishop, with you I am a Christian. The former is a title of duty, the latter is one of grace. The former is a danger, the latter is a title to salvation."[1]

33. The laity, gathered together in the people of God and established in the one body of Christ under a single head, whoever they are, are called as living members to work with all the strength they have received from the goodness of the

Creator and the grace of the Redeemer for the growth of the church and its continual sanctification.

The apostolate of the laity is a sharing in the church's mission of salvation, and everyone is commissioned to this apostolate by the Lord himself through baptism and confirmation. By the sacraments, especially by the sacred eucharist, there is communicated and nourished that love for God and for people which is the soul of the entire apostolate. The laity, however, have the specific vocation to make the church present and active in those places and circumstances where only through them can it become the salt of the earth.[2] In this way every lay person, because of the gifts received, is at the same time a witness and a living instrument of the church's mission "according to the measure of Christ's gift" (Eph 4, 7).

This apostolate concerns every one of Christ's faithful, but in addition the laity can also be called in various ways to a more immediate cooperation in the apostolate of the hierarchy,[3] like those men and women who assisted the apostle Paul in the gospel, working hard in the Lord (see Ph 4, 3; Rm 16, 3 ff.). They may also be appointed by the hierarchy to carry out certain ecclesiastical offices which have a spiritual aim in view.

It is, therefore, the glorious task of all the faithful to work for the ever greater extension of the divine plan of salvation to all people everywhere and of every period. So then let every opportunity be given them to share zealously in the saving work of the church in accordance with their ability and the needs of the times.

34. Jesus Christ, the supreme and eternal priest, wants to continue his witness and service also through the laity. So he gives them life through his Spirit and unceasingly urges them on to every good and perfect work.

He associates them intimately with his life and mission and has also given them a share in his priestly office of offering spiritual worship, so that God may be glorified and human beings be saved. The laity, therefore, dedicated as they are to Christ and anointed by the holy Spirit, are wonderfully called and instructed so that ever more abundant fruits of the Spirit may be produced in them. For all their works, if done in the Spirit, become spiritual sacrifices acceptable to God through Jesus Christ: their prayers and apostolic works, their married and family life, their daily work, their mental and physical recreation, and even life's troubles if they are patiently borne (see 1 Pt 2, 5). In the eucharistic celebration these are offered with very great piety to the Father along with the offering of the body of the Lord. In this way the laity too, as worshippers carrying out their holy activity everywhere, consecrate the world itself to God.

35. Christ, the great prophet, who by the witness of his life and the power of his word, proclaimed the Father's kingdom, continues to carry out his prophetic task, until the full manifestation of his glory, not only through the hierarchy who teach in his name and by his power, but also through the laity whom he constitutes his witnesses and equips with an understanding of the faith and a grace of speech (see Ac 2, 17–18; Ap 19, 10) precisely so that the power of the gospel may shine forth in the daily life of family and society. The laity show that they are children of the promise, if strong in faith and hope they make full use of the present moment (see Eph 5, 16; Col 4, 5) and await with patience the glory that is to come (see Rm 8, 25). This hope, however, is not to be hidden in the depths of their hearts. It has also to be expressed through the structures of secular life, through their continual conversion and their struggle "against the world

rulers of the present darkness, against the spiritual hosts of wickedness" (Eph 6, 12).

Just as the sacraments of the new law, by which the life and apostolate of the faithful are nourished, foreshadow the new heaven and the new earth (see Ap 21, 1), so the laity become effective heralds of faith in the things we hope for (see Heb 11, 1) if they firmly combine the profession of faith to a life of faith. This evangelisation—that is, the message of Christ proclaimed by word and the witness of life—takes on a special quality and a particular effectiveness from the fact that it is carried out in ordinary worldly situations.

In this task, that state of life is of great value which is sanctified by a special sacrament, namely married and family life. Here, where the christian religion pervades the whole structure of life and increasingly transforms it day by day, there is both the practice and the outstanding school of the lay apostolate. Here husband and wife have their particular vocation to be witnesses to each other and to their children of their faith and love of Christ. The christian family proclaims aloud both the virtues of the kingdom of God here and now and the hope of a blessed life to come. In this way, by example and by witness, it accuses the world of sin and enlightens those who seek the truth.

Therefore, even when occupied with temporal cares, the laity can and must perform the valuable task of evangelising the world. Some lay people, when there is a shortage of sacred ministers or when these are impeded by a persecuting government, supply some of the sacred offices in so far as they can; a greater number are engaged totally in apostolic work. It is, however, the duty of all to work together for the extension and growth of the kingdom of Christ on earth. Consequently the laity have a duty to try diligently to deepen their knowledge of revealed truth and earnestly to pray to God for the gift of wisdom.

36. Christ, obedient unto death and for this reason exalted by the Father (see Ph 2, 8–9), has now entered into the glory of his kingdom. To him all things are made subject until he subjects himself and all created things to the Father, so that God may be all in all (see 1 Cor 15, 27–28). This power he has communicated to his disciples so that they too may be constituted in a royal freedom, and through self-denial and a holy life may overcome the reign of sin within themselves (see Rom 6, 12), and indeed that serving Christ also in others, they may through humility and patience lead their sisters and brothers to the King to serve whom is to reign. For the Lord desires that the faithful laity also should extend his kingdom, the kingdom of "truth and life, the kingdom of holiness and grace, the kingdom of justice, love and peace"; [4] in which creation itself will be set free from its bondage to decay and obtain the glorious liberty of the children of God (see Rm 8, 21). It is certainly a great promise that is given to the disciples, a great commandment: "All things are yours; and you are Christ's; and Christ is God's" (1 Cor 3, 23).

The faithful have, therefore, a duty to acknowledge the inner nature and the value of the whole of creation and its orientation to the praise of God; they must help each other towards greater holiness of life even through their secular activity, so that the world may be penetrated with the spirit of Christ and more effectively attain its purpose in justice, in love and in peace. In the universal fulfilment of this task the laity have the principal role. So through their competence in secular disciplines and their activity, interiorly raised up by the grace of Christ, they are to work effectively so that the goods of creation, in accordance with the plan of the Creator and the light of his word, through human work, technical skill and civilisation, may be developed for the good of everyone without exception, that there be a more equitable distribution of these goods and that they may lead in their own way to universal progress in human and christian freedom. In this way, through the members of the church, Christ will increasingly enlighten the whole of human society with his saving light.

Moreover, the laity should even band together to improve those secular structures and conditions which constitute an inducement to sin, in such a way that all these things are brought into harmony with the rules of justice and become an encouragement to the practice of virtue rather than an obstacle. By acting in this way they will imbue human work and culture with a moral value. In this way too the field of the world is better prepared for the seed of the divine word, and the doors of the church are opened more widely for the entry into the world of the proclamation of peace.

Because of the economy of salvation itself, the faithful must learn carefully to distinguish between the rights and duties which are theirs in so far as they are members of the church, and those which belong to them as members of human society. They are to labour carefully that both of these work harmoniously together, remembering that temporal matters are to be guided by their christian conscience, since there is no human activity—not even in temporal matters—that can be withdrawn from God's dominion. However, it is particularly important in this our time that this distinction and at the same time this harmony should be very clearly evident in the conduct of the faithful, so that the mission of the church may be more able to meet the particular needs of the modern world. And just as one must recognise that the earthly city, rightly taken up with secular cares, is governed by its own principles, so also must that misguided teaching be rightly rejected which claims to construct society without any reference to religion, and which attacks and undermines the religious freedom of the citizens.[5]

37. The laity have the right, as do all the faithful, to receive abundant help from the sacred pastors out of the spiritual goods of the church, especially the help provided by the word of God and the sacraments;[6] and they should make known to these pastors their needs and desires with that freedom and confidence which befits children of God and sisters and brothers in Christ. In accordance with the knowledge, competence or authority that they possess, they have the right and indeed sometimes the duty to make known their opinion on matters which concern the good of the church.[7] If possible this should be done through the institutions set up for this purpose by the church; and it should always be done with respect for the truth, with courage and with prudence, and in a spirit of reverence and love towards those who by reason of their sacred office represent Christ. The laity, like all the faithful, should be prompt to accept in a spirit of christian obedience those decisions that the sacred pastors make as teachers and governors of the church and as representatives of Christ; in doing so they follow the example of Christ, who by his obedience unto death opened to all people the blessed way of the freedom of the children of God. Nor should they neglect to commend to God in their prayers those who have been placed over them, that they may do their work with joy and not sadly (see Heb 15, 17), they are after all keeping watch as persons who will have to give an account for our souls.

However, the sacred pastors are to acknowledge and promote the dignity and the responsibility of the laity in the church; they should willingly make use of their prudent counsel; they should confidently entrust to them offices in the service of the church and leave them freedom and space to act. Indeed they should encourage them to take up work on their own initiative. With a father's love they should pay careful attention in Christ to the projects, the requests and the desires put forward by the laity.[8] The pastors must, moreover, carefully acknowledge that just freedom which belongs to all in the earthly city.

From this familiar relationship between laity and pastors many advantages for the church can be expected: for in this way there is strengthened in the laity a sense of their own responsibility, their enthusiasm is fired, and the strengths of the laity are more easily joined to the work of the pastors. The pastors, for their part, helped by the experience of the laity, are able to make clearer and more suitable decisions both in spiritual and in temporal affairs. In this way the whole church, strengthened by all its members, is able more effectively to carry out its mission for the life of the world.

38. Every individual lay person ought to be a witness to the world of the resurrection and life of the lord Jesus and a sign of the living God. All of them together, and each for her or his own part, should nourish the world with the fruits of the Spirit (see Gal 5, 22), and spread throughout the world that spirit which is the life of the poor, the meek and the peacemakers, whom the Lord proclaimed blessed in the gospel (see Mt 5, 3–9). In a word, "Christians should be in the world what the soul is in the body."[9]

Chapter 5. The universal call to holiness in the church

39. The church, whose mystery is being set forth by this synod, is held to be indefectibly holy as a matter of faith. For Christ, the Son of God, who with the Father and the Spirit "alone is holy,"[1] loved the church as his bride and delivered

himself up for it that he might sanctify it (see Eph 5, 25–26), and he joined it to himself as his body and bestowed on it the gift of the holy Spirit to the glory of God. For this reason everyone in the church is called to holiness, whether he belongs to the hierarchy or is cared for by the hierarchy, according to the saying of the apostle: "This is the will of God, your sanctification" (1 Th 4, 3; see Eph 1, 4). This holiness of the church is shown continuously, and it should be shown, in those fruits of grace which the Spirit produces in the faithful; it is expressed in many different ways in the lives of those individuals who in their manner of life tend towards the perfection of charity and in so doing are a source of edification for others. In a particularly appropriate way it can be seen in the practice of those counsels which are customarily called evangelical. Through the inspiration of the holy Spirit the practice of the counsels has been undertaken by many Christians, either privately or in some condition or state authorised by the church, and provides in the world, as it should, an outstanding witness and example of this holiness.

40. The lord Jesus, the divine master and model of all perfection, preached holiness of life, which he himself both initiates and perfects, to each and every one of his disciples no matter what their condition of life: "You, therefore, must be perfect, as your heavenly father is perfect" (Mt 5, 4–8).[2] To all of them he sent the holy Spirit to inspire them from within to love God with all their heart, all their soul, all their mind, and with all their strength (see Mk 12, 30) and to love one another even as Christ has loved them (see Jn 13, 34; 15, 12). The followers of Christ, called by God not for their achievements but in accordance with his plan and his grace, and justified in the lord Jesus, by their baptism in faith have been truly made children of God and sharers in the divine nature, and are therefore really made holy. This holiness, therefore,

which they have received by the gifts of God, they must maintain and perfect by their way of life. They are warned by the apostle to live "as is fitting among saints" (Eph 5, 3), "as God's chosen ones, holy and beloved," to put on "compassion, kindness, lowliness, meekness and patience" (Col 3, 12); to possess the fruits of the Spirit for sanctification (see Gal 5, 22; Rom 6, 22). And since all of us commit many faults (see Jas 3, 2), we are in continuous need of the mercy of God and our daily prayer has to be: "And forgive us our trespasses" (Mt 6, 12).[3]

It is therefore evident to everyone that all the faithful, whatever their condition or rank, are called to the fullness of the christian life and the perfection of charity.[4] And this sanctity is conducive to a more human way of living even in society here on earth. To attain this perfection the faithful should exert their strength in the measure in which they have received this as Christ's gift, so that following in his footsteps and forming themselves in his likeness, obedient in all things to the Father's will, they may be wholeheartedly devoted to the glory of God and the service of their neighbour. In this way the holiness of the people of God will produce fruit in abundance, as is clearly shown in the history of the church by the lives of so many saints.

41. In the different kinds of life and its different duties, there is one holiness cultivated by all who are led by the Spirit of God; obeying the voice of the Father and worshipping God the Father in spirit and in truth, they follow Christ poor and humble in carrying his cross so that they may deserve to be sharers in his glory. All, however, according to their own gifts and duties and without hesitation, must commit themselves to that pathway of living faith which stirs up hope and works through love.

In the first place the pastors of Christ's flock, in accordance with the pattern set by the eternal high priest, must carry out their ministry with holiness and zeal, with humility and courage. Fulfilled in this way their ministry will be also for themselves an excellent means of sanctification. Called to the fullness of the priesthood, they receive a sacramental grace which enables them perfectly to fulfil their duty of pastoral love through prayer, the offering of the holy sacrifice and preaching and through everything that calls for episcopal care and service.[5] Nor need they be afraid to give their lives for their sheep and, making themselves an example for their flock (see 1 Pt 5, 3), they should lead the church, also by their own example, to a daily higher level of holiness.

Priests form the spiritual crown of the bishop;[6] and like the order or bishops they share in their grace of office through Christ the unique and eternal mediator. Through the daily performance of their office they should grow in the love of God and of their neighbour, safeguard the bond of priestly communion, abound in every spiritual good and give to all a living witness to God,[7] rivalling those priests who down through the centuries have left a glorious pattern of holiness, often in a form of service that was humble and hidden. Their praise lives on in the church. For their own people and for the whole people of God they have a duty to pray and offer sacrifice, realizing what they are doing and imitating what they are handling;[8] and far from being held back by their apostolic cares, dangers and tribulations, by these very means they should rise to greater heights of sanctity, nourishing and fostering their action from the rich source of meditation, to the delight of the whole of God's church. All priests, especially those who because of their particular title of ordination are called diocesan priests, should bear in mind how much loyal union and generous cooperation with their bishop contributes to their sanctification. In the mission and grace of the supreme priest, those persons also participate in a particular way who belong to a lower order of the ministry, in the first place deacons. Since they are servants of the mysteries of Christ and of the church,[9] they must keep themselves from all vice, be pleasing to God and be a source of all good in the sight of people (see 1 Tm 3, 8–10 and 12–13). Clerics, who have been called by the Lord and set apart for his service, should prepare themselves for the duties of the ministry under the pastors' watchful care; they are bound to keep their hearts and minds in harmony with such a glorious vocation by being assiduous in prayer, fervent in love, and with their mind intent on all that is true, just and of good repute, and doing everything for the glory and honour of God. There are in addition those chosen lay people who are called by the bishop to dedicate themselves completely to apostolic works; these persons work very fruitfully in the Lord's field.[10]

Christian married couples and parents should follow their own way, supporting one another in grace all through life with faithful love. They should imbue their children, lovingly welcomed from God, with christian truths and gospel virtues. Thus they offer to all an example of untiring and generous love, they build up the community of love, and they bear witness to and cooperate in the fruitfulness of mother church. They are a sign of and share in the love with which Christ loved his bride and gave himself to her.[11] A similar example is given, in a different way, by widows and single people, who can make a great contribution towards holiness and activity in the church. Those who engage in work, which is often toilsome, can through their labours perfect themselves, help their fellow citizens, and raise up all of society and creation itself to a better state. Indeed by their active charity, rejoicing in hope and bearing one another's burdens, they imitate Christ who worked as a carpenter and is always working with the Father for the salvation of all; by their daily work they may rise to a higher and truly apostolic holiness.

As for those also who are crushed by poverty, weakness, disease or various other hardships, or who suffer persecution for the sake of justice, they should realize that they are united in a special way with Christ in his suffering for the world's salvation. In the gospel the Lord called these people blessed, and after they "have suffered a little while, the God of all grace, who has called us to his eternal glory in Christ Jesus, will himself restore, establish and strengthen" them (1 Pt 5, 10).

All the faithful, therefore, whatever their condition of life, their duties or their circumstances, and through all of them, will grow daily in holiness if they accept all these things in faith from the hand of their heavenly Father and if they cooperate with the divine will by making manifest to all, even as they carry out their work here on earth, that love with which God has loved the world.

42. "God is love, and whoever abides in love abides in God, and God abides in him" (1 Jn 4, 16). God has poured out his love in our hearts by the holy Spirit who has been given to us (see Rm 5, 5). Therefore the first and most necessary gift is that charity by which we love God above all things and our neighbour for God's sake. However if charity is to grow in the soul like good seed and bear fruit, each individual believer must give the word of God a willing hearing and with the help of his grace do God's will, take part often in the sacraments, especially the eucharist, and in the sacred liturgy. He should apply himself constantly to prayer, self-denial, active fraternal service and the practice of all the virtues. For charity, as the bond of perfection and fullness of the law (see Col 3, 14; Rm 13, 10), directs all the means of sanctification,

gives them their form and brings them to their goal.[12] The true disciple of Christ is, therefore, characterized by his love for God and for his neighbour. Since Jesus, the Son of God, has shown his love by laying down his life for us, no one has greater love than he who lays down his life for Christ and for his sisters and brothers (see 1 Jn 3, 16; Jn 15, 13). Right from the beginning, therefore, some Christians have been called to bear this highest witness of love in the sight of all and especially of persecutors; and some Christians will always be called to do this. Through martyrdom the disciple is made like his master in willing acceptance of death for the salvation of the world and resembles him by the shedding of his blood. For this reason, therefore, martyrdom is held by the church to be the highest gift and the supreme proof of love. This is given to few, yet all must be prepared to confess Christ before people and to follow him along the ways of the cross amid the persecutions which the church never lacks.

The holiness of the church is also nourished in a special way by the manifold counsels the observance of which the Lord in the gospel commends to his disciples.[13] Outstanding among these is that precious gift of divine grace which is granted to some by the Father (see Mt 19, 11; 1 Cor 7, 7), that in the state of virginity or celibacy they may more easily devote themselves to God alone with an undivided heart (see 1 Cor 7, 32–34).[14] This perfect continence for the sake of the kingdom of heaven has always been held in particular esteem by the church as a sign and a stimulus of charity and as a singular source of spiritual fruitfulness in the world. The church reflects too on the advice of the apostle who, in urging the faithful to charity, exhorted them to have the same sentiments as Christ Jesus who "emptied himself, taking the form of a servant . . . and became obedient unto death" (Ph 2, 7–8), and for our sake "though he was rich, he became poor" (2 Cor 8, 9). The disciples must always imitate this charity and humility of Christ and bear witness to it. Therefore mother church rejoices that it has within itself many men and women who follow more closely this self-emptying of the Saviour and show it forth more clearly by undertaking poverty with the freedom of God's children and by renouncing their own will; that is to say, they make themselves subject to another person for the love of God, going beyond what is of precept in the matter of perfection so that they may resemble more closely the obedient Christ.[15]

All the faithful are, therefore, invited and bound to strive towards holiness and the perfection of their particular state of life. Consequently all must be careful to keep due control over their emotions, so as not to be held back from the pursuit of perfect charity by using this world's goods and being attached to riches in a way that is against the spirit of evangelical poverty; as the apostle warns us: "Those who deal with the world must not be attached to it, for the form of this world is passing away" (see 1 Cor 7, 31 Greek text).[16]

Chapter 6. Religious

43. The evangelical counsels of chastity consecrated to God, poverty and obedience constitute a divine gift which the church has received from its Lord and maintains always with the help of his grace. For they have their foundation in the words and example of the Lord and are recommended by the apostles and fathers, by the doctors of the church and its pastors. The authority of the church, under the guidance of the holy Spirit, has taken on the task of interpreting these counsels and regulating their practice as well as establishing stable forms of living according to them. And so it has come about that, like a tree growing from a seed planted by God

and spreading out its branches in a wonderful and varied way in the field of the Lord, there has grown up a variety of forms of solitary or community life and different families which increase their resources both for the progress of their members and the good of the whole body of Christ.[1] These families provide their members with the support of greater stability in their way of life, a proven doctrine that is able to lead to perfection, a fellowship in the army of Christ, and a freedom strengthened by obedience. And so they are able to live up to their religious profession without anxiety, maintain fidelity to it and, rejoicing in spirit, make progress along the way of charity.[2]

If one considers the divine and hierarchical constitution of the church, the religious state is not an intermediate condition between the clerical and the lay. But some faithful, from each of these two conditions (clerical and lay), are called by God to enjoy a particular gift in the life of the church and, each in their own way, to help the church in its mission of salvation.[3]

44. By the vows, or other sacred bonds which of their nature resemble vows, by which some of the faithful bind themselves to these three evangelical counsels that have just been mentioned, they consecrate themselves totally to God whom they love above all things, in such a way that by a new and particular title they are committed to the service and honour of God. Certainly by baptism they have died to sin and have been dedicated to God; however, in order to draw more abundant fruit from that baptismal grace, by profession in the church of the evangelical counsels they aim to free themselves from obstacles which could hinder the fervour of love and the pursuit of perfection in divine worship, and they consecrate themselves more closely to the service of God.[4] And this consecration will be the more perfect in

as much as by firmer and more stable bonds Christ is more clearly seen to be united to his bride the church by an indissoluble bond.

By the charity to which they lead,[5] the evangelical counsels in a special way unite those who make profession of them with the church and its mystery. Consequently, the spiritual life of these persons must be dedicated to the good of the whole church. This is the source of their duty to strive, so far as they can and according to their own particular vocation, through prayer or active works, to implant and strengthen the reign of Christ in souls and to extend it everywhere. Therefore the church both protects and encourages the particular character of the different religious institutes.

The profession of the evangelical counsels is seen, therefore, as a sign which can and should effectively draw all the members of the church to carry out zealously the duties of the christian vocation. The people of God have here no abiding city; they seek rather one that is to come. Therefore the religious state, while giving its followers greater freedom from earthly cares, also makes clearer to all believers the heavenly goods that are already present in this world. It both bears witness to the new and eternal life won through Christ's redemption and foretells the resurrection that is to come and the glory of the heavenly kingdom. Moreover, the religious state imitates more closely and shows forth in the church unceasingly the form of life that the Son of God took on when he came into the world to do the will of the Father and which he proposed to the disciples who followed him. And it makes clear in a particular way how the kingdom of God surpasses all earthly things and how high are its requirements. It demonstrates to all people the incomparable grandeur of the power of Christ the king and the infinite power of his Spirit which is wonderfully active in the church.

This state, therefore, which is constituted by the profession of the evangelical counsels, although it does not belong to the hierarchical structure of the church, does, however, belong unquestionably to its life and holiness.

45. Since it is the duty of the ecclesiastical hierarchy to feed the people of God and lead them to the richest of pastures (see Ez 34, 14), it is the task of the same hierarchy wisely to regulate by law the practice of the evangelical counsels by which perfect charity towards God and one's neighbour is encouraged in a special way.[6] Moreover, in docile submission to the inspiration of the holy Spirit, the hierarchy accepts rules put forward by outstanding men and women and, once these have been further revised, gives them official approval. It also provides vigilant and protective authority to see that institutes that have been set up here and there for the building up of the body of Christ develop and flourish in accordance with the spirit of their founders.

To meet the needs of the whole of the Lord's flock more effectively, any institute of perfection and its individual members can, for the general good of the church, be exempted by the supreme pontiff from the jurisdiction of local ordinaries and subjected to him alone; this is possible by reason of his primacy over the universal church.[7] Similarly they can be left or committed to their own patriarchal authorities. The members themselves, in carrying out their duty towards the church which arises from their particular form of life, have a duty of reverence and obedience, in accordance with the canon laws, towards the bishops, because of their authority in the particular churches and because of the need for unity and harmony in apostolic work.[8]

However, not only does the church by its authority raise religious profession to the dignity of a canonical state, it also shows through its liturgical action that it is a state consecrated to God. For it is the church, through the authority committed to it by God, which receives the vows of persons making profession, by its public prayer asks of God help and grace for them, commends them to God, imparts to them its spiritual blessings and links their self-oblation to the eucharistic sacrifice.

46. Religious should try hard to ensure that through them the church more effectively shows forth the real Christ—to believers and unbelievers—in prayer on the mountain, or announcing the kingdom of God to the crowds, or healing the sick and the wounded and turning sinners to a better life, or blessing children and doing good to everybody, always, however, in obedience to the will of the Father who sent him.[9]

Finally, all should realize clearly that although profession of the evangelical counsels entails the renunciation of goods which are without doubt to be held in high esteem, nevertheless it is not an obstacle to the development of the human person but by its very nature is highly conducive to this development. For the counsels, willingly undertaken in accordance with the personal vocation of each individual, contribute not a little to the purification of the heart and to spiritual freedom; they keep ablaze continuously the fervour of charity, and, as is confirmed by the example of so many holy founders, are able to bring the Christian into greater conformity with that kind of virginal and poor life which Christ the lord chose for himself and which his virgin mother embraced. Nor should anyone think that religious by their consecration become either alienated from humanity or useless in the earthly city. For even if at times they do not assist directly their contemporaries, yet in a deeper way they hold them present in the bowels of Christ and cooperate spiritually with them, so that the building up of the earthly city may be always founded in the Lord and directed towards him, lest those who are constructing it may have laboured in vain.[10]

Therefore the holy synod confirms and praises the men and women, the brothers and sisters, who in monasteries or in schools and hospitals, or in the missions, by their persevering and humble fidelity in the above-mentioned consecration honour the spouse of Christ and provide all humankind with generous and very diverse forms of service.

47. Let all, then, who have been called to the profession of the counsels make every effort to persevere and make greater progress in the vocation to which God has called them, for the richer holiness of the church and the greater glory of the one and undivided Trinity, which in Christ and through Christ is the source and origin of all holiness.

Chapter 7. The eschatological character of the pilgrim church and its union with the heavenly church

48. The church, to which we are all called in Christ Jesus and in which through the grace of God we attain sanctity, will reach its completion only in the glory of heaven, when the time for the restoration of all things will come (see Ac 3, 21) and along with the human race the whole universe, which is intimately united to humanity and through it attains its goal, will be established perfectly in Christ (see Eph 1, 10; Col 1, 20; 2 Pt 3, 10–13).

Christ, when he was lifted up from the earth, drew all people to himself (see Jn 12, 32 Greek text); rising from the dead (see Rm 6, 9), he sent his lifegiving Spirit down on his disciples and through him he constituted his body which is the church as the universal sacrament of salvation; sitting at the right hand of the Father he is continuously at work in the world to lead people to the church and through it to join them more closely to himself; and he nourishes them with his own body and blood to make them sharers in his glorious life. The promised restoration, therefore, which we await, has already begun in Christ, is advanced through the mission of the holy Spirit and by means of the Spirit continues in the church in which, through faith, we are instructed concerning the meaning of our temporal life, while we, as we hope for the benefits that are to come, bring to its conclusion the work entrusted to us in the world by the Father and work out our salvation (see Ph 2, 12).

Already, therefore, the end of the ages has reached us (see 1 Cor 10, 11) and the renewal of the world has been irrevocably constituted and is being anticipated in this world in a real sense: for already on earth the church is adorned with true though imperfect holiness. However, until the arrival of the new heavens and the new earth in which justice dwells (see 2 Pt 3, 13), the pilgrim church in its sacraments and institutions, which belong to this age, carries the figure of this world which is passing and it dwells among creatures who groan and till now are in the pains of childbirth and await the revelation of the children of God (see Rm 8, 19–22). Joined, therefore, to Christ in the church and sealed by the holy Spirit "who is the guarantee of our inheritance" (Eph 1, 14), we are called and really are children of God (see 1 Jn 3, 1), but we have not yet appeared with Christ in glory (see Col 3, 4), in which we will be like God, for we shall see him as he is (see 1 Jn 3, 2). So, "while we are at home in the body, we are away from the Lord" (2 Cor 5, 6); and possessing the first fruits of the Spirit we groan within ourselves (see Rm 8, 23) and desire to be with Christ (see Ph 1, 23). But we are urged on by this same love to live more for him who died for us and rose again (see 2 Cor 5, 15). We try therefore in all things to please God (2 Cor 5, 9), and we put on the armour of God, so that we can stand up against the snares of the devil and resist in the evil day (see Eph 6, 11–13). Since, however, we know neither the day nor the hour, at the Lord's warning we must be constantly on the watch so that, at the end of our single course of life on earth (see Heb 9, 27), we may deserve to enter the nuptial celebration with him and be counted among the blessed (see Mt 25, 31–46), and not be ordered, like the evil and lazy servants (see Mt 25, 26), to go down into the eternal fire (see Mt 25, 41), into the exterior darkness where "there will be weeping and gnashing of teeth" (Mt 22, 13 and 25, 30). For before we reign with Christ in glory we must all appear "before the judgment seat of Christ, so that each one may receive good or evil, according to what he has done in the body" (2 Cor 5, 10); and at the end of the world "they will come forth, those who have done good to the resurrection of life, and those who have done evil to the resurrection of judgment" (Jn 5, 29; see Mt 25, 46). Considering, therefore, that "the sufferings of this time are not worth comparing with the glory that is to be revealed in us" (Rm 8, 18; see 2 Tm 2, 11–12), strong in faith we await "our blessed hope, the appearing of the glory of our great God and Saviour Jesus Christ" (Tt 2, 13), "who will change our lowly body to be like his glorious body" (Ph 3, 21); and he will come "to be glorified in his saints and to be marvelled at in all who have believed" (2 Th 1, 10).

49. Until, therefore, the Lord comes in his majesty and all his angels with him (see Mt 25, 31) and, when death has been destroyed, all things will have been made subject to him (see 1 Cor 15, 26–27), some of his disciples are pilgrims on earth, others who have departed this life are being purified, while others are in glory gazing "clearsighted on God himself as he is, three in one";[1] all of us, however, though in a different degree and manner, communicate in the same love of God and

our neighbour and sing the same hymn of glory to our God. For all who are in Christ, possessing his Spirit, are joined together into one church and united with each other in him (see Eph 4, 16). The union, therefore, of those who are still pilgrims with their sisters and brothers who have gone to sleep in the peace of Christ is by no means broken, indeed according to the perennial faith of the church it is strengthened through participation in spiritual benefits.[2] Because those who are in heaven are more intimately united with Christ, they bring greater consolidation to the holiness of the whole church, they ennoble the worship offered to God by the church here on earth and in a variety of ways contribute to the greater building-up of the church (see 1 Cor 12, 12–27).[3] For, since they have been admitted into their homeland and are present before the Lord (see 2 Cor 5, 8), through him and with him and in him they do not cease to intercede for us to the Father,[4] displaying the merits they gained on earth through the one mediator between God and humanity, Christ Jesus (see 1 Tm 2, 5), in all things serving the Lord and fulfilling in their flesh all that is lacking in the sufferings of Christ for the sake of his body which is the church (see Col 1, 24).[5] Therefore by their fraternal solicitude our weakness is helped in many ways.

50. Fully acknowledging this communion of the whole mystical body of Jesus Christ, right from the very early period of the christian religion the pilgrim church has with great respect honoured the memory of the dead[6] and, since "it is a holy and wholesome thought to pray for the dead that they may be loosed from their sins" (2 Mc 12, 46), it has also offered prayers for them. The church has, however, always believed that the apostles and martyrs of Christ, who have given the supreme witness to their faith and charity by the shedding of their blood, are more closely united to us in

Christ, has honoured them as well as the blessed virgin Mary and the holy angels with a special affection,[7] and has piously implored the help of their intercession. To these there were soon added those others who had imitated more closely the virginity and the poverty of Christ,[8] and finally there were added others whom the outstanding practice of the christian virtues[9] and the divine charismata recommended to the pious devotion and imitation of the faithful.[10]

For when we look at the lives of those men and women who have faithfully followed Christ, we are spurred on by a new reason to seek after the city that is to come (see Heb 13, 14 and 11, 10), and at the same time we are educated in the safest way by which, through the world's changing patterns, in accordance with the state and condition of each individual, we will be able to attain perfect union with Christ and holiness.[11] In the lives of those who, while sharing our humanity, are nevertheless more perfectly transformed into the image of Christ (see 2 Cor 3, 18), God makes vividly manifest to humanity his presence and his face. He himself speaks to us in them and provides us with a sign of his kingdom[12] towards which we are powerfully drawn, having before us so great a cloud of witnesses (see Heb 12, 1) and such an affirmation of the truth of the gospel. However, we cultivate the memory of the saints in heaven not by reason of their example only, but still more so that through the practice of fraternal charity the union of the whole church in the Spirit may be strengthened (see Eph 4, 1–6). For just as christian communion among pilgrims brings us closer to Christ, so our communion with the saints joins us to Christ, from whom as from the source and the head flows all grace and life of the people of God itself.[13] It is therefore most fitting that we love these friends and coheirs of Jesus Christ who are also our sisters and brothers and outstanding benefactors, that we give due thanks to God for them,[14] "that we invoke them and that we have recourse to their prayers and helpful assistance to obtain blessings from God through his Son our lord Jesus Christ, who is our sole Redeemer and Saviour."[15] For every authentic testimony of love that we offer to the saints, by its nature tends towards Christ and finds its goal in him who is "the crown of all the saints,"[16] and through him to God, who is wonderful in his saints and in them is glorified.[17]

Our union with the church in heaven is realized in a most noble way when, especially in the sacred liturgy, in which the power of the holy Spirit acts on us by means of the sacramental signs, we celebrate together in common exultation the praise of the divine majesty,[18] and all who have been redeemed in the blood of Christ from every tribe and tongue and people and nation (see Ap 5, 9) and gathered together into one church, in one canticle of praise glorify God who is one and three. When we celebrate, therefore, the eucharistic sacrifice we join very closely the worship of the heavenly church, communicating and celebrating the memory in the first place of the glorious and ever virgin Mary, and also of blessed Joseph and blessed apostles and martyrs and all the saints.[19]

51. This venerable faith of our forefathers concerning the living communion with our brothers and sisters who are in heavenly glory or still being purified after death, this holy synod accepts with great respect, and it reiterates the decrees of the sacred councils of Nicaea II,[20] Florence[21] and Trent.[22] At the same time, however, in its pastoral solicitude it exhorts all whom it concerns to do their best to get rid of or to correct any abuses, excesses or deficiencies that may have crept in here and there and to restore all to the fuller praise of Christ and of God. Let them, therefore, teach the faithful that the genuine cult of the saints does not so much consist

in a multiplicity of external acts but rather in the intensity of our active love by which, for the greater good of ourselves and of the church, we ask of the saints "example from their way of life, a sharing in their communion and help from their intercession."[23] On the other hand, let them instruct the faithful that our relationship with the saints in heaven, provided this is conceived in the fuller light of faith, in no way weakens the latreutic cult given to the Father through Christ in the Spirit, but on the contrary it greatly enriches it.[24]

For, all of us who are children of God and constitute one family in Christ (see Heb 3, 6), while we communicate with each other in mutual love and in the one praise of the most holy Trinity, are responding to the intimate vocation of the church and getting a foretaste of the liturgy of consummated glory.[25] For when Christ appears and the glorious resurrection of the dead takes place, the brightness of God will illuminate the heavenly city and the lamb will be its lamp (see Ap 21, 23). Then the whole church of the saints in the supreme happiness of love will adore God and "the lamb who was slain" (Ap 5, 12), with one voice proclaiming: "To him who sits upon the throne and to the lamb be blessing and honour and glory and might for ever and ever" (Ap 5, 13).

Chapter 8. The blessed virgin Mary, mother of God, in the mystery of Christ and the church

I. Introduction

52. God in his very great goodness and supreme wisdom wishing to bring about the redemption of the world, "when the time had fully come, sent forth his Son, born of a woman . . . so that we might receive adoption as children" (Gal 4, 4–5). He was the Son "who for us human beings and for our salvation came down from the heavens and was made

incarnate by the holy Spirit of the virgin Mary."[1] This divine mystery of salvation is revealed to us and continues in the church, which the Lord constituted as his body and in which the faithful, adhering to Christ their head and in communion with all his saints, must venerate also the memory "first of all, of the glorious Mary ever virgin, mother of Jesus Christ, our lord and God."[2]

53. For the virgin Mary, who at the message of an angel received the word of God in her heart and her body and brought forth life for the world, is recognised and honoured as the true mother of God and of the Redeemer. In view of the merits of her Son, redeemed in a more sublime manner and united to her Son by a tight and indissoluble bond, she is enriched by this supreme office and dignity of being the mother of God the Son, and therefore she is the specially loved daughter of the Father and the shrine of the holy Spirit; and by this gift of pre-eminent grace she surpasses by far all other creatures in heaven and on earth. At the same time, however, she is united in Adam's race with all human beings who are to be saved, indeed she is "clearly mother of the members [of Christ] . . . for she has cooperated with love in the birth of the faithful in the church, who are members of its head."[3] Therefore she is also acknowledged as the supereminent and uniquely special member of the church as well as its model in faith and love and its most outstanding exemplar; and the catholic church, instructed by the holy Spirit, with the affection of filial piety, treats her as its most loving mother.

54. Therefore the holy synod, while it expounds the doctrine of the church in which the divine Redeemer effects salvation, intends to illustrate carefully both the role of the blessed virgin Mary in the mystery of the incarnate Word and of the mystical body, and the duties of redeemed humanity towards

the mother of God, mother of Christ and mother of humankind, especially of the faithful, without however intending to
put forward a complete doctrine concerning Mary or of settling questions which have not yet been brought fully to light
through the work of theologians. The right remains therefore to discuss those opinions, which are freely put forward
in catholic schools, concerning her who in holy church oc-
cupies the place that is highest after Christ and nearest to us.[4]

II. The role of the blessed Virgin in the economy of salvation
55. The sacred books of the old and the new Testament and
venerable tradition show ever more clearly the role of the
mother of the Saviour in the economy of salvation and, in
a manner of speaking, put it forward for our consideration.
The books of the old Testament describe the history of salvation in which the coming of Christ into the world is slowly
prepared. These ancient documents, as they are read in the
church and understood in the light of the later and full revelation, gradually put forward ever more clearly the figure
of the woman, the mother of the Redeemer. In this light she
is already prophetically adumbrated in the promise, made
to the first parents when they had fallen into sin, concerning
the victory over the serpent (see Gn 3, 15). Similarly, she is
the virgin who will conceive and bring forth a son whose
name will be Emmanuel (see Is 7, 14; compare Mi 5, 2–3;
Mt 1, 22–23). She is outstanding among the humble and the
poor of the Lord, who await with confidence and receive salvation from him. With her, finally, the exalted daughter of
Sion, after the long wait for the fulfilment of the promise,
the ages come to fulfilment and the new economy is begun,
when the Son of God took from her his human nature so
that through the mysteries of his flesh he might free humanity from sin.

56. The Father of mercies willed that the acceptance of her, who was predestined to be the mother, should precede the incarnation so that just as a woman contributed to the coming of death so also a woman should contribute to the coming of life. This is pre-eminently true of the mother of Jesus who brought into the world life itself that renewed all things, and was enriched by God with gifts worthy of such a role. Consequently it is no surprise to find that the custom grew up among the fathers by which they called the mother of God all holy and free from all stain of sin, as though fashioned by the holy Spirit and made a new creature.[5] Enriched from the first instant of her conception by the splendour of a most singular holiness, the virgin from Nazareth is greeted by the angel of the annunciation, at God's command, as "full of grace" (see Lk 1, 28), and she replies to the messenger from heaven: "Behold I am the handmaid of the Lord; let it be to me according to your word" (Lk 1, 38). And so Mary, the daughter of Adam, by consenting to the divine word, became the mother of Jesus, and embracing the salvific will of God wholeheartedly and without being held back by any sin, dedicated herself totally as the handmaid of the Lord to the person and work of her son, putting herself under him and with him, by the grace of almighty God, at the service of the mystery of redemption. Rightly, therefore, the holy fathers maintain that Mary was not simply a passive instrument in the hands of God, but that she cooperated in the salvation of the human race with free faith and obedience. In fact, as St. Irenaeus says, "by her obedience she became the cause of salvation for herself and for the whole human race."[6] Consequently not a few of the ancient fathers in their preaching willingly join him in asserting: "The knot of Eve's disobedience was untied through the obedience of Mary; what the virgin Eve had bound up through her lack of faith,

the virgin Mary untied by her faith";[7] and taking over this comparison with Eve, they call Mary "the mother of the living"[8] and frequently assert that "death came through Eve, but life through Mary."[9]

57. This union of the mother with the Son in the work of redemption is manifest from the instant of the virginal conception of Christ right on to his death. First of all when Mary, rising up in haste to visit Elizabeth, was proclaimed blessed by her because of her faith in the salvation that had been promised, and the precursor leapt in his mother's womb (see Lk 1, 41–45); at the nativity, when the mother of God was happy to show to the shepherds and the Magi the Son, her first-born, who did not diminish her virginal integrity but consecrated it.[10] And when she presented him to the Lord in the temple with the offering of the poor, she heard Simeon foretell at one and the same time that the Son would become a sign of contradiction and that a sword would pierce the soul of his mother, so that the intimate thoughts of many hearts would be revealed (see Lk 2, 34–35). And after having lost the child Jesus and searched for him anxiously, his parents found him in the temple occupied in his Father's business, and they did not understand the words of the Son. His mother kept all these things in her heart to meditate on (see Lk 2, 41–51).

58. In the public life of Jesus his mother appears in a significant role: at first when she was moved by compassion at the wedding feast at Cana in Galilee, and by her intercession caused the first of the signs of Jesus the Messiah (see Jn 2, 1–11). During his preaching she accepted the words by which the Son exalted the kingdom above the reasons and ties of flesh and blood and called those people blessed who hear and guard the word of God (see Mk 3, 35; Lk 11, 27–28), just as she herself was doing faithfully (see Lk 2, 19 and 51). In this

way even the blessed Virgin made progress in her pilgrimage of faith, and maintained faithfully her union with the Son right up to the cross where, in keeping with the divine plan, she stood (see Jn 19, 25), suffering very profoundly with her only begotten son, and associated herself with a mother's heart with his sacrifice, lovingly consenting to the immolation of the victim that had been born from her; and finally by the same Christ Jesus, when he was dying on the cross, was given to the disciple as his mother in these words: "Woman, behold your son" (see Jn 19, 26–27).[11]

59. Since it pleased God not to make a solemn manifestation of the mystery of the human race's salvation before he had poured forth the Spirit that had been promised by Christ, before the days of Pentecost we see the apostles "with one accord devoting themselves to prayer, together with the women and Mary the mother of Jesus, and with his brethren" (Ac 1, 14), and Mary also imploring by her prayers the gift of the Spirit who had already overshadowed her at the annunciation. And finally the immaculate Virgin, preserved free from every stain of original sin,[12] when the course of her earthly life was completed, was taken up body and soul to heavenly glory,[13] and exalted by the Lord as queen of all so that she might be more fully conformed to her son, the lord of lords (see Ap 19, 16) and victor over sin and death.[14]

III. The blessed Virgin and the church

60. According to the words of the apostle, our mediator is unique: "There is one God, and there is one mediator between God and human beings, the man Christ Jesus who gave himself as a ransom for them all" (1 Tm 2, 5–6). Now the maternal role of Mary towards humanity in no way obscures or diminishes this unique mediation of Christ; rather

it shows forth its power. For every saving influence that the blessed Virgin has on humanity arises not from any natural necessity but from the divine good pleasure; it flows forth from the superabundance of Christ's merits, is founded on his mediation, completely depends on this and from this draws all its power; it in no way hinders the direct union of believers with Christ, rather it fosters this union.

61. The blessed Virgin, predestined from eternity as the mother of God along with the incarnation of the divine Word, by the design of divine providence was the loving mother of the divine Redeemer here on earth, a singularly generous companion beyond others, and the humble handmaid of the Lord. She conceived Christ, gave birth to him and nourished him, presented him to the Father in the temple, and suffered with her son as he was dying on the cross; in doing all this she cooperated in a very special way in the work of the Saviour—through her obedience, faith, hope and burning charity—towards the restoration of the supernatural life of souls. For this reason she has become our mother in the order of grace.

62. This motherhood of Mary in the economy of grace goes on without interruption from the consent she faithfully gave at the annunciation, which she upheld without wavering at the foot of the cross, right on to the perpetual consummation of all the elect. For assumed into heaven she has not put aside this saving role, rather she continues by her many prayers of intercession to obtain for us gifts of eternal salvation.[15] In her motherly love she looks after the sisters and brothers of her son who are still on their pilgrimage and placed amidst dangers and difficulties, until they are led to their happy homeland. Therefore in the church the blessed Virgin is invoked by the titles of advocate, benefactress,

helper and mediatrix.[16] This, however, must be understood in such a way that it takes away nothing from the dignity and power of Christ the one mediator, and adds nothing on to this.[17] For no creature can ever be counted along with the incarnate Word and Redeemer; but just as the priesthood of Christ is shared in a variety of ways both by ministers and by the faithful people, and just as the one goodness of God is really poured out on creatures in diverse ways, so also the one mediation of the Redeemer does not rule out, but rouses up among creatures, participated cooperation from the one unique source.

This subordinate task of Mary the church does not hesitate to profess. The church experiences it continually and commends it to the heart of the faithful, so that supported by this motherly protection they may be more closely united to their mediator and Saviour.

63. The blessed Virgin, through the gift and office of the divine motherhood which unites her with the Son the Redeemer, and by reason of her singular graces and gifts, is also intimately united to the church: the mother of God is the type of the church, as already St. Ambrose used to teach, that is to say, in the order of faith, charity and perfect union with Christ.[18] For in the mystery of the church, which is also rightly called mother and virgin, the blessed virgin Mary has taken precedence, providing in a pre-eminent and singular manner the exemplar both as virgin and as mother.[19] For by her faith and obedience she brought forth on earth the very Son of the Father, and this without sexual intercourse but under the shadow of the holy Spirit, believing like a new Eve not the ancient serpent but the messenger of God with a faith that was not adulterated by any doubt. She brought forth the Son whom God placed as the first-born among many brothers and sisters (see Rm 8, 29), that is to say, of the

faithful in whose birth and education she cooperates with motherly love.

64. The church, contemplating her hidden holiness and imitating her love, and faithfully carrying out the will of the Father, by faithfully accepting the word of God also becomes a mother: for by preaching and baptism it brings forth to new and immortal life children conceived of the holy Spirit and born of God. The church is also a virgin who keeps integral and pure the faith she has given to her spouse; and in imitation of the mother of its Lord, by the power of the holy Spirit, it preserves virginally intact its faith, solid its hope and sincere its love.[20]

65. While in the most blessed Virgin the church has already attained the perfection by which it is without stain or wrinkle (see Eph 5, 27), the faithful continue to strive by overcoming sin to grow in holiness; therefore they lift up their eyes to Mary who shines out to the whole community of the elect as the model of virtues. The church, when it thinks of her piously and contemplates her in the light of the Word made man, enters with reverence more deeply into the inmost mystery of the incarnation and becomes more and more like its spouse. For Mary, who has entered deeply into the history of salvation, in a certain way unites within herself the greatest truths of the faith and echoes them; and when she is preached about and honoured she calls believers to her son, to his sacrifice and to the love of the Father. And the church in giving glory to Christ is made more like its exalted model, making continuous progress in faith, hope and love and seeking and obeying the divine will in all things. Even in its apostolic work, therefore, the church rightly looks to her who brought forth Christ so conceived by the holy Spirit and born of the virgin, that through the church he may also be born and grow in the hearts of the faithful. For this virgin in

her life was the model of that motherly love which should inspire all who work together in the church's apostolic mission for the regeneration of humanity.

IV. The cult of the blessed Virgin in the church

66. Mary, exalted by the grace of God, after the Son, above all angels and human beings because she is the most holy mother of God who took part in the mysteries of Christ, is rightly honoured by the church with a special cult. Clearly from the most ancient times the blessed Virgin has been honoured with the title of "mother of God," to whose protection the faithful run in all their dangers and needs.[21] Especially from the council of Ephesus the cult of the people of God for Mary has grown wonderfully in love and veneration, in invocation and in imitation, in accordance with her own prophetic words: "All generations will call me blessed; for he who is mighty has done great things for me" (Lk 1, 48–49). This cult, as it has always existed in the church, although it is a very special cult, differs essentially from the cult of adoration which is given to the incarnate Word and equally to the Father and the holy Spirit, and it very greatly fosters this cult of adoration. The church has approved a variety of forms of devotion to the mother of God within the limits of sound and orthodox doctrine and according to circumstances of time and place and the temperament and character of the faithful; but these devotions are such that, while the mother is honoured, the Son for whom all things exist (see Col 1, 15–16), and in whom it was the eternal Father's "good pleasure to let all fullness dwell" (Col 1, 19), should be duly known, loved and glorified and his commandments observed.

67. The holy synod expressly teaches this catholic doctrine and at the same time exhorts all the members of the church generously to foster the cult, especially the liturgical cult, of

the blessed Virgin, to hold in high esteem those pious practices recommended down the centuries by the magisterium, and carefully to observe what has been laid down in the past concerning the cult of images of Christ, of the blessed Virgin and of the saints.[22] It earnestly exhorts theologians and preachers of the divine word carefully to avoid all false exaggeration and equally a too narrow mentality in considering the special dignity of the mother of God.[23] Through the study of holy scripture, of the holy fathers and doctors and of the liturgies of the church, under the guidance of the magisterium, they should explain correctly the gifts and privileges of the blessed Virgin, which always have Christ in view, who is the origin of all truth, holiness and piety. They should sedulously avoid, both in what they say and in what they do, anything that might lead our separated brothers and sisters or any other people into error concerning the true teaching of the church. Let the faithful also bear in mind that true devotion consists neither in sterile and passing feelings nor in an empty credulity, but that it arises out of that true faith by which we are brought to acknowledge the excellence of the mother of God and urged on towards filial love for our mother and imitation of her virtues.

V. Mary, the sign of sure hope and comfort for the pilgrim people of God

68. Meanwhile, however, the mother of Jesus, as already glorified in body and soul in heaven she is the image and the beginning of the church which will receive fulfilment in the age that is to come, so here on earth until the day of the Lord arrives (see 2 Pt 3, 10) she shines forth as a sign of sure hope and comfort for the pilgrim people of God.

69. It brings great joy and consolation to this holy synod that people are not lacking among our separated sisters and

brothers who duly honour the mother of our Lord and Saviour, especially among eastern Christians who honour the ever virgin mother of God with fervour and devotion.[24] Let all Christians pour forth insistent prayers to the mother of God and mother of the human race that she who stood by the primitive church with her prayers, now also, exalted in heaven above all the blessed and the angels, in communion with all the saints may intercede with her son so that all the families of peoples, both those that are honoured by the christian name and those who do not yet know their Saviour, may be happily gathered together in peace and harmony into one people of God to the glory of the most holy and undivided Trinity.

—November 21, 1964

Clarifications
Made by the secretary-general of the council at the 123rd general congregation on 16 November 1964
A question has been asked concerning the *theological note* that should be given to the teaching that is put forward in the schema *The Church (De Ecclesia)* and is submitted for voting.

The doctrinal commission has replied to the question by evaluating the *amendments* proposed to the third chapter of the schema *The Church,* as follows:

"As is self-evident, the council text is always to be interpreted according to general rules that are known by all."

On this occasion the doctrinal commission refers to its *Declaration* of 6 March 1964. We reproduce the text of this here:

"Taking into account conciliar custom and the pastoral aim of the present council, this holy synod defines as binding on the church only those matters concerning faith and morals which it openly declares to be such.

The other matters which the synod puts forward as the teaching of the supreme magisterium of the church, each and every member of the faithful should accept and embrace according to the mind of the synod itself, which is clear either from the subject matter or from the way it is said, in accordance with the rules of theological interpretation."

Then at the command of higher authority there is communicated to the fathers a preliminary explanatory note concerning the amendments proposed to the third chapter of the schema *The Church*. The doctrine set forth in this third chapter must be understood and explained in accordance with the mind and the statement of this note.

Preliminary Explanatory Note
"The commission has decided to preface its appraisal of the amendments with the following general observations.

1. *College* is not understood in its *strict juridical* meaning, that is as a group of equals who might hand over their power to their president, but as a stable group whose structure and authority must be deduced from revelation. For this reason, in reply to amendment 12 it is explicitly stated concerning the twelve that the Lord constituted them 'like a college or a *stable group*.' For the same reason, concerning the college of bishops sometimes the words *order* or *body* are also used. The parallelism between Peter and the rest of the apostles on the one hand, and the supreme pontiff and the bishops on the other, does not imply that the extraordinary power of the apostles is transmitted to their successors, nor, as is evident, does it imply *equality* between the head and the members of the college, but only a *proportionality* between the first relationship (Peter—apostles) and the second (pope—bishops).

Hence the commission decided to write in no. 22, not *the same* but a *similar* relationship. See amendment 57.

2. A person becomes a *member of the college* by reason of episcopal consecration and hierarchical communion with the head of the college and the members. See no. 22 §1 at the end. In the *consecration* there is given an *ontological* participation in the *sacred* functions, as is undoubtedly clear from tradition, including the liturgical tradition. The word *functions* is used deliberately, and not *powers*, because the latter word could be understood as power *all ready for action*. But to have such power ready for action there has to be added, through hierarchical authority, the *canonical* or *juridical determination*. This determination can consist in the granting of a particular office or in the assignment of subjects, and it is given in accordance with *rules* approved by the supreme authority. A further rule of this kind is required *by the nature of the case* because it is a question of functions which have to be exercised *by a plurality of subjects* cooperating hierarchically by the will of Christ. It is evident that this 'communion' was applied *in the life* of the church according to circumstances before it became codified, so to speak, *in the law*.

For this reason it is expressly stated that *hierarchical* communion is required with the church's head and members. *Communion* is a notion which was held in high esteem in the ancient church (as it is also today especially in the east). It is understood, however, not as consisting in some vague *disposition*, but as an *organic reality* which requires a juridical form and at the same time is animated by charity. Therefore the commission decided almost unanimously that 'in *hierarchical* communion' should be written. See what is said concerning *canonical mission* under no. 24.

The documents of recent supreme pontiffs concerning

the jurisdiction of bishops are to be interpreted in accordance with this necessary determination of powers.

3. The college, which does not exist without its head, is said to be '*also the subject of supreme and full power* over the universal church.' This was necessarily to be admitted lest the Roman pontiff's plenitude of power be endangered. For the college necessarily and always presupposes its head, *who in the college fully retains his function as vicar of Christ and pastor of the universal church.* In other words, the distinction is not between the Roman pontiff and the bishops taken together, but between the Roman pontiff taken separately and the Roman pontiff together with the bishops. And because the Roman pontiff is the *head* of the college, he alone can perform certain acts which are in no way within the competence of the bishops, for example, to call together and direct the college, to approve the rules of procedure, etc. The care of the whole of Christ's flock has been committed to the supreme pontiff and it is his prerogative, in accordance with the changing needs of the church in the course of time, to determine the way this care should be exercised either personally or collegially. In setting up, encouraging and approving collegial activity the Roman pontiff takes into consideration the good of the church and proceeds according to his own discretion.

4. The supreme pontiff, as supreme pastor of the church, can exercise his power at all times as he thinks best, as is required by his very function. The college, however, while always in existence, does not for that reason permanently act by *strictly* collegial action, as is clear from the church's tradition. In other words, it is not always 'fully active,' indeed only periodically does it act in a strictly collegial way and then only *with the consent of the head.* The expression '*with the consent of the head*' is used to avoid any idea of *dependence,*

as though on someone who is *outside;* on the contrary, the expression *'with the consent of'* brings out the *communion* between head and members and entails the need of the *act* which is the prerogative of the head. The matter is expressly stated in no. 22 §2 and is explained there at the end. The negative formula *'only with'* covers all cases: so it is evident that the *rules* approved by the supreme authority must always be observed.

Everywhere it is clear that it is a question of *union* of the bishops *with their head,* and it is never a question of the bishops acting *independently* of the pope. In this case, if the action of the head is missing, the bishops cannot act as a college, as is evident from the idea of a 'college.' This hierarchical communion of all the bishops with the supreme pontiff is certainly hallowed by tradition.

N.B. Without hierarchical communion the sacramental-ontological function, which is to be distinguished from the canonico-juridical aspect, *cannot* be exercised. The commission decided that they should not get into the questions about *liceity* and *validity;* these are left for the discussion of theologians, especially with regard to the power that is in fact exercised among our eastern separated brothers and sisters, and there is a variety of opinions on how this is to be explained."

Pericles Felici
Titular Archbishop of Samosata
Secretary-General of the Council

Pastoral Constitution on the Church
in the Modern World
(Gaudium et Spes)

The Pastoral Constitution on the Church in the Modern World was the only document of Vatican II that was born during the council itself. Toward the end of the first session—with tensions exposed and frustration spreading—Cardinal Léon-Joseph Suenens rose to address the assembly. He urged his brother bishops not to let the council become so preoccupied with the internal affairs of the church that it ignored the rest of the world. The church must reach out and engage pressing questions of social justice, evangelization, poverty, and peace. He spoke of the need for a triple dialogue: a dialogue among the church's own members, a dialogue with other Christians, and a dialogue with "the modern world." His remarks were followed by sustained applause. The next day Cardinal Giovanni Battista Montini, who would soon become Pope Paul VI, endorsed Suenens's proposal. The seeds of Gaudium et Spes *were planted.*

Though its introduction to the assembly was dramatic, Suenens's proposal did not fall out of the sky. Suenens was writing about his hopes for Vatican II long before his December 1962 speech. Particularly important was a 1962 Lenten letter that he devoted to the upcoming council. This letter attracted the attention of Pope

John XXIII and led to a series of exchanges between the two men. When Suenens complained about the disorganized nature of the preparatory work and the overwhelming number of draft texts, Pope John asked him to develop an overall plan for the council. Suenens responded with enthusiasm. He identified a central theme, "the church of Christ, light to the world" (Ecclesia Christi, lumen gentium), and then broke this theme down into two basic parts: the church in and of itself (ad intra) and the church in relationship to the world at large (ad extra). Suenens shared his plan with the pope and with a small group of leading cardinals. All of this came too late to influence the agenda for the first session, but the cardinal's intervention in December 1962 was decisive in focusing the work of the council for the sessions that were still to come.

At its January 1963 meeting, the central Coordinating Commission decided to add a new document to the end of its sixteen-point agenda for the council. Thus the text on the church in the modern world earned the temporary nickname Schema 17. After a subsequent reordering of texts, the document became widely known as Schema 13. It was to be prepared by a mixed group composed of members from both the Doctrinal Commission (headed by Cardinal Alfredo Ottaviani) and the Commission on the Apostolate of the Laity (headed by Cardinal Fernando Cento). They faced a daunting task. Nothing like this had ever been done before. There was no preparatory text to work with. The closest model would have been the great social encyclicals of the late nineteenth and early twentieth centuries, which dealt with just a few of the aspects to be considered under the broad heading "the church in the world." More problematic for some, however, was the belief that dialogue with the modern world contradicted other papal teaching—particularly Pius IX's condemnations of modernity in his 1864 Syllabus of Errors.

Still, the drafters found encouragement in the resurgence of lay initiatives before the council; in recent theologies that sought to overcome the separation of nature and grace; in Pope John XXIII's 1963 encyclical on peace, Pacem in Terris; and in those bishops from developing nations who pressed for greater attention to the church of the poor. Dozens of drafts were produced—with at least four complete rewrites—in a process that stretched across almost three years.

A draft was eventually ready for debate at the council's third session. In introducing the text, Cardinal Cento emphasized that dialogue ought to be the church's preferred way of relating to the world. Cento cited Pope Paul VI's encyclical on the church, Ecclesiam Suam, which, along with the pope's earlier speeches, helped to spread the language of dialogue throughout the council texts. Thus the four short chapters of the document stressed dialogue as a necessary component in the church's mission of promoting human dignity and human solidarity.

The main text was followed by five appendixes that dealt with specific issues: (1) the human person in society, (2) marriage and the family, (3) culture, (4) economic issues, and (5) peace. Most of the debate—which lasted almost three weeks and included over 150 speeches—focused here. In the course of this wide-ranging debate, two issues garnered the most attention: nuclear war and birth control. Vatican II opened in the midst of the Cuban Missile Crisis. Thus the threat of nuclear annihilation loomed large for the bishops gathered in Rome. Some argued that modern war's potential for total devastation made traditional Catholic discussions of "just war" irrelevant. They called for a condemnation of modern war in all circumstances—following the prophetic vision of Pope John's Pacem in Terris. Others, particularly those from the United States and Great Britain, wanted to avoid such a blanket condemnation. In the end, Gaudium et Spes charted a middle course. It called the indiscriminate destruction of whole cities or areas "a crime against God and humanity" but still recognized the legitimate right of nations to their own self-defense.

If the context of the debate on war and peace was the Cold War, the context of the debate on marriage and family was the sexual revolution. The invention of the birth control pill had put unprecedented pressure on traditional prohibitions against contraception, just as a new personalism in philosophy was challenging the church's legalistic definition of marriage as a contract between two parties. The draft before the bishops did two things that scandalized the more conservative members of the assembly. First, it avoided the standard seminary textbook distinction between the "primary" and "secondary" ends of marriage—in which the primary end (or purpose) of marriage is the procreation of children and the secondary end is the mutual help marriage offers to the spouses. Instead, the document spoke in equal terms of the goodness of the love between husband and wife, and the goodness of children as the fulfillment of that love. Second, the draft did not explicitly condemn birth control, seeming to suggest that individual conscience was the deciding factor. While some bishops raised concerns about birth control, the council never fully debated the issue. Pope Paul VI announced that a special commission had been established to advise him on this issue, and that he would reserve to himself any final decision on it. He had, in effect, taken birth control off the agenda. Four years later (July 25, 1968), Paul VI issued the encyclical Humanae Vitae, in which he reaffirmed the church's traditional ban on artificial contraception.

Amid the debates on particular issues was a larger critique leveled against Schema 13. This critique was articulated concisely by Cardinal Josef Frings of Cologne when he said that the document did not give sufficient attention to Christ crucified. The treatment of the human person seemed more sociological than theological. Its view of the world seemed overly optimistic. Needed was a greater emphasis on the cross, which reminds us of the sinfulness of humanity, the necessity of sacrifice, and the value of abstaining from worldly goods. According to Frings, what the world needs from the church is not primarily dialogue but the proclamation of Jesus, who died for all. Here Frings was articulating a concern about the theological weakness of the text that was shared by a number of German-speaking bishops and theologians—including his own adviser Joseph Ratzinger.

As the document on the church in the world moved into revisions between the third and the fourth sessions—revisions that entailed another complete rewrite—these concerns remained. Archbishop Karol Wojtyla of Krakow (who would later become Pope John Paul II) joined the Germans in criticizing the text as too sanguine about a world torn between two dangerous extremes: consumeristic materialism on the one hand, and atheistic communism on the other. Cardinal Frings kept up the pressure. Even Karl Rahner complained about the theological balance of the text. As the document took final shape, Part I ("The Church and Humanity's Vocation") addressed some of these concerns by concluding each of its four chapters with a substantive Christological section, in which Jesus Christ is lifted up as the church's distinctive contribution to dialogue with the world. The five chapters of Part II go on to treat particular contemporary issues (family life, culture, economics, politics, and peace) in light of this foundation.

In the end, Pope Paul VI's overriding call for an approach rooted in dialogue prevailed—guided by a clear recognition of what the church has to offer to this conversation. The Pastoral Constitution on the Church in the Modern World celebrates the dignity of the human person and, at the same time, acknowledges the reality of human sin. It describes our place within a rapidly changing society and yet lifts up eternal truths. It affirms our shared humanity but singles out one man, Jesus Christ, as the goal of all human striving. It calls the church both to dialogue with others and to proclaim the Gospel to all.

Gaudium et Spes

Pastoral Constitution on the Church in the Modern World[1]

TRANSLATED BY JOHN MAHONEY, S.J.

Preface

1. (*The close link between the church and the whole human family*) The joys and hopes and the sorrows and anxieties of people today, especially of those who are poor and afflicted, are also the joys and hopes, sorrows and anxieties of the disciples of Christ, and there is nothing truly human which does not also affect them. Their community is composed of people united in Christ who are directed by the holy Spirit in their pilgrimage towards the Father's kingdom and who have received the message of salvation to be communicated to everyone. For this reason it feels itself closely linked to the human race and its history.

2. (*Those whom the council addresses*) Accordingly, after exploring the mystery of the church more deeply, the second Vatican council now immediately addresses itself not just to the church's own daughters and sons and all who call on the

name of Christ but to people everywhere, in its desire to explain to all how it understands the church's presence and activity in today's world. This world it sees as the world of men
and women, the whole human family in its total environment; the stage of human history notable for its toil, its tragedies and its triumphs; the world which Christians believe
has been established and kept in being by its Creator's love,
has fallen into the bondage of sin but has been liberated by
Christ, who was crucified and has risen to shatter the power
of the evil one, so that it could be transformed according to
God's purpose and come to its fulfilment.

3. (*The service to be offered to humanity*) Although the human
race today is proud of its achievements and its abilities, it
is frequently concerned about modern developments in the
world, about humanity's place and role on the planet, about
the meaning of individual and corporate endeavours, and
about the ultimate purpose of things and of human beings.
The council, in witnessing and giving expression to the faith
of the whole of God's people brought together by Christ,
cannot give more striking evidence of this people's feelings
of oneness, concern and love towards the whole human family, of which it is a part, than by entering into conversation
with it on these various problems, contributing enlightenment derived from the gospel and supplying the human race
with the saving resources which, under the guidance of the
holy Spirit, the church receives from its founder. For it is the
human person that is to be saved, and human society to be
restored. It is around humankind therefore, one and entire,
body and soul, heart and conscience, mind and will, that our
whole treatment will revolve.

Thus it is that the holy synod proclaims the noble calling of humanity and the existence within it of a divine seed,
and offers the human race the sincere cooperation of the

church in working for that universal community of sisters and brothers which is the response to humanity's calling. The church is not motivated by any earthly considerations, but has in mind only, with the guidance of the Paraclete, to continue the work of Christ who came into the world to give witness to the truth,[2] to save and not to judge, to serve and not to be served.[3]

Introduction
The condition of humanity in today's world
4. (*Hopes and anxieties*) To discharge this function, the church has the duty in every age of examining the signs of the times and interpreting them in the light of the gospel, so that it can offer in a manner appropriate to each generation replies to the continual human questionings on the meaning of this life and the life to come and on how they are related. There is a need, then, to be aware of, and to understand, the world in which we live, together with its expectations, its desires and its frequently dramatic character. Some of the more outstanding features of today's world can be outlined as follows.

The human race finds itself today in a new stage of its history, in which fundamental and rapid changes are gradually extending to the whole globe. These have come about through human intelligence and creative effort, and they redound on women and men, on their individual and collective judgments and wishes, and on their ways of thinking and acting both in material and in human affairs. So much so that we can speak of a real social and cultural transformation which has its effects also on the life of religion.

As is the case in any crisis of growth, this transformation is introducing considerable difficulties. Thus while human beings are increasingly extending their power, they are not always able to control it in their own service. They are intent on exploring the depths of the mind, yet they often appear more unsure of themselves. They are gradually uncovering the laws of their life in society, but uncertain about how to give it direction.

Never has the human race possessed such an abundance of wealth, resources and economic power, and yet a large part of the world's population is still racked by hunger and need, and very many are illiterate. Never has humanity had so intense a feeling for freedom as today, but new forms of social and psychological slavery are on the increase. The world is keenly aware of its unity and interdependence in essential solidarity, while it is seriously polarised by opposing forces; and in fact bitter political, social, economic, racial and ideological dissensions remain, together with the risk of a war which will annihilate everything. Communication of ideas is on the increase, but the very words to express ideas take on quite different meanings in competing ideologies. And there is concern to improve the temporal order without there being any comparable spiritual progress.

Caught up in such complexities, very many of our contemporaries are prevented from identifying permanent values and from reconciling them with recent discoveries. They fluctuate between hope and anxiety, question themselves about the current course of events and are deeply disquieted. Such a development calls for, and even demands, an answer from men and women.

5. (*The profound change of conditions*) The spiritual unease of today and the change in living conditions are part of a greater upheaval, which comes from the growing importance accorded at the intellectual level to the mathematical, natural and social sciences, and at the practical level to the repercussions of these sciences upon technology. This

scientific mentality is affecting human culture and ways of thinking, and technology is going so far as to transform the face of the earth and even to attempt to conquer extraterrestrial space.

The human mind is extending its sway over time also: over the past with the aid of historical information, and over the future through projection and planning. The advancing biological, psychological and social sciences are not only enabling human beings to know themselves better but are also helping them to have a direct influence through technology on the lives of societies. At the same time the human race is giving increasing thought to forecasting and controlling its own demographic growth.

History itself is accelerating at such a pace that individuals can scarcely keep up with it. Humanity's fate is becoming one rather than being divided into different historical movements. The human race is moving from a more static view of things to one which is more dynamic and evolutionary, giving rise to new combinations of problems which call for new analyses and syntheses.

6. (*Changes in the social order*) Because of this, local traditional communities, such as patriarchal families, clans, tribes, villages and the various groupings and relationships in society are daily experiencing change.

The industrial type of society is gradually spreading, leading some nations to economic wealth and utterly transforming age-old ideas and conditions of social living. Similarly the desire for urban life is on the increase, whether by the growth of cities and their inhabitants or by the trend to urbanise rural people.

New and improved media of social communication are contributing to knowledge of events and to the rapid spread of ways of thinking and reaching, with all the consequences which follow.

Of considerable significance also are the numbers of people who are led by a variety of reasons to migrate and change their manner of living.

Thus people's relationships are multiplying continually, and at the same time *socialisation* is introducing new relationships without necessarily promoting *personalisation*, or a maturing of the person and genuinely personal relationships.

This evolution is more clearly apparent in countries which already enjoy the advantages of economic and technological progress, but it also affects peoples who are struggling for progress and are eager to secure the benefits of industrialisation and urbanisation for their regions. And at the same time these peoples, particularly those committed to older traditions, are experiencing an advance towards a more mature and more personal exercise of freedom.

7. (*Psychological, moral and religious changes*) A change in mentality and structures is frequently challenging traditional values, especially on the part of the young who are at times impatient, if not in revolt, and who have become aware of their importance to society and wish to be active in it at an earlier age. The result is that quite often parents and teachers find their tasks increasingly difficult.

Inherited institutions, laws and ways of thinking and feelings do not always appear easily adaptable to modern conditions, and the result is disruption in the manner, and even the norms, of behaving.

The new conditions also affect the living of religion. On the one hand, a more critical judgment is purifying it of a magical approach to the world and of still widespread superstitions and is increasingly demanding a more personal and active commitment of faith, such that many people are coming to a more appreciative awareness of God. On the other hand, more groups of people are giving up the practice of religion. In contrast to earlier generations it is not now unusual or just an individual matter to deny God or religion or to abandon them: today it is not infrequent for this to be considered as demanded by scientific progress or a new humanism. All of this finds expression in several parts of the world not just in the opinions of philosophers but is widespread in literature and the arts, in the interpretation of the human sciences and of history, and in the laws of society; and it is disturbing many individuals.

8. (*Imbalances in modern society*) Such rapid and often uneven change and a keener awareness of the discrepancies which already exist in society give rise to, or aggravate, contradictions and imbalances.

In the human person there quite often arises an imbalance between the modern practical mentality and the theoretical way of thinking which is unable to control or synthesise the totality of knowledge. Similarly there arises an imbalance between concern for practical results and the demands of the moral conscience, and often between the collective conditions of living and the requirements for personal thought and contemplation. Finally, there arises an imbalance between the specialisations of human activity and a global view of things.

In the family, imbalances arise from demographic, economic and social pressures, or from the resulting tensions between generations, or from new relationships between men and women in society.

Considerable imbalances also arise between races and various classes of society; between rich nations and the weaker and more needy ones; and between the international institutions which have been born of the desire of nations for peace, and the desire to spread ideologies or the collective ambition to further one's own interests which exists among nations and other groups.

Hence the mutual mistrust and enmity, the conflicts and hardships, of which humanity is both cause and victim.

9. (*The wider aspirations of humanity*) Meantime there is a growing realisation not just that the human race can and should daily increase its control over created things, but in addition that its task is to establish a political, social and economic order which will daily be of better service to humanity and will enable individuals and groups to assert and cultivate the dignity which is theirs.

Hence considerable numbers insistently demand those advantages of which they feel very conscious of being deprived, whether through injustice or inequality of distribution. Nations on the road to progress and those that have recently become independent wish to share in the advantages of modern civilisation in the economic as well as the political sphere and to play their own part freely in the world, and yet so often they are increasingly outdistanced and dependent economically in relation to nations richer than themselves and progressing more rapidly. Peoples oppressed by hunger appeal to the wealthier peoples. Women claim equality with men in law and in reality, where they have not yet achieved it. Labourers and agricultural workers want not just to produce the necessities of life but to cultivate their personal resources at work and to take their place in economic, social, political and cultural life. Now, for the first time in human history, whole peoples are convinced that the benefits of culture really can and should extend to everyone.

Underlying all these demands there is a deeper and more widespread wish: people and groups are thirsting for a life which is full and free and worthy of human beings, by applying to their own advantage all that today's world can provide for them in such abundance. Nations are continually aiming to bring about a universal community.

In such circumstances the world of today is showing both its strength and its weakness, the capacity to produce the best and the worst as it faces the road leading to freedom or to slavery, advance or retreat, fellowship or hatred. Men and women are becoming conscious of having to give direction to the powers which they have created, which can either enslave or serve them, and as a result are questioning themselves.

10. (*Deeper human questions*) The imbalances affecting the world today are in fact connected with a deeper imbalance rooted in the human heart where various elements are in opposition. On the one hand, human beings as creatures experience considerable limitations, while on the other hand they are aware of being unlimited in their desires and of being summoned to a higher life. They are subject to many attractions and constantly compelled to choose between them and renounce some of them. And being weak and sinful, they frequently do what they would rather not, and fail to do what they would.[4] They experience internal disunity within themselves, from which so many disharmonies in society also originate. Many whose life is infected with practical materialism are prevented from clearly perceiving this dramatic situation; others are so crushed by wretchedness that they cannot appreciate it. Many consider they can find peace through various ways of interpreting events.

Some, for instance, look to a true and complete liberation of humanity resulting from human effort alone and are persuaded that the future kingdom of women and men on earth will fulfil all their hearts' desires. Others despair of any meaning to life and admire the boldness of those who consider human existence completely devoid of significance and who struggle to give it significance by their own efforts. And yet, faced with today's evolving world, an increasing number are asking the really basic questions or feeling them with a new urgency: What is man and woman? What is the meaning of the suffering, evil and death which persist even in the midst of such progress? What is the point of these expensive conquests? What can people contribute to society or expect from society? What comes after this earthly existence?

It is the church's belief that Christ, who died and was raised for everyone,[5] offers to the human race through his Spirit the light and strength to respond to its highest calling; and that no other name under heaven is given to people for them to be saved.[6] It likewise believes that the key and the focus and culmination of all human history are to be found in its Lord and master. The church also affirms that underlying so many changes there are some things which do not change and are founded upon Christ, who is the same yesterday and today and forever.[7] It is accordingly in the light of Christ, who is the image of the invisible God and first-born of all creation,[8] that the council proposes to elucidate the mystery of humankind and, in addressing all people, to contribute to discovering a solution to the outstanding questions of our day.

Part 1

The church and humanity's vocation
11. (*Responding to the promptings of the Spirit*) Impelled by its belief that it is being led by the Spirit of the Lord who

fills the whole earth, God's people works to discern the true signs of God's presence and purpose in the events, needs and desires which it shares with the rest of modern humanity. It is faith which shows everything in a new light and clarifies God's purpose in his complete calling of the human race, thus pointing the mind towards solutions which are fully human. The council's first aim is to subject the values most highly regarded today to this light and to relate them to their divine source, since these values are very good insofar as they proceed from the God-given character of the human person, but are in need of purification from the distortion they often receive from the corruption of the human heart.

What is the church's view of woman and man? What does it consider is to be commended in constructing today's society? What is the ultimate significance of human activity in the world as a whole? These questions require answers which will show more clearly that the people of God and the human race of which it is a part are of service to each other, and that the church's mission is seen to be a religious one and by that very fact an outstandingly human one.

Chapter 1. The dignity of the human person

12. (*Humanity in God's image*) Believers and unbelievers are almost at one in considering that everything on earth is to be referred to humanity as its centre and culmination.

But what is humanity itself? It has proposed, and continues to propose, a variety of sometimes contradictory views about itself, which often either hold it up as the absolute measure of all things or cast it into despair as divided and fear-ridden. Aware of these difficulties but instructed by God's revelation, the church can offer an answer to them which describes the true human condition, provides an explanation for its weakness and recognises its dignity and calling.

For scripture teaches that humankind was created "in the image of God," with the capacity to know and love its Creator, and was divinely appointed with authority over all earthly creatures,[1] to rule and use them and glorify God.[2] "What is humankind that you are mindful of it, and the human family that you care for it? Yet you have made it little less than God, and you crown it with glory and honour. You have given it dominion over the work of your hands; you have put all things under its feet" (Ps 8, 5–7).

God, however, did not create the human person a solitary: from the very beginning "male and female God created them" (Gn 1, 27), and their coming together brings about the first form of the communion of persons. For by natural constitution the human person is a social being who cannot live or develop without relations with others.

Accordingly, as scripture again states, God saw "everything that God had made, and behold, it was very good" (Gn 1, 31).

13. (*Sin*) Although constituted in righteousness by God, humanity was persuaded by the evil one, and at the dawn of history abused its freedom, raising itself up against God and seeking to find its destiny apart from God. Although they were aware of God, they did not give the glory befitting God, but their foolish hearts were darkened and they served the creature rather than the Creator.[3] What is known to us through God's revelation is consonant with our experience. Looking into our hearts, we also find ourselves with a leaning towards evil and submerged in a multitude of evils which cannot originate in our good Creator. Frequently declining to acknowledge God as our source, we also disrupt our right

relationship to God as our ultimate destination, as well as our whole relationship to ourselves or to others or to created things.

Thus the human being is divided interiorly, and the whole of human life, whether singly or shared, is shown to be a dramatic struggle between good and evil, light and darkness. People find themselves incapable of overcoming the onslaughts of evil by themselves, and individuals feel bound and helpless. But the Lord has come to liberate them and strengthen them, renewing them interiorly and expelling the prince of this world (see Jn 12, 31), who kept them in the slavery of sin.[4] For sin diminished them and prevented them from attaining their fulfilment.

In the light of this revelation both the noble calling and the profound dejection experienced by human beings find their ultimate explanation.

14. (*The human constitution*) Being a unity of body and soul, humanity concentrates in its physical dimension the elements of the material world, which reach their peak in the human and raise their voice in free praise of the Creator.[5] Women and men may not therefore despise their bodily life, but on the contrary are bound to consider the body, created by God and to be raised on the last day, as good and worthy of honour. And yet, being wounded by sin, they experience the rebelliousness of the body. Thus human dignity itself requires them to glorify God in the body[6] and not to permit the body to serve the evil inclinations of the heart.

Humankind is not mistaken in recognising its superiority over bodily things and in considering itself not just as a particle of nature or an impersonal element of human society. By its interior life it far exceeds the totality of things, and it experiences this deep interiority when it enters into the heart where God, the searcher of hearts,[7] is waiting and where it decides its own destiny in the sight of God. Thus, in acknowledging a spiritual immortal soul within them, human beings are not misled by some deceptive construct of merely physical or social conditions but on the contrary they are penetrating to the truth of reality.

15. (*The dignity of the mind; truth; wisdom*) As sharers in the light of the divine mind, human beings are correct in judging that by their intellect they are superior to the totality of things. Through the ages the human mind has been unceasingly active and has made progress in the empirical sciences, technology and the liberal arts. In modern times it has achieved remarkable successes in investigating and harnessing the world of matter. And yet it has always sought and discovered a deeper truth. For its understanding is not bound simply by appearances but is capable of grasping intelligible reality with true certainty, even if it is partly dimmed and weakened as a result of sin.

The intellectual nature of the human person reaches its final perfection, and needs to do so, through the wisdom which gently draws the human mind to seek and love what is true and good, and which leads it through visible realities to those which are invisible.

The present age more than ever requires such wisdom to humanise its new discoveries. The future of the world is at risk if wiser people are not forthcoming. And it may be noted that several nations which are less rich in economic resources are more endowed with wisdom, and can make a unique contribution to others.

By the gift of the holy Spirit humankind attains in faith to the contemplation and savouring of the mystery of God's design.[8]

16. (*The dignity of the moral conscience*) Deep within their conscience individuals discover a law which they do not make

for themselves but which they are bound to obey, whose voice, ever summoning them to love and do what is good and to avoid what is evil, rings in their heart when necessary with the command: Do this, keep away from that. For inscribed in their hearts by God, human beings have a law whose observance is their dignity and in accordance with which they are to be judged.[9] Conscience is the most intimate centre and sanctuary of a person, in which he or she is alone with God whose voice echoes within them.[10] In a marvellous manner conscience makes known that law which is fulfilled by love of God and of neighbour.[11] In their faithfulness to conscience, Christians are united with all other people in the search for truth and in finding true solutions to the many moral problems which arise in the lives of individuals and in society. And the more a correct conscience prevails, so much the more do persons and groups abandon blind whims and work to conform to the objective norms of morality. Not infrequently, however, conscience can be mistaken as a result of insuperable ignorance, although it does not on that account forfeit its dignity; but this cannot be said when a person shows little concern for seeking what is true and good and conscience gradually becomes almost blind from being accustomed to sin.

17. (*The excellence of freedom*) It is only in freedom, however, that human beings can turn to what is good, and our contemporaries are right in their evaluation and assiduous pursuit of such freedom, although often they cultivate it in wrong ways as a licence to do anything they please, even evil. Genuine freedom is an outstanding manifestation of the divine image in humans. For God willed to leave them in the hands of their own counsel,[12] so that they would seek their Creator of their own accord and would freely arrive at full and blessed perfection by cleaving to God. Their human dignity there-

fore requires them to act through conscious and free choice, as motivated and prompted personally from within, and not through blind internal impulse or merely external pressure. They achieve such dignity when they free themselves from all subservience to their feelings, and in a free choice of good pursue their own end by effectively and assiduously marshalling the appropriate means. Wounded as it is by sin, human freedom cannot fully realise this orientation towards God without the help of God's grace. Everyone will have to give an account of his or her life before God's judgment seat according as she or he has done good or evil.[13]

18. (*The mystery of death*) The enigma of the human condition is most evident when face to face with death. Humankind is tortured not just by progressive suffering and physical pain but also, or more, by the fear of perpetual extinction. Its instinctive judgment is correct in recoiling from and rejecting the total destruction and complete departure of the person. The seed of eternity which it bears cannot be reduced to mere matter and it revolts against death. All the efforts of technology, however beneficial, cannot allay human anxiety, and the prolongation of biological life cannot assuage the essential longing of the human heart for further life.

The imagination fails before death, but the church learns from divine revelation to affirm that men and women have been created by God for a blessed destiny beyond the boundary of earthly unhappiness. And christian faith teaches that the bodily death, from which they would have been immune had they not sinned,[14] will be vanquished when they are restored by an all-powerful and merciful Saviour to the salvation lost through their own fault. For God has called women and men and is calling them to cleave to God with all their being in the everlasting communion of an incorruptible divine life. It was Christ who gained this victory when he freed them from death by his own death and rose again to life.[15] Thus, to anyone who thinks about it, faith is proposed with solid arguments to provide the answer to human concern about fate, and at the same time it affords the opportunity of being in communion in Christ with beloved sisters and brothers who have already been taken away by death, imparting the hope that they have attained true life with God.

19. (*The forms and foundations of atheism*) The outstanding feature of human dignity is that human beings have been called to communion with God. From its first moment a human being is invited to encounter God. It exists solely because it is continually kept in being by the love of the God who created it out of love, and it cannot live fully and truly unless it freely acknowledges that love and commits itself to its Creator. Many of our contemporaries, however, either completely fail or explicitly refuse to accept this intimate and vital relationship with God, with the result that atheism is to be viewed as one of the most serious of contemporary phenomena and merits close consideration.

The term "atheism" covers a range of things, including the explicit denial of God, the human incapacity to say anything about God, and the methodological claim that the question of God is meaningless. Many unjustifiably exceed the bounds of the positive sciences in claiming that everything is to be explained in these scientific terms or else in admitting that there is no such thing as absolute truth. Some so exalt the human as to empty faith in God of all content, being apparently more preoccupied with the affirmation of human beings than with denial of God. Others so conceive of God that the image which they then reject bears no resemblance to the God of the gospel. Others again do not even address themselves to questions about God since they apparently do not feel any religious stirrings or see why they should be interested in religion. It is not infrequent for atheism to follow from a powerful reaction against evil in the world, or from the absolutism wrongly conferred upon certain human values which become substitutes for God. And modern civilisation, not of necessity but insofar as it is excessively taken up with earthly considerations, can often make access to God much more difficult.

Those who attempt to expel God deliberately from their hearts and to avoid religious questions, ignoring the command of their conscience, are not devoid of guilt; but believers often bear some responsibility for this. Considered as a whole, atheism is not something which arises spontaneously; it is the result of a variety of causes, including a critical reaction to religions and, especially in some areas, to Christianity. And no small part in the rise of atheism is attributable to believers who may be described more as concealing the true features of God and religion than as revealing them, through the neglect of education in the faith or false explanations of its doctrines or even through the faults in their religious, moral and social lives.

20. (*Systematic atheism*) Modern atheism frequently takes a systematic form which, among other elements, makes so much of the wish for human autonomy that it creates difficulties for any degree of dependence on God. Those who profess this type of atheism claim that freedom consists in humanity's constituting its own end as the sole fashioner and agent of its own history, and they assert that such an attitude is irreconcilable with recognising a lord who is originator and goal of all things, or at least makes such an assertion quite unnecessary. And support is forthcoming for this doctrine from the sense of power conferred on humanity by modern technological progress.

One form of modern atheism which may not be ignored

is that which looks especially to people's economic and social liberation for their liberation, and claims that religion of its nature is an obstacle to such liberation in raising people's hope towards a future illusory life which would discourage them from building the earthly city. Consequently, when those who hold such a doctrine come to govern their country, they strongly oppose religion and propagate atheism, especially in the education of the young, even applying the pressures of public authority.

21. (*The church's attitude to atheism*) In its loyalty to both God and the human race the church cannot refrain from strongly and strenuously deploring, as it has in the past,[16] those destructive doctrines and actions which contradict the reason and shared experience of human beings and deprive them of their inherent grandeur.

Yet the church seeks to identify the causes in the minds of atheists which underlie their denial of God, and it is sensitive to the gravity of the questions which atheism raises. In its love for all people it considers that these questions demand serious and deeper examination.

The church holds that the acknowledgement of God is in no way at odds with human dignity, since this has God for its basis and fulfilment. Humankind is constituted in society intelligent and free by God the Creator, but above all we are called as daughters and sons to communion with God and to a share in the divine happiness. The church also teaches that the importance of earthly tasks is not diminished by eschatological hope but that on the contrary their fulfilment is strengthened by additional motives. But when the divine foundation and the hope of eternal life are missing, human dignity is seriously impaired, as frequently occurs today, and the mysteries of life and death, and of guilt and grief, remain unsolved, often resulting in people's sinking into despair.

Meantime each individual remains to himself or herself an unsolved question which is dimly perceived. For nobody can entirely escape such questioning at some time, particularly in the major events of life. To this question only God, who calls us to a higher level of thought and a humbler search, can provide the answer completely and with full certainty.

The answer to atheism is to be sought in the appropriate exposition of the church's teaching and in the total life of the church and its members. For the church's function is to make God the Father and his incarnate Son present and almost visible by continually renewing and cleansing itself under the guidance of the holy Spirit.[17] This is brought about in the first place by the witness of a faith which is living and mature, and which is educated to be able to view difficulties clearly and overcome them. Outstanding evidence of such faith has been given, and is being given, by numerous martyrs. It should show its fruitfulness in permeating the entire life of believers, including their secular life, and in stimulating them to justice and love, especially towards the needy. And the greatest contribution to making God's presence manifest lies in the brotherly and sisterly love of believers who are united in spirit to collaborate in the faith of the gospel[18] and to provide a sign of unity.

While completely rejecting atheism, the church nonetheless honestly proclaims that all women and men, believers and unbelievers, have a duty to contribute to the fitting construction of this world which they share; and this cannot be done without honest and prudent dialogue. Hence it protests at the discrimination between believers and unbelievers unjustly applied by some governments which ignore the basic rights of the human person. It demands for believers an effective liberty to be allowed to build God's temple also in this world. And it gently invites atheists to consider Christ's gospel with open hearts.

For the church is fully aware that its message is in harmony with the deepest desires of the human heart when it champions the dignity of the human calling and restores hope to those despairing of any higher destiny. Far from diminishing humankind, this message spreads light, life and liberty for its progress, and nothing less can satisfy the human heart. "It is for yourself that you have made us," Lord, "and our hearts are restless, until they repose in you."[19]

22. (*Christ, the new human being*) In fact, it is only in the mystery of the Word incarnate that light is shed on the mystery of humankind. For Adam, the first human being, was a representation of the future,[20] namely, of Christ the lord. It is Christ, the last Adam, who fully discloses humankind to itself and unfolds its noble calling by revealing the mystery of the Father and the Father's love. It is not therefore to be wondered at that it is in Christ that the truths stated here find their source and reach their fulfilment.

He who is "the image of the invisible God" (Col 1, 15),[21] is the perfect human being who has restored to the offspring of Adam the divine likeness which had been deformed since the first sin. Since the human nature which was assumed in him was not thereby destroyed,[22] it was by that fact raised to a surpassing dignity in us also. For by his incarnation the Son of God united himself in some sense with every human being. He laboured with human hands, thought with a human mind, acted with a human will,[23] and loved with a human heart. Born of Mary the virgin he truly became one of us and, sin apart, was like us in every respect.[24]

In freely shedding his blood as the innocent lamb, he merited life on our behalf and in him God has reconciled us together with himself[25] and rescued us from slavery to the devil and sin, so that each one of us can say with St. Paul: the Son of God "loved me and gave himself for me" (Gal 2, 20). Suffering for us, he not only set us an example to follow in his footsteps,[26] but he also opened for us a way in which life and death are sanctified and given a fresh significance.

Christians conformed to the image of the Son, who is the first-born of many brothers and sisters,[27] receive "the first fruits of the Spirit" (Rm 8, 23) which enable them to fulfil the new law of love.[28] Through the Spirit who is the "guarantee of our inheritance" (Eph 1, 14), the whole person is renewed within, even to "the redemption of our bodies" (Rm 8, 23): "If the Spirit of him who raised Jesus from the dead dwells in you, he who raised Christ Jesus from the dead will give life to your mortal bodies also through his Spirit which dwells in you" (Rm 8, 11).[29] Christians are certainly subject to the need and the duty to struggle against evil through many tribulations and to suffer death; but they share in the paschal mystery and are configured to the death of Christ, and so are strengthened in the hope of attaining the resurrection.[30]

This applies not only to Christians but to all people of good will in whose hearts grace is secretly at work.[31] Since Christ died for everyone,[32] and since the ultimate calling of each of us comes from God and is therefore a universal one, we are obliged to hold that the holy Spirit offers everyone the possibility of sharing in this paschal mystery in a manner known to God.

Such is the great mystery of humankind which is illuminated for believers through the christian revelation. It is through Christ and in Christ that light is shed on the enigma of suffering and death, which would overwhelm us were it not for his gospel. Christ is risen, by his death destroying death, and has bestowed life on us[33] so that, as children in the Son, we cry in the Spirit, "Abba, Father!"[34]

Chapter 2. The human community

23. (*The council's intention*) One of the outstanding features of the modern world to which modern technological progress has vastly contributed is the growth in contacts among people. Attitudes of kinship are not, however, brought about by such progress but come about at a deeper level by a community of persons which calls for mutual respect for the full spiritual dignity of each. The christian revelation has much to contribute to promoting this community between persons and at the same time it leads to a higher appreciation of the laws of social life which have been written by the Creator in our spiritual and moral nature.

Recent statements of the church's teaching authority have dealt in some detail with christian social doctrine,[1] and so the council recalls only some of its more fundamental truths and expounds their basis in the light of revelation, as a prelude to considering some of the more important conclusions for the present day.

24. (*The communal nature of the human vocation in God's design*) God has a parent's care for every individual and has willed that all should constitute a single family treating each other as brothers and sisters. All have been created in the image of God who "made from one every nation of humankind to live on the whole face of the earth" (Ac 17, 26), and all have been called to one and the same end, God himself.

This is why the first and greatest commandment is love of God and of neighbour. We are taught by scripture that love for God cannot be separated from love for neighbour: ". . . and any other commandment, are summed up in this sentence, 'You shall love your neighbour as yourself' . . . Therefore love is the fulfilling of the law" (Rm 13, 9–10; see 1 Jn 4, 20). The immense importance of this is becoming evident as people become increasingly interdependent and the world increasingly one.

Indeed, when the lord Jesus prays to his Father that "they may all be one . . . , even as we are one" (Jn 17, 21–22), disclosing prospects unattainable to human reason, he indicates a certain similarity between the union of the divine persons and the union of God's children in truth and love. And this similarity indicates that the human, the only creature on earth whom God willed for its own sake, can attain its full identity only in sincere self-giving.[2]

25. (*The interdependence of the human person and human society*) The social character of human beings indicates that the advancement of the human person and the growth of society are dependent on each other. For the origin, the subject and the purpose of all social institutions is and should be the human person, whose life of its nature absolutely needs to be lived in society.[3] And since social life is not something accidental to us, it is through our dealings with others, mutual duties and exchange with our sisters and brothers, that we grow in all our endowments and can respond to our vocation.

Of the social ties which are needed for humanity's development some, such as the family and the political community, correspond more closely to our inner nature while others follow more from our free decision. Today, for various reasons, there is a continual growth in mutual relationships and dependence, giving rise to a variety of associations and institutions of a public and private nature. This phenomenon of "socialisation" is not without its dangers but it also has great advantages in strengthening and increasing the qualities of the human person and in safeguarding his and her rights.[4]

If human persons are helped, however, by this life in society to fulfil their vocation, including their religious vocation, it is nevertheless undeniable that they are often deterred from doing good and encouraged to do evil by the social conditions in which they live and by which they are surrounded from childhood. Certainly the disturbances which occur so often in the social order arise partly from the tensions of economic, political and social structures. But at a deeper level they originate in the pride and selfishness of men and women which also pervert the social environment. And where the order of things is affected by the consequences of sin, there woman and man who are born prone to evil find fresh incentives to sin, which can only be resisted by continual struggle with the help of grace.

26. (*Promoting the common good*) The increasingly close interdependence which is gradually encompassing the entire world is leading to an increasingly universal common good, the sum total of the conditions of social life enabling groups and individuals to realise their perfection more fully and readily, and this has implications for rights and duties affecting the whole human race. Any group must take into account the needs and legitimate desires of other groups and the common good of the entire human family.[5]

There is also increasing awareness of the exceptional dignity which belongs to the human person, who is superior to everything and whose rights and duties are universal and inviolable. Consequently, everything should be rendered to a person which is required to lead a truly human life, such as food, clothing, shelter, the rights to free choice of one's state of life and to found a family, to education, to work, to one's good name, to respect, to appropriate information, to act in accordance with the right norm of conscience, to the protection of one's private life and to a just freedom, including religious freedom.

The social order and its progress ought, then, continually to favour the good of people since the order of things should be subordinated to the order of persons, and not the other way round, as the Lord indicated in saying the sabbath was made for us and not we for the sabbath.[6] It is an order which must increasingly evolve, founded on truth, built in justice and activated in love; and it must find an increasingly human balance in freedom.[7] To achieve all this needs renewal of minds and major changes in society.

The Spirit of God, who with marvellous foresight directs the course of the ages and renews the face of the earth, is present in this evolution. And the leaven of the gospel has stimulated and stimulates in the human heart the irresistible demand of dignity.

27. (*Respect for the human person*) Turning to practical and urgent consequences, the council stresses respect for human beings such that individuals look upon each neighbour without exception as another self, paying particular attention to his and her life and what they need in order to live it in a worthy manner,[8] so as not to imitate the rich man who had no concern for poor Lazarus.[9]

Today particularly there is a pressing obligation on us to be a neighbour to every single individual and to take steps to serve each individual whom we encounter, whether she or he be old and abandoned, or a foreign worker unjustly despised, or an exile, or an illegitimate child innocently suffering for the sin of others, or a hungry person appealing to our conscience with the Lord's words: "as you did it to one of the least of my brothers or sisters, you did it to me" (Mt 25, 40).

Moreover, whatever is hostile to life itself, such as any

kind of homicide, genocide, abortion, euthanasia and voluntary suicide; whatever violates the integrity of the human person, such as mutilation, physical and mental torture and attempts to coerce the spirit; whatever is offensive to human dignity, such as subhuman living conditions, arbitrary imprisonment, deportation, slavery, prostitution and trafficking in women and children; degrading conditions of work which treat labourers as mere instruments of profit and not as free responsible persons: all these and the like are a disgrace, and so long as they infect human civilisation they contaminate those who inflict them more than those who suffer injustice, and they are a negation of the honour due to the Creator.

28. (*Respect and love for enemies*) Respect and love should extend also to those who think or act differently from us in social, political and even religious matters. The more we understand with courtesy and love their ways of thinking, the more easily shall we be able to enter into dialogue with them.

Such love and friendliness should not make us in any way indifferent towards what is true and good. And it is love which drives Christ's disciples to proclaim the saving truth to everyone. Nevertheless, a distinction has to be made between error, which should always be rejected, and the person in error, who retains the dignity of a person even when contaminated by false or inaccurate religious ideas.[10] Only God is the judge and searcher of hearts, and God forbids us to judge the inner guilt of anyone.[11]

Christ's teaching demands that we forgive even injuries and extends the command of love to all our enemies as the commandment of the new law: "You have heard that it was said, 'You shall love your neighbour and hate your enemy,' but I say to you, 'Love your enemies, do good to those who hate you, and pray for those who persecute and calumniate you'" (Mt 5, 43–44).[12]

29. (*The essential equality of all people and social justice*) Since all men and women possessed of a rational soul and created in the image of God have the same nature and the same origin, and since they have been redeemed by Christ and enjoy the same divine calling and destiny, the basic equality which they all share needs to be increasingly recognised.

Not everyone is identical in physical capacity and in mental and moral resources. But every type of discrimination affecting the fundamental rights of the person, whether social or cultural, on grounds of sex, race, colour, class, language or religion, should be overcome and done away with, as contrary to the purpose of God. It is matter for deep regret that these basic personal rights are still not universally recognised and respected, as when women are denied the choice of a husband or a state of life, or opportunities for education and culture equal to those of men.

Moreover, although there are just differences among individuals, the equal dignity of persons demands access to more human and equal conditions of life. And the excessive economic and social inequalities among members or peoples of the same human family are a scandal and are at variance with social justice, equity, the dignity of the human person and, not least, social and international peace.

Human institutions, whether they be private or public, should aim to serve the dignity and the goal of human beings, opposing any social or political slavery and safeguarding the basic rights of all under every form of government. And such institutions should gradually align themselves with spiritual interests which are the highest of all, even if sometimes considerable time is required to reach this desired goal.

30. (*Transcending the ethics of individualism*) The profound and rapid change of affairs gives urgency to the demand that no one should, through disregard for events or lethargy, indulge in a merely individualist morality. The duties of justice and charity are increasingly fulfilled when everyone contributes to the common good according to his or her own resources and the needs of others, and also promotes and supports public and private institutions which serve to improve human living conditions. There are some people who are bountiful and generous in their views but who behave in fact as if they had no care for society's needs. In various parts of the world quite a number make light of society's laws and statutes. A considerable sector does not shrink from fraudulent and deceitful behaviour to escape the just taxes and other contributions which are due to society. Others show little concern for some of the regulations of social life, relating for instance to the protection of health or to speed-limits, not realising that by such carelessness they are endangering their own and others' lives.

All should agree in acknowledging that social relationships are among the most important responsibilities of all of us today, and in respecting them. The more united the world is, the more our responsibilities transcend our particular groups and gradually extend to the entire world. This cannot be achieved unless both as individuals and as groups we cultivate the moral and social virtues among ourselves and propagate them throughout society to produce, with the indispensable help of God's grace, really new people and builders of a new humanity.

31. (*Responsibility and participation*) To help individuals exercise more care in discharging their conscientious duty towards themselves, as well as towards the various groups to which they belong, there is a need for a fuller type of cul-

tural education utilising the immense aids available to the human race today. There is special need for the education of youth of all social origins to be undertaken in such a way that it produces men and women who are not just cultivated people but who are also, as is urgently required today, generous in spirit.

People will have difficulty in attaining this sense of responsibility, however, unless their conditions of life allow them to be aware of their dignity and to respond to their calling of applying themselves to God and to others. Human freedom is often enfeebled when people fall into extreme need, just as it is cheapened when they take all that life has to offer and enclose themselves in splendid isolation. But it is strengthened when they recognise the unavoidable requirements of life in society, accept the variety of needs arising from human relationships and devote themselves to serving the human community.

All should therefore be encouraged to play their part in enterprises of a community nature. The arrangement obtaining in some countries, where as many citizens as possible freely participate in public affairs, is to be commended; although the actual situation of each people and the need for a strong public authority should be respected. To encourage all citizens to share in the life of the various groups which make up the body social, it is important that in such groups they should find benefits for themselves which also dispose them to help others. We may rightly judge that the future of humanity is in the hands of those who can hand on to posterity grounds for living and for hope.

32. (*The incarnate Word and human solidarity*) Just as God did not create human beings to live separately but to form a united society, it also "pleased God . . . not to sanctify and save them individually, without mutual relationships, but

224 | Vatican II

to make them into a people which would recognise God in truth and serve God in holiness."[13] From the very beginning of the history of salvation God chose men and women not just as individuals but as members of a community. In revealing this plan God called those whom he had chosen "my people" (Ex 3, 7–12), with whom God also made a covenant at Sinai.[14]

This community characteristic is being perfected and completed by the work of Jesus Christ. For the incarnate Word chose to share in human society. He took part in the wedding at Cana, he visited Zacchaeus, he ate with publicans and sinners. He revealed his Father's love and the unique vocation of women and men in terms of the most ordinary of social events and through expressions and illustrations from everyday life. He sanctified human relationships, especially those of the family, from which society takes its origin, and he was willingly subject to the laws of his country. He chose the life of a workman appropriate to his age and situation.

In his preaching he explicitly commanded God's children to behave towards each other as sisters and brothers. In his prayer he asked that all his disciples should be one. And he offered himself, even unto death, for all, as the Redeemer of all. "Greater love has no one than this, of laying down one's life for one's friends" (Jn 15, 13). He instructed the apostles to preach the gospel message to all peoples so that the human race should become God's family in which the law would be fulfilled by love.

As the first-born of many brothers and sisters, by giving his Spirit after his death and resurrection he set up among those who accept him in faith and love a new communion of kinship, his body, which is the church, in which all as members of each other would serve each other in accordance with the various gifts imparted to them.

This solidarity must continually increase until the day of its accomplishment when women and men saved by grace will give perfect glory to God as the family beloved of God and of Christ its brother.

Chapter 3. Human activity throughout the world

33. (*Description of the problem*) By effort and ingenuity the human race has always attempted to develop its life. Today, particularly with the aid of science and technology, it has extended and continues to extend its control over almost the whole of nature, and especially with the help of increased international activity the human family is gradually recognising and realising its identity as a single worldwide community. As a result it is now providing itself through its own resources with many of the things which formerly it largely expected would come from powers above.

In the presence of this vast enterprise, in which the whole human race is now involved, many questions are emerging. What precisely is the meaning and the value of this effort? How are all these resources to be utilised? What is the goal to be set for individual and collective enterprises? The church, as guardian of the deposit of God's word, draws religious and moral principles from it, but it does not always have a ready answer to particular questions, wishing to combine the light of revelation with universal experience so that illumination can be forthcoming on the direction which humanity has recently begun to take.

34. (*The value of human activity*) Believers are agreed that individual and collective human activity, the massive endeavour of humanity throughout history to improve the conditions of life, corresponds in principle to God's design. Created in God's image, humankind was commissioned to subdue the

earth and all it contains, to rule the world in justice and holiness,[1] and, recognising God as the Creator of all things, to
refer itself and the totality of things to God so that, with everything subject to God, the divine name would be admired
through all the earth.[2]

This also applies to everyday activities. Men and women
who are providing for themselves and their families, and are
thus performing an appropriate service in society, can rightly
regard themselves as furthering the Creator's work by their
labour, as being concerned for the wellbeing of their fellows
and as making a personal contribution to the achievement of
the divine plan in history.[3]

Far from thinking, then, that the achievements of human enterprise and ability are in opposition to the power of
God, or that the rational creature is a rival to God, Christians
are of the view that the successes of the human race are a
sign of God's greatness and a result of God's marvellous design. The more the power of women and men increases, the
greater becomes their individual and collective responsibility. The christian message is seen, then, not as discouraging
them from building the world, or as leading them to neglect
the wellbeing of their fellows, but as strictly obliging them
to this as their duty.[4]

35. (*Organising human activity*) Proceeding as it does from human beings, human activity is for them. When they are active, they are not just changing things and society; they are
also perfecting themselves. They are learning much, exercising their abilities, going outside and beyond the self. And
this kind of expansion, rightly understood, is of more worth
than the accumulation of wealth. People are more valuable
for what they are than for what they have.[5] Similarly, all that
they do to bring about greater justice, more extensive kin-

ship and a more human structure of human relationships, is of more value than technological progress. Such progress can provide the raw material for human betterment, but it can never achieve it on its own.

The norm, then, of human activity is that, in accordance with God's design and will, it should really be of benefit to the human race and should enable people, both individually and in society, to pursue and fulfil their total calling.

36. (*The just autonomy of earthly realities*) Many of our contemporaries, however, seem to fear that a closer connection between human activity and religion will prejudice the autonomy of humanity, of societies or of the sciences. If we take the autonomy of earthly realities to mean that created things, and societies also, have their own laws and values which are to be gradually discovered, utilised and ordered by us, then it is perfectly proper to claim such autonomy as not only demanded by people today but as in harmony with the will of the Creator. From the fact of being created, every thing possesses its own stability, truth and goodness, and its own laws and order, which should be respected by us in recognising the methods which are appropriate to the various sciences and arts. Therefore methodical inquiry in all disciplines, if it is conducted in a really scientific manner and according to moral norms, can never really be at variance with faith, since secular realities and the realities of faith have their origin in the same God.[6] And whoever tries humbly and perseveringly to explore the hidden depths of reality is being led, even unawares, by the hand of God who upholds everything and makes it what it is. One can therefore legitimately regret attitudes to be found sometimes even among Christians, through an insufficient appreciation of the rightful autonomy of science, which have led many people to

conclude from the disagreements and controversies which such attitudes have aroused, that there is opposition between faith and science.[7]

If, however, the autonomy of earthly realities is taken to mean that created things are not dependent on God and that we can use them without reference to their Creator, then anyone who acknowledges God realises the falsity of such opinions. For without its Creator the creature simply disappears. And all believers of whatever religion have always sensed the voice and manifestation of the Creator in the utterances of creatures. If God is ignored the creature itself is impoverished.

37. (*Human activity corrupted by sin*) Scripture, confirmed by the experience of centuries, teaches the human family that although human progress is of great advantage to us it brings great temptations with it: the order of values is upset, evil is mixed with good, and individuals and groups consider only their own interests and not those of others. As a result the world is no longer a place for true fellowship, and our increased power is now threatening to destroy the human race itself.

The whole of human history is permeated with an arduous struggle against the powers of darkness which started at the world's beginning and will continue to the last day, as the Lord tells us.[8] Finding ourselves in this conflict, we have continually to fight to ally ourselves with good, and only with great effort and the help of God's grace can we achieve unity within ourselves.

This is why, while the church trusts in the Creator's plan and recognises that human progress can be of service to the true happiness of human beings, it can only echo the injunction of Paul, "do not be conformed to this world" (Rm 12, 2), namely, to the spirit of vanity and badness which distorts human activity, ordained for the service of God and of men and women, into an instrument of sin.

If anyone asks how such a state of affairs can be overcome, Christians proclaim that all human activity, which is daily jeopardised through pride and distorted self-love, needs to be purified and completed by the cross and resurrection of Christ. Redeemed by Christ and made a new creature in the holy Spirit, humankind can and should love the things which God has created. We receive them from God and regard and respect them as flowing from the hand of God. We thank our benefactor for them, and in using and enjoying creatures in poverty and freedom of spirit we attain to a true possession of the world, as having nothing yet possessing everything.[9] "All are yours, and you are Christ's, and Christ is God's" (1 Cor 3, 22–23).

38. (*Human activity brought to perfection in the paschal mystery*) When the Word of God, through whom all things were made, was himself made flesh and dwelt on earth among us[10] he entered into the world's history as the perfect human being and assumed and summed it all up in himself.[11] It is he who reveals to us that "God is love" (1 Jn 4, 8) and at the same time teaches us that the fundamental law of human perfection, and therefore of the world's transformation, is the new command of love. He gives those who believe in divine love the conviction that the way of love is open to all people and that the attempt to establish worldwide fellowship is not a delusion. At the same time he enjoins that this love is to be pursued not just in great matters but above all in the ordinary circumstances of life. Undergoing death on behalf of all of us sinners,[12] he teaches us by his example the need to carry the cross which the flesh and the world lay upon those who pursue peace and justice. Established as lord by his resurrection and given all power in heaven and on earth,[13] Christ is

now at work in human hearts through the strength of his Spirit, not only instilling a desire for the world to come but also thereby animating, purifying and reinforcing the noble aspirations which drive the human family to make its life one that is more human and to direct the whole earth to this end. The gifts of the Spirit vary: some people the Spirit calls to give clear witness to the desire for a heavenly dwelling and to keep this before the eyes of the human family; while others the Spirit calls to devote themselves to the earthly service of humanity, in this ministry making preparations for the heavenly kingdom. To all the Spirit gives the freedom to deny self-love and to direct all earthly resources towards human life, stretching out towards the future when humanity itself will become an offering acceptable to God.[14]

An earnest of this hope and sustenance for the journey have been left by the Lord to his followers in the sacrament of faith, in which natural elements cultivated by human hands are turned into his glorious body and blood, the supper of brotherly and sisterly communion and the foretaste of the heavenly banquet.

39. (*A new earth and a new heaven*) We do not know the hour of earth's and humankind's consummation,[15] nor how the universe is to be transformed. The form of this world which has been deformed by sin is passing away,[16] but we are taught that God is preparing a new habitation and a new earth in which justice resides,[17] and whose happiness will fulfil and surpass all the longings for peace which arise in human hearts.[18] Then death will have been defeated, the daughters and sons of God will be raised up in Christ, and what was sown in weakness and corruption will put on incorruptibility,[19] love and the work of love will abide,[20] and the whole of creation which God created for our sake will be freed from its bondage to decay.[21]

We are warned that it is of no profit to us if we gain the whole world but lose ourselves.[22] And yet the expectation of a new earth should not weaken, but rather stimulate, the resolve to cultivate this earth where the body of the new human family is increasing and can even now constitute a foreshadowing of the new age. Although earthly progress must be carefully distinguished from the growth of Christ's kingdom, nevertheless its capacity to contribute to a better ordering of human society makes it highly relevant to the kingdom of God.[23]

For the values of human dignity, of fellowship and of freedom, those valuable fruits of nature and of our own energy which we shall have produced here on earth in the Spirit of the Lord and in obedience to God's command, will all be cleansed from all disfigurement and be shining and transformed, to be regained by us when Christ hands over to the Father an eternal and universal kingdom: "a kingdom of truth and life, of holiness and grace, a kingdom of justice, love and peace."[24] Here on earth that kingdom is already mysteriously present; at the Lord's coming it will be consummated.

Chapter 4. The church's task in today's world

40. (*The interrelation between the church and the world*) Everything that we have said about the dignity of the human person, the community of women and men and the significance of human activity provides ground for the relationship between the church and the world and a basis for mutual dialogue.[1] In this chapter we presuppose all that the council has already stated about the mystery of the church, and we turn our attention to the church as it actually exists in this world and lives and acts with it.

The church was initiated by the love of the eternal Father,[2] was founded in history by Christ the Redeemer and was made one by the holy Spirit,[3] and it has a saving and eschatological function which can be fully discharged only in the age to come. Yet it is now present on earth, composed of people who are members of the earthly city and are summoned to constitute, even now in human history, the family of God's children which must ever increase until the Lord's coming. United for heavenly values and endowed with them, this family has been "constituted and set up as a society in this world" by Christ,[4] and equipped with "the appropriate means of visible and social union."[5] Thus the church, as at the same time "an identifiable group and a spiritual community,"[6] proceeds on its way with the whole of humanity and shares the world's earthly lot, while also being a leaven and a sort of soul of human society,[7] which is to be renewed in Christ and transformed into God's family.

This interpenetration of the heavenly and earthly cities can be grasped only by faith, and remains in fact the mystery of human history which will be disturbed by sin until the brightness of God's children is fully revealed. The church pursues its saving purpose not only by communicating divine life to humanity but also by reflecting the light of that life throughout the world, particularly in healing and ennobling the dignity of the human person, strengthening the fabric of human society and investing the daily activity of men and women with a deeper sense and significance. In this way the church believes that through its individual members and as a whole it can contribute much to making the human family and its history more human.

The catholic church is pleased, moreover, to recognise the contributions made and being made in these areas by other christian churches or ecclesiastical communities working together. And it is convinced that in preparing the way for the gospel it can be greatly helped in various ways by the world, whether by individuals or by society and their resources and activities. It now proposes some general principles to promote this mutual activity and aid in areas which are common in some degree to the church and the world.

41. (*The help offered by the church to individuals*) Contemporary humanity is in the process of developing its personality and of increasingly identifying and claiming its rights. Since the church has been entrusted with making manifest the mystery of God, which is our ultimate goal, at the same time it discloses to us the meaning of our existence, or the intimate truth about ourselves. The church is fully aware that only the God whom it serves corresponds to the deepest hunger of the human heart, which can never be satisfied with earthly nourishment. It is also aware that humanity is being continually stirred by the Spirit of God and can therefore never be completely indifferent to the problems of religion, as is borne out by the experience of previous centuries as well as by the varied witness of our own times. People will always, at least indistinctly, want to know what meaning to give to their life, their activity and their dying. The church's presence reminds us of such problems. Only God, who created us in the divine image and redeemed us from sin, can give a complete answer to these questions; and God does this through his revelation in the Son who became human. Whoever follows Christ, the perfect human being, becomes more of a human being.

By this faith the church is able to preserve the dignity of human nature from all changing views which, for instance, either devalue the human body or unduly concentrate on it. No human law is able to safeguard the personal dignity and freedom of humans as fittingly as the gospel which Christ has entrusted to his church. The gospel announces and proclaims the liberty of God's children, rejects every slavery as ultimately resulting from sin,[8] reverently respects the dignity of conscience and its free decision, continually teaches that all human talents should be devoted to God's service and the wellbeing of women and men, and commends all to the love of all.[9] This gospel message corresponds to the fundamental law of the christian dispensation. For although it is the same God who is Creator and Saviour, lord of human history and of salvation history, far from this divine order depriving creation and especially humanity of its just autonomy it reinstates this autonomy and strengthens its dignity.

And so the church is empowered by the gospel entrusted to it to proclaim the rights of humanity and to recognise and value the modern movement to promote these rights everywhere. This movement must, however, be imbued with the spirit of the gospel and be protected from all appearance of mistaken autonomy. We are tempted to consider our personal rights as fully protected only when we are free of every norm of divine law; but following this road leads to the destruction rather than to the maintenance of the dignity of the human person.

42. (*The help offered by the church to human society*) The union of the human family is greatly strengthened and brought to completion by the unity of the family of God's children which is based on Christ.[10]

The particular mission which Christ entrusted to his church is not in the political, economic or social order; the goal which he set it is in the religious order.[11] And yet this mission of a religious nature produces a function, enlightenment and resources which can be of service in constructing and strengthening the human community in accordance with the divine law. And when necessary, according to circumstances of time and place, this mission can, and even should, initiate works to serve everyone, especially the needy, such as the works of mercy and the like.

The church also recognises whatever good is to be found in the modern social movement, especially the development of unity and the process of healthy socialisation and of civil and economic association. The encouraging of unity is in accord with the church's central mission since it is "a sacrament, or sign and instrument, in Christ of intimate union with God and of the unity of the whole human race."[12] It demonstrates to the world that genuine exterior social union has its origin in the union of minds and hearts, in the faith and love on which its unity is indissolubly founded in the holy Spirit. The influence which the church can inject into modern society consists in that faith and love being put into practice and not in some external power exercised in merely human ways.

Since its mission and nature do not identify the church with any particular form of human culture or any political, economic or social system, its universality can make the church a close bond between the different human communities and peoples, so long as they trust it and really respect its genuine freedom to fulfil this mission. For this reason the church enjoins its sons and daughters, and all people, that in this family spirit of God's children they should transcend all disagreements between nations and races and provide an internal strength to just human associations.

Whatever truth, goodness or justice is to be found in the great variety of institutions which have been formed, and continue to be formed, by the human race is regarded by the council with respect. It also states that the church wants to help and encourage all such institutions so far as this depends on the church and is compatible with its mission. In serving the wellbeing of all, it wants nothing more than to develop in freedom under any government which recognises the fundamental rights of the person and the family and the requirements of the common good.

43. (*The help offered by the church through Christians to human activity*) The council exhorts Christians as citizens of both cities to be attentive in faithfully discharging their earthly duties, led by the spirit of the gospel. Those who think that, because we do not have here a lasting city but seek the city which is to come,[13] they can therefore neglect their earthly duties, are in error and do not appreciate that their faith obliges them even more to perform them according to the vocation with which each one is called.[14] A similar mistake is committed by those who consider that they can thus become immersed in earthly undertakings, as if these were totally foreign to their religious life which they regard as consisting solely of acts of worship and the fulfilling of certain moral obligations. The split between the faith which they profess and the daily lives of many people is to be counted as among the more serious misconceptions of our day. It was a scandal attacked by the prophets in the days of the old Testament,[15] and in the new Testament it was threatened even more with serious sanctions by Jesus Christ himself.[16] No false opposition should be set up between professional and social activities on the one hand and the life of religion on the other. Christians who neglect their temporal duties are neglecting their duties to their neighbour and even to God and are endangering their eternal salvation. On the contrary, Christians should rejoice that, following the example of Christ who practised a craft, they are in a position to engage in all their earthly activities and they should bring their human, domestic, professional, scientific and technical activities into

a living synthesis with religious values which orient and co-ordinate everything to the glory of God.

It is to the laity that secular duties and activities belong, although not exclusively. When they act as citizens of the world, whether singly or together, they will not only be observing the conditions appropriate to each sphere but they will also be acquiring real expertise in those areas. They will willingly cooperate with others who have the same goal. In their awareness of what faith demands, and in the strength of that faith, they should immediately introduce whatever initiatives are required and bring them to fruition. It is a matter for their properly formed conscience that God's law be impressed on the life of the earthly city. The laity may expect enlightenment and spiritual help from the clergy. But they should not consider that their pastors always have the expertise needed to provide a concrete and ready answer to every problem which arises, even the most serious ones, or that this is their mission. The laity, as enlightened with christian wisdom and paying careful attention to the teaching of the magisterium,[17] have their own part to play.

Sometimes the christian world-view will dispose them to favour one particular solution in certain circumstances, while others of the faithful who are no less sincere will take a different line on the same matter, as is not uncommon and quite permissible. And if the solutions proposed from one side or another are considered by many as simply following from the gospel, even though their proponents do not intend this, they should bear in mind that in such cases no one is allowed to claim the church's authority for his or her view alone. They should always work to enlighten each other in honest dialogue and maintain mutual love while concentrating on the common good.

The laity have an active part to play in the entire life of the church, and are not just obliged to give the world a christian spirit, but are also called to be witnesses to Christ in all they do within human society.

The bishops, who have been entrusted with the function of governing God's church, should preach Christ's message along with their priests in such a way that all the earthly activities of the faithful are illuminated by the gospel. And all pastors should remember that in their daily behaviour and concerns[18] they are presenting the face of the church to the world, and that people judge from that the force and the truth of the christian message. In their lives and their words, along with religious and the faithful, they should show that simply by its presence, with all its endowments, the church is the inexhaustible source of those virtues of which today's world stands most in need. They should study carefully to equip themselves to play their part in entering into dialogue with the world and with people of every persuasion. Above all, they should take to heart these words of the council, "since the human race is today becoming more and more of a civil, economic and social unity, it is all the more necessary for priests to share their concern and resources under the guidance of the bishops and the supreme pontiff and eliminate all forms of division, so that the whole human race may be brought into the unity of the family of God."[19]

Although by the power of the holy Spirit the church has remained a faithful spouse to her Lord and has never ceased to be a sign of salvation in the world, it is well aware that in the course of its long history it has not lacked members,[20] both clerical and lay, who have been unfaithful to the Spirit of God. Even at present the church is not blind to the large gap which exists between the message which it delivers and the human frailty of those who are entrusted with the gospel.

Whatever may be the verdict of history on these failings, we ought to be aware of them and assiduously combat them to prevent their harming the spread of the gospel. The church is equally conscious of how much it needs to learn from the experience of centuries in cultivating its relationship to the world. Guided by the holy Spirit, mother church continually exhorts her children "to purification and renewal, so that the sign of Christ may shine more clearly on the face of the church."[21]

44. (*The help the church receives from the modern world*) Just as it is important for the world to recognise the church as a social reality and agent in history, so the church also is aware of how much it has received from the history and development of the human race.

The experience of past centuries, the advances in the sciences and the treasures hidden in the various forms of human culture, which disclose human nature more completely and indicate new ways to the truth, are of benefit also to the church. From the beginning of its history it has learned to express Christ's message in the concepts and languages of various peoples, and it has also tried to throw light on it through the wisdom of philosophers, aiming so far as was proper to suit the gospel to the grasp of everyone as well as to the expectations of the wise. This adaptation in preaching the revealed word should remain the law of all evangelisation. In this way, in every nation, the capacity to express Christ's message in its own fashion is stimulated and at the same time a fruitful interchange is encouraged between the church and various cultures.[22] To develop such an exchange, especially in a time characterised by rapid change and a growing variety in ways of thought, the church has particular need of those who live in the world, whether they are believers or not, and who are familiar with its various institutions and disciplines and understand them intimately. It is for God's people as a whole, with the help of the holy Spirit, and especially for pastors and theologians, to listen to the various voices of our day, discerning them and interpreting them, and to evaluate them in the light of the divine word, so that the revealed truth can be increasingly appropriated, better understood and more suitably expressed.

Since the church has a visible social structure, as a sign of its unity in Christ, it can and does benefit from the development of human life in society, not in the sense that anything is lacking in the constitution given it by Christ, but in order to gain a deeper appreciation of that constitution and to express it in better terms and to adapt it more successfully to the present day. The church gratefully acknowledges the variety of help which it receives as a whole, as well as in its individual children, from people of every class and condition. Whoever gives encouragement to the human community in the sphere of the family, culture, economic and social life, and political life at the national or international level, is in God's design contributing no little help to the community of the church insofar as this relies upon externals. And indeed the church affirms that it has derived, and can derive, much benefit from the opposition of its opponents and persecutors.[23]

45. (*Christ, the alpha and omega*) While it helps the world and receives much from the world, the church has only one goal, namely the coming of God's kingdom and the accomplishment of salvation for the whole human race. Whatever good God's people can contribute to the human family, in the period of its earthly pilgrimage, derives from the church's being "the universal sacrament of salvation,"[24] which shows forth and at the same time brings into effect the mystery of God's love for humanity.

For the Word of God, through whom all things were made, was made flesh so that as perfectly human he would save all human beings and sum up all things. The Lord is the goal of human history, the point on which the desires of history and civilisation turn, the centre of the human race, the joy of all hearts and the fulfilment of all desires.[25] He it was whom the Father raised from the dead, exalted and placed at his right hand, making him judge of the living and the dead. It is as given life and united in his Spirit that we make our pilgrimage towards the climax of human history which is in full accord with the design of his love, "to unite all things in him, things in heaven and things on earth" (Eph 1, 10).

Part 2

Some urgent problems

46. (*Introduction*) Having outlined the dignity of the human person and the individual and social task which he and she is called to fulfil in the world as a whole, the council now draws attention in the light of the gospel and of human experience to certain urgent contemporary needs which particularly affect the human race.

Among the many causes for universal concern today the outstanding ones are: marriage and the family, human culture, socio-economic and political life, union within the family of nations, and peace. It is hoped that each of these will become clearer through the principles and the light which come from Christ and which will lead the faithful and enlighten all humanity in the search for solutions to such a multitude of complex problems.

Chapter 1. Promoting the dignity of marriage and the family

47. (*Marriage and the family in the modern world*) The well-being of the person and of human and christian society is intimately connected with the healthy state of the community of marriage and the family. That is why Christians and all who value this community derive real satisfaction from the various supports being developed today in promoting this community of love and caring for its life as well as in helping married couples and parents in their outstanding task. They also look for further benefits and desire to encourage them.

The dignity of this institution, however, is not in evidence to the same degree everywhere, being obscured by polygamy, the plague of divorce, free love and other deformities. And married love is often demeaned by selfishness, pleasure-seeking and wrongful practices against having children. In addition, modern economic, socio-psychological and public conditions are seriously disrupting families, and in some regions the problems arising from increasing population are causing anxiety. All these factors are disturbing the consciences of people. And yet the power and vigour of marriage and the family are also to be seen in the fact that, whatever difficulties the profound changes in modern society may entail, they also frequently bring to light in various ways the true character of this institution.

Accordingly, by highlighting some major features of the church's teaching, the council aims to enlighten and encourage Christians and all people who are working for the protection and fostering of the inherent dignity and the noble and sacred significance of the state of matrimony.

48. (*The holiness of marriage and the family*) The covenant, or irrevocable personal consent, of marriage sets up an intimate sharing of married life and love as instituted by the Creator

and regulated by God's laws. Thus, the human action in which spouses give themselves to each other and accept each other results in an institution which is stable by divine ordinance and also in the eyes of society. This sacred bond, aimed at the good of the couple and their children and of society, does not depend on human decision. It is God who is the author of marriage and its endowment with various values and purposes,[1] all of which are of such vital importance for the continuance of the human race, the personal development and eternal destiny of the individual members of the family, and the dignity, stability, peace and prosperity of the family itself and of human society as a whole. The institution of marriage and married love are, of their nature, directed to the begetting and upbringing of children and they find their culmination in this. Thus it is that a man and a woman, who "are no longer two but one flesh" (Mt 19, 6) in their marital covenant, help and serve each other in their intimate union of persons and activities, and from day to day experience and increase their sense of oneness. Such intimacy, as a mutual giving of two persons, as well as the good of their children require complete faithfulness between the partners, and call for their union being indissoluble.[2]

Christ the Lord has richly blessed this varied love, which has sprung from the divine fountain of love, to be a reflection of his union with the church. As God once approached his people with a covenant of love and faithfulness,[3] so now the Saviour of women and men, and husband of the church,[4] comes to meet christian couples through the sacrament of matrimony. God abides with them so that, as he loved the church and gave himself for it,[5] likewise marriage partners may love each other with everlasting fidelity in their dedication to each other. Genuine married love is taken up into the divine love and is directed and endowed by the redeeming power of Christ and the saving action of the church, so that married couples may be successfully led to God and be helped and strengthened in their noble task as father and mother.[6] For this reason christian partners are fortified and in a sense consecrated for the duties and dignity of their state by a special sacrament,[7] by virtue of which they fulfil their marital and parental tasks, imbued with the Spirit of Christ who fills their whole life with faith, hope and love, and increasingly attain to their own perfection, their mutual sanctification and their joint glorying of God.

With parents leading them by example and family prayer, children and all who live within the family circle will more readily discover the way to humanity, salvation and holiness. And married couples, honoured with the dignity and duty of parenthood, will diligently discharge their responsibility of education, especially in religion, which belongs to them before anyone else.

As active members of the family, children contribute in their own way to the sanctification of their parents. They will respond with gratitude, respect and trust to what their parents do for them and will help them, as children should, in their difficulties and the loneliness of old age. Widowhood accepted bravely as an extension of the vocation of marriage will be respected by all.[8] The family will generously make its spiritual resources available to other families. And the christian family, springing as it does from marriage as reflecting and sharing in the covenant of the love of Christ and the church,[9] will reveal to all people the active presence of the Saviour in the world and the genuine nature of the church, in the love, the generous fruitfulness, the unity and the faithfulness of husband and wife, and the loving cooperation of all the members.

49. (*Married love*) The word of God regularly invites engaged

and married couples to nurture and cherish their betrothal with a love which is chaste, and their marriage with a devotion which is undivided.[10] And many people today value true love between husband and wife as this finds expression in various ways according to the honourable practices of different peoples and times. Fully human as it is, in being willed by one person for another, such a love embraces the good of the entire person and is therefore capable of endowing human expressions with a particular dignity and of ennobling them as special features and manifestations of married friendship. The Lord deigned to heal, perfect and raise this love by a special gift of grace and charity. Such love, bringing together the human and the divine, leads couples to a free and mutual self-giving shown in tender feelings and actions, and permeates the whole of their lives,[11] being itself also perfected and increased by its own generosity. Thus it is vastly more than mere eroticism which is selfishly stimulated and quickly and disappointingly vanishes.

This devoted love finds its unique expression and development in the behaviour which is proper to marriage. The acts by which married couples are intimately and chastely united are honourable and respectable, and when they are carried out in a truly human way they express and encourage a mutual giving in which a couple gladly and gratefully enrich each other. This love sincerely confirmed by mutual fidelity, and made especially sacrosanct by the sacrament of Christ, is indissolubly faithful physically and mentally in prosperity and adversity, and is therefore far removed from all adultery and divorce. The unity of matrimony confirmed by the Lord is also clearly apparent in the equal personal dignity of the wife and the husband which is recognisable in mutual and full love. Outstanding virtue, however, is needed to fulfil the duties of this christian vocation with constancy. This is why married couples, strengthened by grace for a holy life, will perseveringly practise, and gain through prayer, endurance in love, generosity of heart and a spirit of sacrifice.

Real marital love will be thought of more highly and held in public esteem if christian married couples are noted for the witness of faithfulness and harmony in their love and for their concern to bring up their children, and if they contribute to the cultural, psychological and social renewal which is required for marriage and the family. Young people should be instructed suitably and in good time on the dignity, duty and details of married love, especially within the family, so that they may acquire the practice of chastity and at a suitable age can make the transition through honourable engagement to marriage.

50. (*The fruitfulness of marriage*) Of their nature marriage and married love are directed towards the begetting and bringing up of children. Children are the supreme gift of a marriage and they contribute greatly to the good of their parents. God who said "it is not good that the man should be alone" (Gn 2, 18) and who "from the beginning made them male and female" (Mt 19, 4), wished to give them a special share in the divine work of creation and blessed the man and woman, saying "be fruitful and multiply" (Gn 1, 28). Thus the true practice of marital love and the whole dimension of family life which results from it, without prejudice to the other purposes of marriage, point towards married couples being courageously prepared to cooperate with the love of the Creator and Saviour who is daily increasing and enriching his family through them.

In the office of transmitting and bringing up human life, which should be considered their special mission, married couples know that they are cooperators with the love of God the Creator and in a sense its interpreters. They will accordingly discharge their task with human and christian responsibility, and will reach a right decision for themselves in humble reverence for God and by shared counsel and endeavour, with an eye to their own good and that of their children, whether those already born or those foreseen, discerning the material and spiritual conditions of the times and of their condition of life, and bearing in mind the good of the family community, of human society and of the church. Ultimately married couples ought to make this decision themselves before God. In reaching it, however, christian couples should be aware that they cannot just do as they please, but ought always to be ruled by a conscience in conformity with the divine law, and be attentive to the church's teaching authority which officially interprets that law in the light of the gospel. That divine law shows the full meaning of marital love, it protects it and encourages it towards its truly human perfection. Thus christian couples who trust in divine providence and practise a spirit of sacrifice[12] are glorifying their Creator and advancing towards perfection in Christ when they discharge their office of procreating with generous, human and christian responsibility. Among the couples who fulfil the task given them by God in this way, special recognition should be accorded those who prudently and jointly decide with open hearts to have a large family which they will bring up in a suitable manner.[13]

Marriage, however, was not instituted just for procreation; the very nature of an unbreakable covenant between persons and the good of the offspring also demand that the mutual love of the partners should be rightly expressed and should develop and mature. And therefore even if children, often longed for, are not forthcoming, marriage remains as a sharing and communion for the whole of life and retains its goodness and indissolubility.

51. (*Reconciling married love with respect for human life*) The council is aware that in living their married life harmoniously, couples can often be restricted by modern living conditions and find themselves in circumstances in which the number of their children cannot be increased, at least for a time, and the constant expression of love and the full sharing of life are maintained only with difficulty. When the intimacy of married life is broken off, the value of fidelity can frequently be at risk and the value of children can be undermined; and then the bringing up of the children and the readiness to have further children are endangered.

Some people take it upon themselves to solve these difficulties by dishonourable solutions, and do not even shrink from killing. But the church reiterates that there cannot be a true contradiction between the divine laws of transmitting life and of promoting genuine married love.

For God, the lord of life, has entrusted to women and men the outstanding service of watching over life and of fulfilling this in a manner worthy of human beings. Therefore from the time of conception life is to be safeguarded with the greatest of care; abortion and infanticide are abominable crimes. The sexual nature of man and woman and the human faculty of reproduction are wonderfully superior to what is possessed in the lower stages of life; consequently those acts which are proper to married life and directed in accordance with true human dignity are to be treated with great respect. When there is, therefore, a question of reconciling marital love with the responsible transmission of life, the moral character of the behaviour does not depend simply on good intention and evaluation of motives, but ought to be determined by objective criteria, derived from the nature of the person and its acts, which take account of the whole meaning of mutual giving and human procreation in the context of true love; and this cannot be achieved if the virtue of marital chastity is not sincerely practised. It is not permitted to daughters and sons of the church who rely on these principles to take steps for regulating procreation which are rejected by the teaching authority in its explanation of the divine law.[14]

All should be aware that the life of human beings, and the office of transmitting that life, cannot be restricted just to this world or be measured and understood by that criterion, but always look to the eternal destiny of humanity.

52. (*Promoting marriage and the family as the concern of all*) The family is a school for a richer humanity. For it to find fulfilment in its life and mission, it needs openness and collaboration on the part of husband and wife and their committed cooperation in raising their children. The involvement of the father can contribute greatly to their formation, and the care of the mother in the home which younger children especially need must be safeguarded, without prejudice to the legitimate advancement of woman in society. Children should be educated in such a way that on reaching adulthood they can exercise full responsibility in following their calling, including a sacred vocation, and in choosing a state of life in which, if they marry, they can found their own family under suitable moral, social and economic conditions. It is for parents or educators to act as guides to young people establishing a family, by their prudent advice which should be willingly listened to, while taking care not to drive them directly or indirectly into marriage or the choice of a partner.

In this way the family, where different generations meet and help each other to increase in wisdom and to reconcile the rights of persons with other requirements of social life, constitutes the basis of society. Therefore all who have influence in communities and social bodies ought to contribute effectively to encouraging marriage and the family. Public authority should consider it its sacred duty to recognise, protect and advance the true nature of marriage and the family, to safeguard public morality and to promote family prosperity. The right of parents to have children and to bring them up in the home should be protected. Legal provision and other initiatives should also protect and provide suitable assistance for those who unfortunately do not have the benefit of a family.

The faithful, redeeming the present time[15] and distinguishing between eternal verities and their changeable expressions, should constantly further the values of marriage and the family, both by the witness of their own lives and by acting in concert with others of good will, and in this way they will overcome difficulties and provide the family with the supports and helps which are suited to our changing times. To this end the christian sense of the faithful, the correct moral conscience of people, and the wisdom and expertise of those who are versed in the sacred disciplines, will be of great help.

Those who are learned in the sciences, especially in the biological, medical, social and psychological fields, can be of considerable service to the good of marriage and the family, and to peace of conscience, if they collaborate in trying to throw more light on the various conditions which favour the virtuous control of procreation.

It is for priests, duly informed in family matters, to foster the vocation of married couples in their married and family life by various pastoral means—preaching God's word, the liturgy, and other spiritual helps—and to strengthen them gently and patiently in their difficulties, and to encourage them in love to produce families which are truly shining examples.

Various bodies, especially family associations, should take steps by their teaching and action to encourage young people and couples, especially those recently married, and to prepare them for family, social and apostolic life.

Married couples themselves, made in the image of the living God and established with the true status of persons, should be united in equal regard, similarity of mind and mutual holiness[16] so that, following Christ the beginning of life[17] in the joys and sacrifices of their vocation, they may become through their faithful love witnesses to that mystery of devoted love which the Lord in his death and resurrection revealed to the world.[18]

Chapter 2. The proper development of culture

53. (*Introduction*) It is a feature of the human person that it can attain to real and full humanity only through culture; that is, by cultivating the goods of nature and values. Wherever human life is concerned, therefore, nature and culture are very intimately connected.

The term "culture" in general refers to everything by which we perfect and develop our many spiritual and physical endowments; applying ourselves through knowledge and effort to bring the earth within our power; developing ways of behaving and institutions, we make life in society more human, whether in the family or in the civil sphere as a whole; in the course of time we express, share and preserve in our works great spiritual experiences and aspirations to contribute to the progress of many people, even of the whole human race.

Human culture thus necessarily takes on a historical and social aspect, and the term "culture" often has a sociological and ethnological connotation. In this sense one can talk of a plurality of cultures. The variety of ways in which objects are utilised, labour is applied, the self is expressed, religion is practised, customary ways of behaving take shape, laws and juridical institutions are established, the sciences and arts develop, and beauty is pursued, all give rise to different conditions of life in common, and different expressions in the structuring of life's resources. In this way the handing on of customs becomes an inheritance peculiar to each human community, and an identifiable historical environment is established to receive people of every race and age and to provide them with the resources to cultivate their human and social life.

Section 1: The conditions of culture in today's world
54. (*New forms of living*) The conditions of life for humanity today have changed profoundly in social and cultural terms, so much so that it is legitimate to speak of a new age in human history.[1] New ways of developing and disseminating culture are opening up, as a result of the enormous expansion of the natural and human sciences, including the social sciences, the increase in technology, and progress in the development and application of means of communication. Culture today thus has certain characteristics: the exact sciences are greatly encouraging critical judgment; recent studies in psychology are explaining human behaviour in depth; the historical disciplines are contributing to examining things from the point of view of their change and evolution; customs and habits are daily becoming more uniform; industrialisation, urbanisation and other factors leading to life in community are creating new forms of mass culture, giving rise to new ways of thinking and behaving and of using leisure; the increasing contacts between nations and groups in society are opening to each and everyone the treasures of the various forms of

culture, and thus a more widespread form of human culture is gradually developing which is extending and expressing the unity of the human race all the more as it gives better recognition to the peculiarities of different cultures.

55. (*Man and woman as the author of culture*) There is a growing number of people in every country who are conscious of being the architects and authors of the culture of their own community. Throughout the world there is a continual increase in the awareness of autonomy as well as of responsibility, which is of the greatest significance for the spiritual and moral maturity of humankind. This is the more evident if we consider the unification of the world and the task laid on us of building a better world in terms of truth and justice. Thus we are witnesses that a new humanism is being born in which the human is defined above all in terms of our responsibility to our sisters and brothers and to history.

56. (*Difficulties and duties*) In these conditions it is not surprising that people, aware of their responsibility for the advancement of culture, have high hopes and yet are also concerned at the many contradictions which exist and which they have to resolve:

What should be done to prevent the more frequent contacts between cultures, which ought to lead to genuine fruitful dialogue between different groups and nations, from disturbing the lives of communities, undermining the wisdom of ancestors, and endangering the native characteristics of peoples?

How is the impetus and expansion of new culture to be supported without loyalty to inherited traditions being destroyed? This is of particular urgency when a culture springing from huge progress in science and technology has to be reconciled with the culture of the spirit nourished by various traditions of classical studies.

How can such rapid progressive diversification of particular disciplines be combined with the need to create a synthesis, or to preserve among men and women capacities for contemplation and wonder which lead to wisdom?

What is to be done to enable everyone in the world to share in cultural values, when at the same time the cultural attainment of the more experienced is continually rising and developing?

And how is the autonomy claimed for culture to be recognised as legitimate without its becoming a purely this-worldly humanism or even one opposed to religion?

In the midst of these tensions, human culture must evolve today to pursue a balanced cultivation of the entire human person, and to help people discharge the duties to which all, especially the faithful, are called, united as sisters and brothers in the one human family.

Section 2: Some principles for the proper development of culture
57. (*Faith and culture*) Christ's faithful on pilgrimage to a heavenly city should seek and value what is above;[2] but far from diminishing, this enhances the importance of their duty to collaborate with all others in building a world of more human construction. In fact, the mystery of the christian faith provides them with greater incentive and help in fulfilling this task more enthusiastically, and especially in uncovering the full significance of the work and according human culture its distinguished place in the complete vocation of humankind.

When by the work of our hands or by technology, we are cultivating the earth to produce fruit and a dwelling place worthy of the whole human family, and when we consciously take part in the life of social groups, we are carrying out the design of God revealed at the beginning of time of subduing the earth[3] and completing creation, and we are cultivating ourselves while at the same time observing Christ's great commandment to devote ourselves to the service of our sisters and brothers.

Moreover, when we devote ourselves to the various disciplines of philosophy, history, mathematics and the natural sciences and engage in the arts, we can greatly contribute to raising the human family to higher planes of truth, goodness and beauty, and to judgments of universal value, thus further enlightening it with the wonderful wisdom which was with God at the beginning, fashioning everything with God, rejoicing in God's inhabited world, and delighting in the inhabitants.[4]

The human mind is thereby more free from enslavement to things and can rise more readily to worship and contemplate the Creator. Under the influence of grace it is in a position to acknowledge the Word of God who, before becoming flesh to save all things and draw them together in himself, was already in the world as "the true light that enlightens everyone" (Jn 1, 9).[5]

Modern progress in science and technology, which by reason of their methods cannot penetrate to the innermost being of reality, can encourage concentration on appearances and agnosticism when the methods of investigation which they apply are unjustifiably taken as the most important rule for discovering all truth. And there is a danger of our trusting too much to modern discoveries and considering ourselves all-sufficient, and of abandoning the search for higher reality.

Such unhappy consequences are not, however, the inevitable result of modern culture nor should they tempt us to deny its positive values, including scientific study and scrupulous respect for truth in scientific enquiry, the need to work in collaboration with others, a feeling of international solidarity, a daily increasing awareness of the responsibility of experts to help and also protect others, and a wish to improve the living conditions of all, especially those who are deprived of responsibility or culturally impoverished. All of these can provide some preparation for receiving the announcement of the gospel, a preparation which can be imbued with divine love by him who came to save the world.

58. (*Multiple connections between the good news of Christ and human culture*) There are many connections between the announcement of salvation and human culture. In revealing himself to his people, even to the extent of showing himself fully in the incarnate Son, God has spoken in terms of the culture peculiar to different ages.

The church likewise, living in various conditions of history, has adopted the discoveries of various cultures to spread and explain the news of Christ in its preaching to all nations, to explore it and understand it more deeply, and to express it better in liturgical celebration and in the life of the varied community of the faithful.

At the same time the church, which has been sent to all peoples of whatever age and region, is not connected exclusively and inseparably to any race or nation, to any particular pattern of human behaviour, or to any ancient or recent customs. Loyal to its own tradition and at the same time conscious of its universal mission, it is able to enter into a communion with different forms of culture which enriches both the church and the various cultures.

The good news of Christ continually renews the life and behaviour of fallen humanity and attacks and dispels the errors and evils which flow from the ever-threatening seduction of sin. It ceaselessly purifies and enhances the ways of peoples. As if from the inside, it enriches with heavenly resources, strengthens, completes and restores in Christ the spiritual endowments and talents of every people and age.[6] Thus, in fulfilling its particular charge,[7] the church thereby encourages and contributes to human and social culture, and by its activity, including the liturgy, it educates people to inner freedom.

59. (*The proper relationships between different forms of human culture*) For these reasons the church recalls to the attention of all that culture should be directed to the total perfection of the human person, and to the good of the community and of human society as a whole. It should cultivate the mind in such a way as to encourage the ability for wonder, for understanding, for contemplation and for forming a personal judgment and cultivating a religious, moral and social sense.

Since culture flows immediately from the rational and social nature of human beings, it continually requires the just freedom to develop and the legitimate opportunity for independence according to its own principles. It rightly calls for respect and enjoys a certain inviolability, without prejudice to the rights of the person and of the particular and general community within the bounds of the common good.

Recalling the teaching of the first Vatican council, this sacred synod declares that there is a distinct "twofold order of knowledge," namely, of faith and of reason, and that the church does not forbid "cultures in the human arts and sciences to have recourse to their own principles and method in their own sphere"; "recognising this just freedom," it affirms the legitimate autonomy of human culture and especially of the sciences.[8]

All this also demands that, while observing the moral order and the common benefit, people should be able to seek the truth freely, to express and publicise their views, to cultivate every art, and finally that they should be informed of the truth of public affairs.[9]

It is not for public authority to determine the particular expressions of human culture, but to encourage the conditions and resources for promoting a cultural life for all, including minorities in any country.[10] Hence it is of the utmost importance that culture should not be diverted from its proper purpose and be forced to serve political or economic interests.

Section 3: Some urgent tasks for Christians affecting culture
60. (*The right to the benefits of culture should be recognised and implemented for all*) Since the possibility now exists to free a great many people from the wretchedness of ignorance, there is a most appropriate duty for our age, especially for Christians, to work for basic decisions to be taken in the economic and political fields and at national and international levels, to recognise and implement throughout the world the right of all to human and civil culture appropriate to the dignity of the person, without discrimination on grounds of race, sex, nationality, religion or social condition. Therefore adequate cultural resources should be made available to all, especially those which constitute a basic culture, so that great numbers of people may not be prevented through illiteracy or the lack of responsible initiative from cooperating in a genuinely human way for the common good.

Attempts should therefore be made to enable people who have the capacity, to reach higher levels of education so that, as far as possible, they may rise in society to the duties, offices and services appropriate to their ability and to the experience they have acquired.[11] In this way each individual, and social groups in every people, will be able to reach the full development of their cultural life in keeping with their gifts and traditions.

Moreover, particular efforts should be devoted to making

all aware of their right to culture, as well as of their responsibility to cultivate themselves and help others to do the same. For sometimes the conditions of life and work stifle the cultural aspirations of men and women and destroy in them the pursuit of culture. This applies particularly to rural people and manual workers, who should be afforded conditions of work which favour rather than hinder their human development. Women are now at work in almost every sphere of life, and it is fitting that they should be able to play their full part according to their disposition. Everyone should recognise and encourage the sharing in cultural life which is suitable and necessary for women.

61. (*Education for a completely human culture*) It is more difficult today than in the past to provide a synthesis of the various disciplines and arts. The scale and diversity of what goes to make up culture are increasing, while the possibility for individuals to be aware of them and unite them is decreasing, with the result that the image of the "universal individual" is gradually disappearing. Yet each individual still has a duty to have regard for the whole human person, in whom the values of understanding, will, conscience and fellowship are preeminent, have their foundation in God the Creator, and have been wonderfully healed and enhanced in Christ.

It is the family above all which is, as it were, the mother and nurse of such education, for children are there lovingly cherished and more easily come to learn the right order of things, imbibing reliable forms of human culture naturally as they grow up.

Modern societies possess opportunities for such education, especially in the increased diffusion of literature and in new means of cultural and social communication which can promote universal culture. For, as the hours of work become shorter everywhere, there is an increase of advantages for many people. Leisure time should be duly devoted to relaxation and mental and physical recreation in pastimes and study, in travel abroad which cultivates one's talents and enriches people through mutual acquaintance, and in sporting activities and events which are helpful for maintaining a balance in life, even in the community, and also for establishing relations of kinship between people of all classes, nationalities and races. Christians should therefore cooperate in instilling a human and christian spirit into the collective cultural expressions and activities of our day.

All these benefits, however, cannot bring people's education to bear on a complete self-development if at the same time they neglect the basic questions about the meaning of culture and knowledge for the human person.

62. (*The correct relationship between human and social culture and christian formation*) Although the church has contributed much to the advancement of culture, it is a fact that for contingent reasons the relationship between culture and christian formation is not always without its difficulties.

Such difficulties are not necessarily harmful to a life of faith and can even stimulate a more accurate and deeper understanding of faith. In fact, recent studies and discoveries in science, history and philosophy give rise to new enquiries with practical implications, and also demand new investigations by theologians. Moreover, while respecting the methods and requirements of theological science, theologians are invited continually to look for a more appropriate way of communicating doctrine to the people of their time; since there is a difference between the deposit or truths of faith and the manner in which—with their sense and meaning being preserved—they are expressed.[12] In pastoral care not just theological principles but also the discoveries of the secular sciences, especially of psychology and sociology, should be recognised and applied so that the faithful may be brought to a more refined and more mature life of faith.

Literature and the arts are also in their own way of great importance for the life of the church. They aim to penetrate our true nature, our problems and our experience as we strive to come to know and to develop ourselves and the world; they endeavour to disclose our situation in history and in the world, to throw light on our distresses and joys, needs and strengths, and to point to a better destiny for humankind. In this way they are capable of enhancing human life as it assumes many forms in time and place.

It follows that steps should be taken so that those who cultivate these arts feel they are recognised by the church in their endeavours and, while enjoying due freedom, develop better relations with the christian community. The church should recognise new forms of art adapted to our contemporaries, according to the variety of nations and regions, and should receive them into the sanctuary when their idiom is suitable and in conformity with the needs of the liturgy and they raise the mind to God.[13]

In this way the knowledge of God is manifested better and the gospel preaching becomes clearer to the understanding of men and women, being seen to find its place in their conditions.

The faithful should live in the closest contact with others of their time, and should work for a perfect understanding of their modes of thought and feeling as expressed in their culture. They should combine the knowledge resulting from the new sciences and teaching, and from recent discoveries, with christian morality and formation in christian teaching, so that their religious worship and uprighteousness go hand in hand with their knowledge of the sciences and increasing technology, and they are thus able to test and interpret everything with full christian awareness.

Those who are engaged in the theological disciplines in seminaries and universities should aim to collaborate and cooperate with experts in the other sciences. Theological investigation should pursue a deep knowledge of revealed truth, while not disregarding the connection with its own day, so that it can help those educated in the various disciplines to gain a fuller knowledge of the faith. This shared activity will be of great benefit for the formation of sacred ministers, enabling them to explain the church's teaching on God, humanity and the world more appropriately to our contemporaries, so that they may be the more willing to receive the word of God.[14] In fact, it is to be desired that more lay people will receive appropriate formation in the sacred disciplines and that many of them will devote themselves to pursuing these studies and developing them. So that they can discharge their task, it should be recognised that the faithful, clerical as well as lay, have a just freedom of enquiry, of thought and of humble and courageous expression in those matters in which they enjoy competence.[15]

Chapter 3. Socio-economic life

63. (*Some aspects of economic life*) The dignity of the human person and of the complete human vocation, and the good of society as a whole, must also be respected and promoted in socio-economic life. For the originator of all socio-economic life, as well as its centre and purpose, is humankind.

No less than the other areas of social life, the modern economy is characterised by our growing mastery over nature, closer and more developed contacts and interdependence among citizens, groups and peoples, and more frequent political intervention. At the same time, advances in productivity and the exchange of goods and services have made the economy an effective instrument to make better provision for the increased needs of the human family.

But there are some reasons for disquiet. Not infrequently, especially in economically developed regions, people appear to be almost ruled by economics and virtually their entire personal and social life is imbued with an economic spirit, both in countries favouring collectivism and in others. At the very time when growth in economic life could reduce the inequalities in society, if it were directed and coordinated in a rational humane manner, more often than not it is increasing them, or even in some cases worsening the social condition of the weak and ignoring the poor. While a vast multitude still wants for the absolute necessities of life, there are some, even in less developed regions, who live lives of opulence or of extravagance. Luxury coexists with wretchedness. And while a few enjoy the highest power of choice, there are many who lack almost all possibility for initiative and responsibility, often also existing in living and working conditions which are not worthy of a human person.

Similar economic and social imbalances exist between agriculture, industry and services, as can be seen even among the different regions of the same country. Between those nations which are more developed economically and those which are not, the contrast is becoming more serious every day, with possible consequences even for world peace.

Our contemporaries have a daily growing awareness of these disparities, being convinced that increased technical and economic resources such as the world enjoys today can and should correct this unfortunate state of affairs. Many reforms, however, are required in socio-economic life as well as a conversion of minds and attitudes on the part of all. To this end the church has developed through the ages in the light of the gospel, and has propounded in recent times especially, principles of justice and equity as demanded by right reason in the conduct of individual and social as well as international life. This holy council aims to corroborate these principles in modern conditions and to propose some directions, with particular reference to the needs of economic advancement.[1]

Section 1: Economic progress

64. (*Economic progress in the service of humanity*) Today more than in the past a growth in agricultural and industrial production and in services is rightly aimed at providing for an increasing population and at satisfying the growing wants of the human race. Hence, encouragement should be given to technical progress, the spirit of innovation, the wish to create and increase new enterprises, adaptation of the means of production, and the activities of all engaged in production: all the factors, namely, which contribute to this advancement. The basic purpose of this production, however, is not the mere growth of products, nor profit, nor domination, but the service of humanity and of the whole human person, taking into account material needs and the requirements of intellectual, moral, spiritual and religious life; and of every person of every group, race and region of the world. Hence, while respecting its own methods and laws, economic activity should be conducted within the limits of the moral order,[2] so that God's purpose for humanity may be brought to completion.[3]

65. (*Economic progress under human control*) Economic progress ought to remain within the control of people and not be committed to the sole decision of a few or of groups pos-

sessing too much economic power, or to the political community or to some more powerful nations. On the contrary, as many people as possible at every stage, and on the international level all nations, ought to play an active part in its direction. Likewise the spontaneous activities of individuals and of free associations need to be coordinated and suitably combined with the enterprises of public authorities.

Growth should not just be left either to some mechanism of economic activity on the part of individuals or to the power of public authority. Hence, doctrines which are opposed to necessary reforms on the grounds of a false freedom are just as mistaken as those which subordinate basic rights of individuals and groups to the collective organisation of production.[4]

Moreover, citizens should remember that they have a right and a duty, which civil powers should recognise, to contribute according to their ability to the genuine progress of their own community. Especially in economically underdeveloped countries, where every resource urgently needs to be mobilised, the common good is seriously endangered by those who keep their resources unproductive or—apart from the personal right of emigration—deprive their community of the material and spiritual supports which it needs.

66. (*Removing vast socio-economic imbalances*) For the demands of justice and equity to be met, strenuous attempts must be made, while respecting the rights of persons and the characters of peoples, to remove as quickly as possible the vast economic inequalities which exist at present and are often on the increase, and which are accompanied by individual and social discrimination. Likewise, in several regions where there are particular difficulties in production and marketing for agriculture, rural people should be helped, whether in increasing and marketing their products or in introducing

the necessary developments and innovations, or in securing a fair return, to prevent them from remaining in the condition of lower class citizens, as is often the case. Agricultural workers, especially the young, should direct their abilities to improving their professional skill, which is essential for progress in agriculture.[5]

Justice and equity also require that the mobility which is needed for economic progress is so arranged that the lives of individuals and their families are not uncertain or unsettled. And all discrimination affecting conditions of pay or work should be carefully avoided in the case of workers coming from another nation or region to contribute their labour to the economic advancement of a people or a province. Moreover, everyone, especially public authorities, ought to consider them not just as mere instruments of production but as persons, and should help them to bring their families to join them and find suitable accommodation, and should encourage their insertion into the social life of the people or region receiving them. However, so far as possible, sources of work should be created in their own regions.

In today's changing economic situation, as in new forms of industrial society, in which, for example, automation is on the increase, care should be taken to provide sufficient work suited to individuals and at the same time the opportunity for appropriate technical and professional formation, and to safeguard the means of living and human dignity especially of those for whom ill health or old age creates serious difficulties.

Section 2: Some principles governing socio-economic life as a whole

67. (*Work, working conditions and leisure*) Human labour, which is exercised in the production and exchange of goods

or in providing economic services, is superior to the other elements of economic life, which are only its instruments.

For such labour, whether undertaken on its own initiative or hired by someone else, proceeds immediately from the person, who puts a personal seal on the elements of nature and submits them to the human will. It is by their labour that people normally support their own and their dependents' lives, unite with their brothers and sisters and serve them, and are able to express a genuine love of their fellows and co-operate in bringing God's creation to its fulfilment. Indeed, we consider that through its labour offered to God humanity is associated with the work of redemption of Jesus Christ, who conferred outstanding dignity on labour in working in Nazareth with his own hands. This is the origin of each person's duty to work faithfully, and also of the person's right to work; while it is society's function, according to prevailing conditions, to help its citizens find the opportunity for adequate work. Finally, labour should be rewarded in such a way as to provide people with the capacity to cultivate in a worthy manner a material, social, cultural and religious life for themselves and their dependents, having regard to the assignment and productivity of each as well as conditions of work and the common good.[6]

Since economic activity is mostly undertaken through people sharing their labour, it is unjust and inhuman to structure and arrange it in a manner harmful to individual workers. Yet it often happens, even today, that workers are in a sense made slaves of their work. This is in no way justified by the so-called laws of economics. Therefore the entire process of productive labour must be adapted to the needs of persons and to considerations of their way of life, particularly home life, and especially as regards mothers of families, and always taking sex and age into account. Workers should also be afforded the opportunity of expressing their own qualities and their personality in their work. And, while applying their time and energy responsibly in their work, all should nevertheless also enjoy sufficient rest and leisure for their family, cultural, social and religious lives. In fact, they should have opportunities freely to develop resources and abilities which perhaps they have little occasion to use in their professional work.

68. (*Sharing enterprises and economic programmes, and disputes*) Economic enterprises are shared by persons, free and independent human beings created in the image of God. Therefore, with due regard to the functions of each, whether as owner, contractor, manager or worker, and while maintaining the unity needed for directing the work, the active participation of everyone should be promoted in ways to be appropriately determined in undertaking enterprises.[7] And since decisions affecting economic and social conditions are frequently taken not in the enterprise itself but at a higher level by higher authorities, on whom the outcome for workers and their children depends, they should also have a say in such decisions, either by themselves or through freely elected delegates.

Among the basic rights of the human person is to be considered the right of workers freely to form associations to represent them and contribute to the proper structuring of economic life, and the right to take part freely in their activities without fear of reprisal. Through such organised participation, in conjunction with developing economic and social formation, there will be a daily increase on the part of all in awareness of their particular function and duty, which can lead them to feel themselves partners, according to their capacities and abilities, in bringing about the whole work of economic and social development and the universal common good.

When socio-economic disputes occur, attempts should be made to bring them to a peaceful solution. Although there should always be recourse above all to genuine dialogue between the parties, nevertheless, even in modern conditions, the strike can remain a necessary, even if ultimate, resort to defend one's rights and to obtain the just demands of workers. But ways should be sought as soon as possible to resume negotiations and conversations aimed at reconciliation.

69. (*The earth's goods destined for all*) God has destined the earth and all it contains for the use of everyone and of all peoples, so that the good things of creation should be available equally to all, with justice as guide and charity in attendance.[8] Whatever forms property may assume, adapted to the legitimate institutions of peoples according to differing and changing situations, attention must always be focused on this universal destiny of goods. For this reason, in making use of them, we ought to regard the exterior things we lawfully possess not just as our own but also as common, in the sense that they can profit not only the owners but others also.[9] However, everyone has the right to have a part of these goods that is sufficient for each and his or her dependents. This was the view of the fathers and doctors of the church in teaching that we are obliged to support the poor, and not just from our surplus.[10] A person who is living in extreme need has the right to procure from the riches of others what is necessary for personal sustenance.[11] Since so many in the world are crushed by hunger, this holy council urges everyone, individuals as well as authorities, to be mindful of the view of the fathers, "Feed those who are dying of hunger, because if you have not fed them you have killed them,"[12]

and actually to share their goods and make them available according to their ability, especially by providing individuals and peoples with aid which can enable them to help and develop themselves.

As is obvious, for correct application of the principle all the conditions that are morally required are to be observed.

In economically underdeveloped societies, the sharing of goods is sometimes satisfied in part by a community's customs and traditions of providing the basic necessities for each member. Some customs, however, should not be considered absolutely unchangeable if they do not correspond to new modern needs; while on the other hand unconsidered action should not be taken against sound customs which are still useful provided they are adapted to modern circumstances. Similarly, in highly developed countries a body of institutions concerned with social security can help to make the common purpose of goods a reality. There needs to be an increase in family and social services, especially those concerned with culture and education. In setting all these up, however, attention should be paid to the danger of making citizens passive towards society or of their avoiding the assumption of responsibility and the idea of service.

70. (*Investment and finance*) So far as investment is concerned, it should aim at creating opportunities for work and returns which are sufficient for a people's present and future. Those who take the decisions about investments and the directing of economic life, whether individuals or groups or public authorities, are obliged to have these aims in mind and to recognise their serious obligation on the one hand to ensure that provision is made for the necessities of a suitable life on the part of individuals and of the community, and on the other hand of looking to the future and striking a just balance between the needs of present individual and collective

consumption and the requirements of investment for the next generation. Attention should also always be paid to the urgent needs of economically less developed countries or regions. In financial matters care should be taken to avoid harming the good of one's own or other countries, and to prevent those who are economically weak from unjustly suffering loss from a change in the value of money.

71. (*Acquiring property and private ownership; estates*) Since property and other forms of private ownership of external goods contribute to expressing the person, and since they provide the person with the opportunity of discharging his or her duty in society and in the economy, it is very important to encourage access to some ownership of external goods on the part of individuals and communities.

Private property or some ownership of external goods affords each person the scope needed for personal and family autonomy, and should be regarded as an extension of human freedom. And because it adds the incentive to exercising duties and responsibilities, it is a condition of civil liberties.[13]

Such ownership or property takes different forms today and increasingly so. Despite social provision and rights and services obtained from society, it remains a basis for security which should not be underestimated. This applies not only to material property but also to non-material goods such as professional abilities.

The right to private ownership is not at variance with the right which resides in various forms of public property. The transfer of goods to public ownership can be undertaken only by the competent authority in accordance with the requirements and limitations of the common good and with the offer of fair compensation. Moreover, public authority should ensure that nobody misuses private property contrary to the common good.[14]

Even private property of its nature also has a social aspect which is based on the law of the common purpose of goods.[15] If this social dimension is neglected, property frequently comes to be an occasion for greed and serious disorder, and provides a pretext for opponents to call the right itself into question.

In several economically underdeveloped regions, large and even vast estates are to be found which are only lightly cultivated or uncultivated for the sake of profit, while the greater part of the people has either no land or only a very little, yet the need to increase agricultural production is obviously seen to be urgent. Often those who are employed as workers by the owners or who rent part of an estate receive nothing but a wage or income unworthy of human beings, are deprived of decent housing, and are exploited by entrepreneurs. Totally lacking in security, they live in such a state of personal servitude that they are deprived of almost every possibility of acting with initiative and responsibility, and are denied any advance in culture and any share in social and political life. Reforms are therefore necessary in various situations: growth in income, improved working conditions, increased security of tenure, incentives for initiative, and even the distribution of insufficiently cultivated lands to those who can make them fruitful. In this case the necessary resources and means should be provided, especially the helps of education, and opportunities for just cooperative arrangements. Whenever the common good demands expropriation, compensation should be calculated fairly and taking all the circumstances into account.

72. (*Socio-economic activity and the reign of Christ*) Christians taking an active part in modern socio-economic progress, and campaigning for justice and charity, should be convinced that they have much to offer to the prosperity of human-

kind and to peace in the world. They should be a shining example in these activities, whether individually or working together. Armed with the skill and experience which are essential, they should preserve right order in earthly activities in fidelity to Christ and his gospel so that their whole lives, individual as well as social, are imbued with the spirit of the beatitudes, especially of poverty.

Whoever in obedience to Christ seeks first the reign of God, gains from that a stronger and purer love to aid all his or her fellows and to bring about the work of justice under the inspiration of charity.[16]

Chapter 4. Life in the political community

73. (*Public life today*) Profound transformations are also evident at the present time in the relationships and institutions of peoples as a result of their cultural, economic and social evolution. These transformations are exerting a powerful influence on the life of the political community, especially as regards the rights and duties of all in the exercise of civil liberty and in achieving the common good, and as regards the relationships of citizens with each other and with public authority.

From a clearer awareness of human dignity there is a movement in various parts of the world to renew the politico-juridical order for the better protection of the rights of the person in public life, such as the rights of free assembly, association, expression of opinion, and religious profession in private and in public. For the safeguarding of the rights of the person is a necessary condition for citizens, individually and together, to be able to take an active part in the life and conduct of the state.

Alongside cultural, economic and social progress the

desire is growing among many people to take a greater share in regulating the life of the political community. In many people's minds there is growing concern to protect the rights of minorities in any country without prejudice to their duties to the political community; there is increasing respect for people professing a different opinion or a different religion; and greater cooperation is being established so that all the citizens, and not just certain privileged ones, can in fact enjoy their personal rights.

There is also condemnation of whatever political structures—such as flourish in some areas—obstruct civil or religious liberty, increase victims of political passions and crimes, and distort the exercise of authority away from the common good to the interests of a particular faction or of those in government.

There is no better way to renew a genuinely human political life than to encourage an inner sense of justice and of good will and service for the common good, and to strengthen basic convictions on the true nature of the political community as well as the purpose, the right use and the limitations of public authority.

74. (*The nature and purpose of the political community*) Individuals, families and the various groups which go to make up the civil community are conscious of their own inadequacy to provide a completely human life, and are aware of the need for a wider community to which all daily devote their energy in order increasingly to bring about the common good.[1] This is why they form a political community taking various expressions. Therefore the political community exists for the sake of that common good in which it finds its entire justification and significance and from which it derives its own primary law. And the common good comprises the sum of the conditions of social life which enable individuals,

families and associations to reach their own perfection more completely and more readily.[2]

The people who join in the political community are many and varied and they can legitimately differ in their views. Therefore, so that the political community is not fragmented through each person pursuing her or his own line, there is a need for authority which will direct the energies of all citizens towards the common good, not in any mechanical or dictatorial manner, but primarily as a moral force which is dependent on freedom and on the awareness of having accepted duties and responsibilities.

It is clear, then, that the political community and political authority have their foundation in human nature and therefore belong to the order established by God, although the form of government and the designation of the rulers are left to the free will of the citizens.[3]

It likewise follows that the exercise of political authority, whether in the community as such or in the institutions representing the state, should always be discharged within the confines of the moral order, to bringing about the common good—and that conceived in a dynamic form—in accordance with a juridical order which has been, or should be, lawfully set up. The citizens are then bound in conscience to obedience.[4] And the responsibility, status and importance of those in charge are also clear.

When citizens are oppressed by a public authority exceeding its competence, they should not withhold what is objectively required by the common good; but it should be legitimate for them to defend their rights and those of their fellow-citizens against the abuse of such authority, while observing the limits laid down by the law of nature and of the gospel.

The actual ways in which the political community struc-

tures its union and authority can vary according to the differing characters of peoples and historical progress; but they
should always be aimed at forming people of culture, peace
and good will towards all, to the advantage of the entire human family.

75. (*Cooperation of all in public life*) It is entirely in accord with
human nature that political and juridical structures be de-
vised which will increasingly and without discrimination
provide all citizens with the genuine opportunity of taking
a free and active share in establishing the juridical foundations of the political community, in determining the form of
government and the functions and purposes of its various
institutions, and in the election of the government.[5] All citizens should therefore be mindful of their right and duty to
use their free vote to further the common good. The church
holds in honour and respect the work of those who devote
themselves to the good of the state for the service of their
fellows by undertaking the burdens of office.

For the cooperation of citizens, and their awareness of
their responsibility to be successful in the daily conduct of
public affairs, there is need for a positive legal system to establish a suitable distinction of offices and institutions of
the public authority and also to provide an effective and
impartial protection of rights. The possession and exercise
of the rights of all persons, families and associations should
be recognised, protected and promoted,[6] together with the
duties binding on all citizens. Among the latter should be
mentioned the duty of providing the state with the material
and personal services which are necessary for the common
good. The government should take care not to hinder family,
social or cultural groups, or intermediate bodies or institutions, nor to prevent their legitimate activities, but rather it
should take steps willingly and in an ordered way to encour-

age them. Citizens individually and together should take care not to concede too much power to the public authority, nor make inappropriate claims on it for excessive benefits and services, in such a way as to weaken the responsibilities of individuals, families and social groupings.

The more complex conditions of our times often compel public authorities to intervene in social, economic and cultural matters in order to create more favourable conditions and provide more help for citizens and groups freely to pursue a complete human wellbeing. The balance between socialisation[7] and personal autonomy and development can be understood differently according to regional diversity and the evolution of peoples. But where the exercise of rights is temporarily restricted for the common good, once the circumstances have changed then freedom should be restored as rapidly as possible. It is inhuman that political authority should take the form of totalitarianism or dictatorship, which are harmful to the rights of the person or of social groups.

Citizens should generously and faithfully practise loyalty to their own country, but without narrow-mindedness, and should always at the same time look to the good of the entire human family which is united by various connections between races, peoples and nations.

All the faithful should feel they have a special vocation in the political community to be a shining example of devotion to duty and of service in promoting the common good, so that they demonstrate in their actions how authority can be reconciled with liberty, personal initiative with sharing and activity in the social body as a whole, and unity, as appropriate, with useful diversity. In the conduct of temporal affairs they should recognise differences of legitimate opinions and respect citizens and groups who defend them in honourable ways. Political parties should promote what they judge is required by the common good, but it is never permissible to put their own interests before the common good.

Civic and political education, which is so necessary today for the people and especially the young, should be undertaken seriously so that all citizens are able to play their part in the life of the political community. Those who are suited or capable should prepare themselves for the arduous but honourable life of politics[8] and should engage in it without any thought for their own advantage or financial gain. They should act with integrity and prudence against injustice and oppression, the arbitrary rule of a single individual or political party, and intolerance; and should sincerely and impartially, and with charity and political courage, devote themselves to the good of all.

76. (*The political community and the church*) It is very important, especially in a pluralist society, to maintain the right attitude towards the relationship between the political community and the church, and to make a clear distinction between what the faithful, acting individually or together and led by their christian conscience, do in their own name as citizens and what they do in the church's name along with their pastors.

By virtue of its commission and competence the church is not identified in any way with political society or bound to any political system, being both a sign and a safeguard of the transcendence of the human person.

The political community and the church are independent of each other and autonomous in their respective spheres of activity. They are both at the service of the personal and social vocation of the same individuals, but under different titles. And both will be successful in discharging their service for the good of all, the more they both develop a healthy cooperation with each other, according to the circumstances of place and time. For human beings are not restricted simply to the temporal order, but while living in human history they still retain their eternal calling. Since it has been founded on the love of the Redeemer, the church's contribution is to increase the spread of justice and charity within nations and between nations. In its preaching of the truth of the gospel, and in the light it throws on every area of human activity through its teaching and the witness of the faithful, it also respects and encourages the political freedom and responsibility of citizens.

Since the apostles and their successors with their helpers are sent to inform men and women of Christ, the world's Saviour, they rely in their apostolate on the power of God who often makes the force of the gospel manifest in the weakness of its witnesses. For those who devote themselves to the ministry of God's word should have recourse to ways and means which befit the gospel and which differ in many respects from the resources of the earthly city.

There is a close connection between the things of earth and what is greater than this world in the human condition, and the church makes use of temporal things so far as is required for its mission. It does not put its hope in privilege tendered by civil authority, and it will even renounce its exercise of some rights which it has lawfully acquired where it has decided that their exercise casts doubt on the sincerity of its witness or that new conditions of life call for a different arrangement. But it should be always and everywhere permitted genuine freedom to preach the faith, to teach its social doctrine, to discharge its task among people unimpeded, and to pass moral judgment even on matters belonging to the political order when this is demanded by the fundamental rights of the person or the salvation of souls, using all and only those means which are appropriate to the gospel and the good of all according to different times and conditions.

In remaining faithful to the gospel and discharging its mission in the world, the church, whose role it is to encourage and enhance whatever truth or goodness or beauty is to be found in the human community,[9] strengthens peace within the human race to the glory of God.[10]

Chapter 5. Promoting peace and encouraging the community of nations

77. (*Introduction*) In these years, when the sufferings and anxieties arising from war or the threat of war still remain extremely serious among us, the whole human family has reached a supreme test in its advancement towards maturity. Gradually coming together and now everywhere more aware of its unity, it is incapable of completing the task facing it of building a really more human world for all, everywhere on earth, unless everyone is renewed in spirit and converted to the truth of peace. As a result, the message of the gospel is at one with the highest desires and aspirations of the human race in throwing a new light on our age when it proclaims the blessedness of peacemakers, "for they shall be called the children of God" (Mt 5, 9).

By proclaiming the truth and the dignity of peace and condemning the horror of war, the council therefore wishes fervently to summon Christians, with the help of Christ the author of peace, to work with all people in order to consolidate peace in mutual justice and love and to prepare instruments of peace.

78. (*The nature of peace*) Peace is not merely the absence of war, nor is it reducible simply to the balance of opposing forces, nor does it arise from despotic domination; it is

rightly and properly called "the work of justice" (Is 32, 17). It is the fruit of the order which has been planted in human society by its divine founder and which is to be brought about by humanity in its thirst for ever more perfect justice. For since the common good of the human race is governed in principle by the eternal law, yet in the process of time is subject to continual change in its actual requirements, peace is never secured once for all but needs continual building. And since the human will is wavering and also wounded by sin, the acquiring of peace demands continual control of each one's passions and the vigilance of lawful authority.

Yet even this is not enough. This peace cannot be obtained in the world unless the good of persons is safeguarded and they trustingly and of their own volition share the resources of their minds and their abilities with each other. A determination to respect other human beings and peoples and their dignity, and a diligent practice of human kinship, are indispensable for the building of peace. Thus peace also emerges as the fruit of love which goes beyond what justice is able to provide.

Earthly peace arising from love of neighbour is an expression and result of the peace of Christ which flows from God our Father. For the incarnate Son, prince of peace, has reunited all of us to God through his cross and has restored the unity of all human beings in one people and one body by putting hatred to death in his own flesh,[1] and by being raised up in the resurrection to pour the Spirit of charity into the hearts of women and men.

This is why all Christians are earnestly called upon "to do the truth in love" (Eph 4, 15) and to unite with true peacemakers to plead and work for the establishing of peace.

Moved by the same spirit, we have nothing but praise for those who renounce violence in claiming their rights, and who have recourse to means of defence which are otherwise available only to weaker parties, provided this can be done without harm to the rights and obligations of others or of the community.

To the extent that we are sinners, the danger of war hangs over us and will continue to do so until the coming of Christ; but to the extent that we are united in charity and overcome sin, then violence too is overcome, until the saying is fulfilled, "they shall beat their swords into ploughshares, and their spears into pruning hooks; nation shall not lift up sword against nation, neither shall they learn war any more" (Is 2, 4).

Section 1: The avoidance of war
79. (*Controlling the barbarity of war*) Although recent wars have inflicted the most serious material and moral damage on our world, still today in some part of the world war continues its devastation. In fact, as scientific weapons of every kind are being used in warfare, its savage character is threatening to lead combatants into barbarity of a kind far greater than hitherto. And the complexity of modern conditions and the network of relations between countries enable covert wars to be pursued with new concealed and subversive methods. In many situations recourse to methods of terrorism is considered a new means of warfare.

Considering this fallen state of humanity, the council wishes first of all to recall the permanent force of the natural international law and its universal principles. The very conscience of the human race is resolutely and increasingly proclaiming these principles. Therefore acts which deliberately violate them and commands ordering such actions are criminal, and blind obedience cannot excuse those who obey them. Foremost among such actions are those, however they are performed, in which an entire people or nation or ethnic minority is exterminated: these are to be condemned in the strongest terms as heinous crimes. And the spirit of those who are not afraid to show open resistance to those who order such actions is greatly to be praised.

There exist various international conventions relating to warfare to which quite a number of countries have subscribed in order to render military actions and their consequences less inhuman: such as conventions concerning the treatment of wounded and prisoners and various agreements of this kind. These treaties must be observed; in fact all, especially governments and experts, are obliged to do all in their power to improve them and thus achieve better and more effective controls on the enormity of wars. It also seems just that laws make humane provision for the case of those who refuse on grounds of conscience to bear arms, provided they consent to another way of serving the human community.

War has obviously not been uprooted from human affairs. And so long as the danger of war is present, and there is no competent international authority with appropriate powers, then, once all means of peaceful negotiation are exhausted, the right of legitimate defence cannot be denied to governments. Rulers and others who share responsibility for the state have a duty, therefore, to protect the safety of the peoples entrusted to them, conducting such serious matters in all seriousness. But it is one thing to engage in military activity for the just defence of a people, and another to want to subjugate other countries. And the capability for war does not legitimise every military and political use of it. Nor does everything automatically become permissible between hostile parties once war has regrettably commenced.

Those also who are dedicated to the service of their

country and are members of the armed forces should regard themselves as ministering to the security and freedom of their peoples, and while they are performing this duty in the right manner they are genuinely contributing to the establishment of peace.

80. (*Total war*) The horror and perversion of war are enormously increased by the proliferation of scientific weapons. Operations with these weapons can inflict extensive indiscriminate destruction far exceeding the bounds of legitimate defence. In fact, if all those means which are now to be found in the arsenals of the great nations were to be utilised, the result would be the almost total mutual destruction of each party by a hostile party, quite apart from the devastation caused elsewhere in the world and the deadly effects following from the use of such arms.

All these considerations force us to submit war to an entirely fresh scrutiny.[2] This generation should realise that it will have to give serious account for its warring activities. On what we decide today largely depends the course of the future.

With all this in mind, this holy synod adopts the condemnations of total war which have already been uttered by recent popes,[3] and declares:

Every operation of war which aims indiscriminately at the destruction of whole cities, or of widespread areas with their inhabitants, is a crime against God and humanity itself which is to be firmly and unhesitatingly condemned.

The peculiar risk of modern warfare lies in the occasion which it offers to those who possess modern scientific weapons of committing such atrocities and the possibility of human minds being led inexorably to the most terrible decisions. To prevent this from ever happening in the future, the bishops of the whole world jointly implore all people, especially the leaders of nations and military commanders, continually to consider their great responsibility before God and the whole of humanity.

81. (*The arms race*) Scientific weapons are not built up simply for use in wartime. Since the security of each party is considered to depend on its destructive capability in retaliation, this build-up of weapons, which is increasing every year, is serving in a new way to deter possible adversaries. This many consider the most effective means of now preserving some peace among nations.

Whatever be the case with regard to this type of deterrence, we should be convinced that the arms race resorted to by several nations is not a safe path to preserving a stable peace, and that the "balance" which results is not a reliable and genuine peace. Far from the causes of war being eliminated, they are gradually threatening to increase. While enormous wealth is being allocated to developing ever new weapons, no adequate remedy can be applied to the many current miseries of the whole world. Rather than disagreements among nations being really and fundamentally resolved, other parts of the world are being drawn into them. New paths, beginning with a change of heart, will have to be chosen to remove this scandal and free the world from its pressing anxiety, thus enabling genuine peace to be restored.

For this reason it must be stated once more that the arms race is a virulent plague affecting humanity and that it does intolerable harm to the poor. And if it continues, then it is greatly to be feared that at some time it will produce all the deadly disasters for which it is now preparing the means.

Alert to the tragedies which the human race has brought within its grasp, we should use the reprieve granted us from above, at which we rejoice, to be more sensitive to our responsibilities and find ways to resolve our differences in a manner more worthy of human beings. God's providence urgently expects us to free ourselves from the age-old slavery to war. If we decline to make this attempt, we do not know the outcome of this wrong path on which we have set foot.

82. (*Total ban on war and international action to prevent it*) It is therefore evident that we must struggle to use all our resources to create a time when nations can agree to a complete ban on all war. This obviously calls for the establishment of a universal public authority, recognised by all, which will possess the effective means on behalf of all to safeguard security, the observance of justice and respect for rights. Before this desirable authority can be set up, the highest international agencies today need to give their close attention to the study of more suitable means of achieving world security. Since peace should be born of mutual trust between peoples rather than imposed on nations by the terror of weapons, all must endeavour to put an end at last to the arms race: for the decrease in weapons actually to begin, it should not proceed unilaterally but in step by agreement, and be protected by genuine effective safeguards.[4] In the meantime the attempts which have already been made, and continue to be made, to remove the risk of war should not be underestimated. Furthermore, there should be encouragement of the good will of the considerable number of individuals burdened by the heavy cares of high office, and motivated by the serious duty incumbent on them, who are working to eliminate the war which they abhor even though they cannot ignore the complexity of the present situation. We must earnestly pray God to give them the strength to persevere, and the determination to accomplish this work of supreme love for humankind, the courageous construction of peace. This most certainly requires of them today the mind and the spirit to transcend the frontiers of their own country, to abandon

national selfishness and the ambition to dominate other countries, and to encourage a profound respect for the whole of humanity as it now proceeds so laboriously towards closer unity.

Examination of the problems of peace and disarmament which has been going on actively and ceaselessly, and the international conferences devoted to the subject, should be looked upon as the first steps to the solution of such serious matters, and should be pursued more urgently in the future to achieve practical results. Nevertheless we should beware of just trusting to the endeavours of some without being concerned about the attitudes of all. Governments, as sponsoring the common good of their own people and at the same time promoting the good of the whole world, are heavily dependent on a multitude of views and feelings. It is useless for them to concentrate on building up peace so long as men and women are divided and at odds with each other through feelings of hostility, contempt and mistrust, or because of racial hatred and ideological obstinacy. There is therefore a great and urgent necessity for re-education and a change in public opinion. Teachers, especially of the young, and those who shape public opinion should consider it a most serious duty to educate everyone in new peaceful attitudes. We must all have a change of heart and direct our attention to the whole world and to those tasks which we can perform together so that our human race can prosper.

We should not be deceived by false hopes. Unless enmity and hatred are laid aside and stable and honourable agreements are struck in the future on universal peace, humankind, which for all its scientific achievements is now in serious danger, may be brought tragically to the point when the only peace it finds will be the dreadful peace of death. And yet in saying so, the church of Christ does not cease from having the strongest hope even amidst the anxieties of the present age. Its aim is to put before our time, again and again, in season and out of season, the message of saint Paul, "Behold, now is the acceptable time" for a change of hearts; "behold, now is the day of salvation."[5]

Section 2: Constructing the international community

83. (*The causes of discord and their remedies*) The first requirement for constructing peace is to remove the causes of discord among people on which war feeds, particularly injustice. Much discord is the result of excessive economic inequalities as well as of delay in applying the remedies needed. Other causes are a spirit of domination and contempt for persons, and, if we look for underlying causes, human envy, mistrust, pride and other selfish feelings. Since humanity cannot bear so many disorders the result is that, even when war is not raging, the world is continually disturbed by human conflicts and by instances of violence. And since the same is to be found in international relations, it is essential to remedy or prevent this and to restrain unlimited acts of violence by better and stronger cooperation and coordination among international institutions, and by continually working to set up bodies to promote peace.

84. (*The community of nations and international bodies*) In order to work effectively and more successfully for the universal common good at a time when the close ties of mutual dependence are on the increase between all citizens and peoples on earth, the community of nations now needs to provide itself with an order which will correspond to modern challenges, particularly those concerning the many regions which are still suffering from intolerable want.

To achieve this, institutions of the international community ought to make provision for the various needs of people, both in the areas of social life covering food, health, education and work, and in some particular situations which can occur in various places, such as the need to encourage general growth in developing countries, to alleviate the distress of refugees dispersed throughout the world, and also to help migrants and their families.

The international institutions which already exist at universal and regional levels deserve the approval of all. They constitute the first attempts to lay the international foundations of the entire human community, to solve the most serious issues of our time, and to further progress throughout the world and prevent wars in any form. In all these spheres the church rejoices at the spirit of true kinship which is at work between Christians and non-Christians and which is struggling to make even greater efforts to alleviate widespread wretchedness.

85. (*International cooperation in the economic field*) The unity of the human race today also calls for instituting greater international cooperation in the economic field. Although almost all countries have now become independent, they are far from being free of excessive inequalities and all forms of undue dependency, and far from immune to all danger of serious internal difficulties.

The growth of a nation depends on human and financial resources. The citizens of every nation should be prepared by education and professional formation to undertake the various duties of economic and social life. But this needs the help of foreign experts, who should not behave as superiors in providing their help but as assistants and partners. Material aid will not be forthcoming for the developing nations unless there are fundamental changes in modern business practice in the world. And other help should be provided by the developed nations in the form of gifts or loans or investment.

These should be offered generously and unselfishly on the one hand, and accepted in all honesty on the other.

The establishing of a true universal economic order requires the abolition of excessive profit-motive, national ambitions, the will to political domination, military considerations, and schemes to spread and impose ideologies. Several economic and social systems are available; it is to be desired that from among them experts will discover a common basis for healthy commerce at world level. This will come about more easily if individuals put aside their own prejudices and show a readiness to engage in honest dialogue.

86. (*Some suitable norms*) The following norms seem suitable for such cooperation:

a) The developing countries should be firmly convinced that the aim of development is the explicit and steady pursuit of the complete human perfection of their citizens. They should bear in mind that development finds its source and increase principally in the work and ability of peoples themselves, since it should not be dependent just on foreign resources but mainly on exploiting their own, and on cultivating their own abilities and tradition. Those who are in positions of influence should give outstanding example of this.

b) There is a very serious obligation on developed countries to aid developing nations to achieve these goals. And they should adapt themselves psychologically and materially to the need for establishing such universal cooperation.

Thus, in negotiating with weaker and poorer nations they should carefully consider what is good for them, since they need the returns from the sale of their products for their own support.

c) The international community's role is to coordinate

and stimulate growth, but in such a way that the disposition of resources for this purpose is as efficient as possible and completely equitable. It is also its function, while respecting the principle of subsidiarity, to coordinate economic programmes throughout the world so that they develop in a just manner.

Appropriate institutions should be set up to encourage and coordinate international trade negotiations, especially with underdeveloped countries, and to compensate for the deficiencies resulting from the undue imbalance of power between countries. This coordination, accompanied by technical, cultural and financial aid, should provide countries which are intent on development with the helps necessary to achieve suitable growth in their own economy.

d) There is a great need in many instances to review economic and social structures, but also to be cautious about technical solutions which are proposed too hastily, especially those which provide people with material advantages but are unfavourable to their spiritual nature and development. For humanity "shall not live by bread alone, but by every word that proceeds from the mouth of God" (Mt 4, 4). Each section of the human family possesses in itself and in its best traditions some part of the spiritual treasury entrusted by God to humanity, even if many are unaware of its origins.

87. (*International cooperation on population growth*) International cooperation is very necessary with regard to those peoples today who, apart from many other difficulties, are quite often particularly burdened as a result of rapid growth in population. There is a pressing need for the full and widespread cooperation of all, especially the richer nations, to explore ways of producing and sharing the necessities of food and of suitable education among the whole human

community. Some countries could considerably improve their conditions of life if they were appropriately instructed on how to transfer from old ways of agriculture to new technical methods and applied these prudently to their conditions, and if a better social order were also established and land more equitably distributed.

Within the limits of its competence, a government has rights and responsibilities respecting population problems among its people, such as concerning legislation affecting society and the family, movement from the countryside to towns, and information about the state and needs of the people. Since there is such anxiety about this problem today, it is also desirable for catholic experts, especially in the universities, to engage in, and develop, specialised study and research in this whole area.

Since many are of the view that the increase in world population, at least in some countries, must be absolutely curtailed by every means and by every kind of state intervention, the council exhorts all to avoid solutions which are publicly and privately promoted, and sometimes enforced, and which are contrary to the moral law. For, according to the inalienable human right to marriage and parenthood, the decision about the number of children to have lies with the right judgment of the parents, and cannot in any way be entrusted to the judgment of public authority. Since the judgment of the parents, however, presupposes a correctly informed conscience, it is important that all be given the opportunity to develop the proper and truly human responsibility, which takes account of the divine law and weighs all the circumstances. This requires that educational and social conditions be improved everywhere and particularly that religious formation, or at least complete moral education, is available. In exploring methods to help couples regulate the number of their children, appropriate information should be given on scientific advances that are well proven and are found to be in accordance with the moral order.

88. (*The responsibility of Christians to offer aid*) Christians should gladly and wholeheartedly cooperate in building an international order with respect for legitimate freedoms and in amicable fellowship, and that all the more since the greater part of the world is still labouring under such insufficiency that Christ himself is appealing in the poor to the love of his disciples. Therefore the scandal should not exist that some countries, most of whose citizens often bear the name of Christian, have an abundance of goods while others are deprived of the necessities of life and are being crucified by hunger, disease and every kind of wretchedness. For the spirit of poverty and of love is the glory and witness of Christ's church.

Praise, therefore, and assistance are due to those Christians, especially the young, who freely volunteer to bring aid to others and to whole peoples. It is, in fact, a task for the whole of God's people, under the leadership of its bishops in word and example, to do all it can to alleviate the wretchedness of these times and to do so, in accordance with an ancient church practice, not just from its surplus but even from its substance.

The manner of collecting and distributing aid should not be rigidly or too uniformly organised, but should be arranged in an orderly manner in dioceses and countries and throughout the world, with Catholics acting in conjunction with their fellow Christians where this seems useful. The spirit of charity imposes rather than discourages a careful and coordinated exercise of social charitable activity. Hence the need also for those who intend to devote themselves to serving the developing countries to receive suitable training from appropriate bodies.

89. (*The active presence of the church in the international community*) When the church, relying on its God-given mission, preaches the gospel and imparts the treasures of grace to all, it is contributing throughout the world to the strengthening of peace and helping to lay what is the firm foundation of human solidarity between individuals and peoples, namely, knowledge of the divine and natural law. For this reason the church certainly ought to be present in the community of nations in order to encourage and stimulate universal cooperation; and to do so through its public institutions as well as through the full and faithful cooperation of all Christians, which is motivated solely by the wish to serve humanity.

This will be more successful if the faithful are sensitive to their human and christian responsibility, and are active each in their own walk of life in creating an attitude of willing cooperation with the international community. Special attention should be devoted to the formation of the young in this regard, in their religious as well as their civic education.

90. (*The part played by Christians in international institutions*) An outstanding expression of international activity on the part of Christians is undoubtedly the joint contribution they have to make, whether individually or together, to the institutions which have been, or should be, set up to further international cooperation. The building of a community of nations in peace and fellowship can also be served in a variety of ways by various catholic international associations, which should be strengthened by an increase in well-formed members, in the helps they require and in the suitable coordination of their resources. For in our time successful activity and the need for dialogue demand joint enterprises.

Moreover, such associations contribute considerably to fostering a sense of universality which is appropriate to Catholics and to creating an awareness of world-wide solidarity and responsibility.

Finally, it is desirable that for Catholics to discharge their function properly in the international community, they should apply themselves to active and positive cooperation with fellow Christians who share their profession of evangelical charity, and with all who thirst after true peace.

In view of the immensity of the sufferings still afflicting the greater part of the human race, and with a view to the universal promotion of justice as well as the love of Christ for the poor, the council considers it most appropriate that an organisation of the universal church should be set up to stimulate the catholic community to the promotion of progress in poor areas and of social justice among nations.

Conclusion

91. (*The task facing individuals and particular churches*) All that this holy synod is proposing from the treasures of the church's teaching is intended to help all people in our day, whether they believe in God or do not recognise him explicitly, to perceive their calling more clearly and to fashion a world more fit for the outstanding dignity of woman and man, to seek a universal fellowship with deeper foundations, and motivated by love to respond generously and in concert to the urgent demands of our age.

In view of the enormous diversities of conditions and human cultures in the world, what is proposed here is in many sections deliberately general in tone; in fact, although it expresses the received doctrine of the church, yet, dealing as it often does with matters in a constant state of evolution, it must be pursued and expounded further. We trust that the many statements we have made, relying on the word of God and the spirit of the gospel, can be of real help to all, especially when they are adapted and applied by the faithful under the guidance of their pastors to individual nations and mentalities.

92. (*Universal dialogue*) In virtue of its mission to spread the light of the gospel's message over the entire globe, and to bring all people of whatever nation, race or culture together into the one Spirit, the church comes to be a sign of that kinship which makes genuine dialogue possible and vigorous.

This requires us first of all to promote mutual esteem, respect and harmony, with the recognition of all legitimate diversity, in the church itself, in order to establish ever more fruitful exchanges among all who make up the one people of God, both pastors and the rest of the faithful. For what unites the faithful is stronger than what divides them: there should be unity in essentials, freedom in doubtful matters, and charity in everything.[1]

We think also of our brothers and sisters who are not yet living in full communion with us, and of their communities, with whom we are nevertheless united in the confession of Father, Son and holy Spirit, and in the bond of charity; and we are mindful that the unity of Christians is something awaited and desired today even by many who do not believe in Christ. The more this unity progresses in truth and charity by the power and strength of the Spirit, so much the more will it be for the whole world an anticipation of unity and peace. Therefore, by uniting our energies and in ways more and more appropriate today to success in this noble purpose, we should endeavour to be daily more conformed to the gospel and work together in fellowship to serve the human family, which is being called in Christ Jesus into the family of the daughters and sons of God.

We next turn our attention to all those who recognise God and whose traditions contain precious religious and human elements, in the desire that open conversations will lead us all to be faithful in receiving, and eager in following, the promptings of the Spirit.

The wish for such conversations, undertaken solely out of love for the truth and with all due prudence, excludes nobody, so far as we are concerned, neither those who cultivate the values of the human spirit while not yet acknowledging their source, nor those who are hostile to the church and persecute it in various ways. Since God our Father is the origin and destiny of all things, we are all called to be sisters and brothers. Therefore, in our common human and divine vocation we can and should work together without violence and deceit, and in true peace, to build the world.

93. (*Building the world and leading it to its destiny*) Mindful of the Lord's words, "by this all will know that you are my disciples, if you have love for one another" (Jn 13, 35), Christians can have nothing more at heart than to be of ever more generous and effective service to humanity in the modern world. That is why, in fidelity to the gospel and drawing on its power, and in union with all who love and pursue justice, they have accepted a vast undertaking on this earth, for which they will have to render an account to the God who will judge everyone on the last day. Not all who say "Lord, Lord," will enter the kingdom of heaven, but those who do the will of the Father[2] and put a strong hand to the task. The Father wishes us to recognise and extend active love in word and deed to Christ our brother in people everywhere, thus witnessing to the truth, and to share with others the

mystery of our heavenly Father's love. In this way human-kind throughout the world will be roused to a living hope, which is the gift of the holy Spirit, of being eventually received into peace and supreme happiness in the homeland which is radiant with the glory of God.

"Now to the God who by the power at work within us is able to do far more abundantly than all we ask or think, to God be glory in the church and in Christ Jesus to all generations, for ever and ever. Amen" (Eph 3, 20–21).

Declaration on Religious Freedom
(Dignitatis Humanae)

The Declaration on Religious Freedom (Dignitatis Humanae) *was one of the most bitterly contested documents of the Second Vatican Council. This fact may seem strange to us today. After all, what could be so controversial about the claim that every individual has the right to practice his or her religion freely? Why did this idea cause so many problems? To put it bluntly, many bishops had trouble endorsing religious freedom because, for much of its history, the Catholic Church had condemned it.*

Ever since the Roman Emperor Constantine granted Christianity official status in the empire (AD 313), the church has sought ways to use the state to promote the faith. Throughout the Middle Ages, a close alignment developed between church and state. This "marriage of throne and altar" was reconfigured by the Reformation, but essentially continued on up until the political revolutions of the eighteenth century, when the Constantinian arrangement finally came under wide-scale attack. With its privileged position called into question, the church was put on the defensive. To protect its interests, the Vatican entered into a number of treaties with secular governments over the course of the nineteenth and early twentieth centuries. The goal of these political arrangements was to salvage some of the special treatment the church had enjoyed for so long.

In the midst of these social and political transformations, a theory grew up to justify the church's special treatment. Catholics argued that, because they possess the truth, they alone have the right to practice and proclaim their faith. Other Christian churches and other religions do not have this right, because they are false, and "error has no rights." The government of a majority Catholic nation could decide to tolerate the religious practices of non-Catholics, if this were necessary in order to keep the peace. But such tolerance was seen as an exception, and not a right that non-Catholics could claim.

Critics were quick to point out the double standard at work here: The church demanded rights and freedoms where it was in the minority but denied the same rights to others where it was in the majority. The French philosopher Jacques Maritain and the American Jesuit John Courtney Murray were—each in his own way— influential and articulate critics of this double standard. Murray argued that instead of focusing on abstract principles like "error" and "truth," the discussion should begin with the nature of the human person, the dignity of conscience, and the freedom of the act of faith. He argued for revision of the traditional teaching. And in the decade before the council, the Vatican silenced Murray for his views. But the arguments he and Maritain presented gradually took hold, coming to inform and influence the debates at Vatican II.

Two groups were central to the story of Dignitatis Humanae. The first was Cardinal Augustin Bea's Secretariat for Promoting Christian Unity; the second was the American hierarchy. The Declaration on Religious Freedom actually started as the fifth chapter of the Decree on Ecumenism. Before the council had even begun, Protestant groups (led by the World Council of Churches) had raised concerns about the Catholic position on religious freedom. They pointed out, for example, that certain governments in Latin

America prohibited Protestants from building churches or schools. What kind of dialogue was possible in the face of this double standard? Bea recognized that the council's ecumenical efforts would be frustrated without a clear affirmation of the right of all Christians to practice their faith. Thus he worked hard to keep the whole issue under the jurisdiction of his Secretariat. But when the debate began on the ecumenism decree at the second session of the council, the decision was made to treat the first three chapters as a unit, setting aside for the time being chapters 4 (on the Jewish people) and 5 (on religious liberty). Time ran out, and discussion of these two chapters had to be postponed until the third session.

Between the second and third sessions, the Coordinating Commission decided that religious freedom should stand on its own as an independent document. When the text was finally debated in September 1964, it was the American bishops who took the lead. Up until this point the Americans had held a low profile in an assembly dominated by strong European voices. But this was their issue. Cardinals Richard Cushing of Boston and Albert Meyer of Chicago each spoke "in the name of almost all the bishops of the United States," arguing that this document would show the world that the church was a champion of human rights. In the meantime, John Courtney Murray had been rehabilitated and brought to the council as an adviser to Cardinal Francis Spellman of New York. Murray's influence on these interventions is clear, and from this point forward he would play an active role in drafting the text.

The Americans were joined by bishops from countries in Soviet-controlled Eastern Europe, from Northern Europe, England, Ireland, New Zealand, and Australia. Most of the resistance came from Spain and Italy, and it was fierce. Cardinals Ernesto Ruffini and Fernando Quiroga y Palacios attacked the text. Cardinal Alfredo Ottaviani was firm in his disapproval. Archbishop Marcel Lefebvre, who would later go into formal schism with the Catholic Church in part over this issue, predicted ruin. They argued not only that the document undermined the Vatican's international treaties—and thus its state-protected privileges—but also that it contradicted church teaching. In the face of what seemed to be the unequivocal condemnation of religious freedom by past popes, how could the council now approve of it? As Lefebvre put it, "If what is being taught is true, then what the church has taught is false." For opponents of the text, to admit that the church had been wrong was to open the door to religious indifference, relativism, and immorality.

Debate ended on September 28, 1964, but controversy continued over who was responsible for revisions—with a minority of powerful bishops seeming intent on killing the document. All of this culminated in a crisis that left a dark cloud over the final days of the council's third session. A vote on the document was scheduled for the next to the last day of the session (November 19, 1964). But when that Thursday arrived, Cardinal Eugène Tisserant, dean of the council presidents, abruptly announced that, because there was not sufficient time to study the newly revised text, there would be no vote. The assembly erupted in protest and confusion. Apparently, the opposition had convinced the council leadership to postpone the vote. As Bishop Josef De Smedt delivered his summary of the document, he was interrupted several times by loud and sustained applause—an effort by the bishops to show their approval for the text. A petition was drafted on the spot, asking Pope Paul VI "urgently, very urgently, most urgently" (instanter, instantius, instantissime) to allow the vote to take place. Many feared that the delay would mean the demise of the document. In the end, the pope stood behind Tisserant's decision. But he promised that religious freedom would be the first item on the agenda when the council reconvened the following fall.

The disappointment and discouragement over this delay was real. But, in hindsight, it may have been for the best. Yves Congar, one of the most progressive theologians at the council, liked the direction of the revised text. But he recognized that it had changed so much that it was only fair to give the bishops more time to review and comment on it. Even John Courtney Murray later admitted that postponing the vote actually helped the document. Further revisions led to a stronger text.

The final document was promulgated on December 7, 1965. It begins with the frank recognition that the church's teaching on this issue has developed. It then goes on, in two short chapters, to ground religious freedom in the dignity of the human person—a dignity we know through both reason (chapter 1) and revelation (chapter 2).

After the council, Murray observed that what made the passage of Dignitatis Humanae so difficult—and, at the same time so important—was that it took up the issue under all the other issues at Vatican II: the development of doctrine. Development, aggiornamento, renewal, reform—these were words used to talk about the reality of change. At its most official level, the council helped the church step into the currents of history. It forced a question that always remains open: How much is the church willing to change?

Dignitatis Humanae
Declaration on Religious Freedom
TRANSLATED BY JOHN COVENTRY, S.J.

On the right of persons and communities to social and civil liberty in religious matters

1. The dignity of the human person is a concern of which people of our time are becoming increasingly more aware.[1] In growing numbers they demand that they should enjoy the use of their own responsible judgment and freedom, and decide on their actions on grounds of duty and conscience, without external pressure or coercion. They also urge that bounds be set to government by law, so that the limits of reasonable freedom should not be too tightly drawn for persons or for social groups. This demand in human society for freedom is chiefly concerned with the values of the human spirit, above all with the free and public practice of religion. Keenly aware of these aspirations, and wishing to assert their consonance with truth and justice, this Vatican synod examines the sacred tradition and teaching of the church from

which it continually draws new insights in harmony with the old.

First, then, this holy synod proclaims that God has himself made known to the human race the way by which, in obedience to him, human beings may reach salvation and blessedness in Christ. We believe that this one and only true religion subsists in the catholic and apostolic church, to which the lord Jesus entrusted the task of spreading it to all people, when he said to the apostles: "Go therefore and make disciples of all nations, baptising them in the name of the Father and of the Son and of the holy Spirit, teaching them to observe all that I have commanded you" (Mt 28, 19–20). But all people are bound to seek for the truth, especially about God and his church, and when they have found it to embrace and keep it.

The synod further proclaims that these obligations touch and bind the human conscience, and that truth imposes itself solely by the force of its own truth, as it enters the mind at once gently and with power. Indeed, since people's demand for religious liberty in carrying out their duty to worship God concerns freedom from compulsion in civil society, it leaves intact the traditional catholic teaching on the moral obligation of individuals and societies towards the true religion and the one church of Christ. Furthermore, in treating of this religious freedom the synod intends to develop the teaching of more recent popes on the inviolable rights of the human person and on the regulating of society by law.

I. The general principle of religious freedom
2. This Vatican synod declares that the human person has a right to religious freedom. Such freedom consists in this, that all should have such immunity from coercion by individuals, or by groups, or by any human power, that no one should be

forced to act against his conscience in religious matters, nor prevented from acting according to his conscience, whether in private or in public, whether alone or in association with others, within due limits. The synod further declares that the right to religious freedom is firmly based on the dignity of the human person as this is known from the revealed word of God and from reason itself.[2] This right of the human person to religious freedom should have such recognition in the regulation of society by law as to become a civil right.

In accordance with their dignity as persons, equipped with reason and free will and endowed with personal responsibility, all are impelled by their own nature and are bound by a moral obligation to seek truth, above all religious truth. They are further bound to hold to the truth once it is known, and to regulate their whole lives by its demands. But people are only able to meet this obligation in ways that accord with their own nature, if they enjoy both psychological freedom and freedom from external coercion. Thus the right to religious freedom is based on human nature itself, not on any merely personal attitude of mind. Therefore this right to non-interference persists even in those who do not carry out their obligation of seeking the truth and standing by it; and the exercise of the right should not be curtailed, as long as due public order is preserved.

3. These truths become even plainer when one reflects that the supreme rule of life is the divine law itself, the eternal, objective and universal law by which God out of his wisdom and love arranges, directs and governs the whole world and the paths of the human community. God has enabled people to share in this divine law, and hence they are able under the gentle guidance of God's providence increasingly to recognise the unchanging truth.[3] Therefore all have both the right

and the duty to search for religious truth, so that they may by the prudent use of appropriate means form for themselves right and true moral judgments.

Truth, however, is to be sought in a manner befitting the dignity and social nature of the human person, namely by free enquiry assisted by teaching and instruction, and by exchange and discussion in which people explain to each other the truth as they have discovered it or as they see it, so as to assist each other in their search. Once the truth is known, it should be embraced by a personal act of assent.

People grasp and acknowledge the precepts of the divine law by means of their own consciences, which they are bound to follow faithfully in all their activity, so as to come to God, their end. They must therefore not be forced to act against their conscience. Nor must they be prevented from acting according to it, especially in religious matters. The practice of religion of its very nature consists principally in internal acts that are voluntary and free, in which one relates oneself to God directly; and these can neither be commanded nor prevented by any merely human power.[4] The social nature of human beings, however, requires that they should express these interior religious acts externally, share their religion with others, and witness to it communally.

Hence wrong is done to the human person and to the order established for people by God, if they are denied the free and corporate practice of their religion within the limits set by due public order.

Furthermore, those private and public acts of religion by which people relate themselves to God from the sincerity of their hearts, of their nature transcend the earthly and temporal levels of reality. So the state, whose proper purpose it is to provide for the temporal common good, should certainly recognise and promote the religious life of its citizens. With equal certainty it exceeds the limits of its authority, if it takes upon itself to direct or to prevent religious activity.

4. The liberty or freedom from coercion in religion which is proper to all as persons must also be allowed them when they act together. For religious community is required by the social nature both of human beings and of religion itself.

Hence such communities, as long as they do not disturb the proper requirements of public order, are entitled to due freedom in conducting their affairs in their own way, in honouring the Deity in public worship, in assisting their members to practise their religion, in nourishing them with instruction and in developing institutions in which their members can cooperate in ordering their lives according to their own religious tenets.

Religious communities also have the right not to be prevented by the state by legal or administrative measures from choosing, training, appointing and transferring their own ministers, from communicating with religious authorities and communities in other parts of the world, from constructing buildings for religious purposes, or from acquiring and using appropriate property.

In addition, religious communities are entitled to teach and give witness to their faith publicly in speech and writing without hindrance. But in propagating their religious belief they must always abstain from any kind of action that savours of undue pressure or improper enticement, particularly in regard to the poor or uneducated. Any such course of action must be held an abuse of their own rights and an infringement of the rights of others.

It is a further component of religious liberty that religious communities should not be prevented from freely expounding the special value of their teaching for the right ordering of society and for the revitalising of all human activity. Finally, the right of those who are stirred by religious ideals freely to hold meetings and to form associations for educative, cultural, charitable and social purposes, is grounded both in the social nature of human beings and in the very character of religion.

5. Any family, since it is a society enjoying its own basic rights, has the right to organise its own religious life at home under the supervision of the parents. These have the right to decide on the kind of religious education to be given to their children, according to the religious convictions of the parents. Hence the state must recognise the right of parents to have a truly free choice of schools or other means of education, and no unjust burdens should be laid on them directly or indirectly as a result of this freedom of choice. The rights of parents are infringed if their children are forced to attend classes which conflict with the religious convictions of the parents, or if a single pattern of education is imposed from which all religious training is excluded.

6. The common good of society is made up of those conditions of social living which enable people to develop their own qualities most fully and easily. It consists chiefly in the safeguarding of the rights and duties of the human person.[5] Hence protection of the right to religious freedom lies with individual citizens and with social groups, with the civil authorities, with the church and other religious communities, each in their own way in view of their obligation towards the common good.

It is an integral part of the duty of every civil authority to safeguard and promote inviolable human rights.[6] The state is therefore obliged to give effective protection to the religious liberty of all citizens by just laws and other suitable means, and to ensure favourable conditions for fostering religious life. By these means citizens will have the real opportunity to exercise their religious rights and fulfil their duties, and society will itself benefit from the fruits of justice and peace which result from people's fidelity to God and his holy will.[7]

If in view of particular demographic conditions special recognition is given in the constitution to one religious community, the right of all citizens and religious communities to religious freedom must at the same time be recognised and upheld.

Finally, the state must ensure that the equality of citizens before the law, which is itself part of the common good of society, should never be impaired either openly or covertly for religious reasons, and that there should be no discrimination against any of them.

It follows from this that it is wrong for a civil power to use force or fear or other means to impose the acceptance or rejection of any religion, or to prevent anyone from entering or leaving a religious body. It is even more against the will of God and contrary to the sacred rights of the human person and of the family of nations, when force of any kind is used to destroy or to repress religion either in the whole human race or in any region or in any particular group.

7. The exercise of the right to religious freedom takes place in human society and is therefore subject to certain modifying principles.

The moral maxim of personal and social responsibility must be followed in the exercise of all liberties: in the use of their rights individuals and social groups are bound by the moral law to have regard to the rights of others, to their own duties towards others and to the common good of all. All should be treated with justice and humanity.

Further, as society has the right to protect itself against the abuses that can occur under the guise of religious liberty, it is chiefly for the state to provide the relevant safeguards. This should be done neither arbitrarily nor with inequitable discrimination, but by legal rules in accord with the objective moral order. Such rules are required for the effective protection and peaceful harmonising of the rights of all citizens. They are required to make adequate provision for that general peace and good order in which people live together in true justice. They are required for the due protection of public morality. These factors together constitute a fundamental part of the common good, and are included in the idea of public order. Nevertheless, that principle of full freedom is to be preserved in society according to which people are given the maximum of liberty, and only restrained when and in so far as is necessary.

8. People today are restricted in various ways and are in danger of being robbed of their power of free decision. At the same time many appear so assertive that in the name of freedom they reject all control and discount every duty of obedience.

Hence this Vatican synod exhorts all, and particularly those who have the charge of educating others, to apply themselves to bringing up people who will respect the moral law, obey legitimate authority and have a love for genuine freedom; that is, people who will use their own judgment to make decisions in the light of truth, plan their activities with a sense of responsibility, and freely combine their efforts with others to achieve all that is just and true. Therefore religious freedom should serve this further purpose, that people should act with greater responsibility in fulfilling their social functions in life.

II. *Religious freedom in the light of revelation*

9. The statements made by this Vatican synod on the right of people to religious freedom have their basis in the dignity of the person, the demands of which have come to be more fully known to human reason from the experience of centuries. But this teaching on freedom also has roots in divine revelation, and is for that reason to be held all the more sacred by Christians. For although revelation does not affirm the right of immunity from external coercion in religious affairs in so many words, it nevertheless makes plain the whole scope of the dignity of the human person; it manifests the respect Christ showed for the freedom of people in fulfilling their duty in believing in the word of God; and it instils in us the spirit that the followers of such a master should always have as their ideal and model. In all these ways light is thrown on the general principles on which the teaching of this declaration on religious freedom is based. And first and foremost religious freedom in the social order fully corresponds with the freedom of the act of christian faith.

10. One of the chief catholic teachings, found in the word of God and repeatedly preached by the fathers of the church,[8] is that the response of people to God in faith should be voluntary; so no one must be forced to embrace the faith against her or his will.[9] Indeed, the act of faith is by its very nature voluntary. Human beings, redeemed by Christ their Saviour and called to adoptive sonship through Jesus Christ,[10] can only respond to God as he reveals himself if, with the Father drawing them,[11] they give to God a free and rational allegiance of faith. It is therefore entirely in accord with the nature of faith that every kind of human coercion should be excluded from religion. And so the ideal of religious freedom greatly helps to produce the conditions in which people can be openly invited to christian faith, and can embrace it

of their own accord and witness to it in action in their whole manner of life.

11. God calls people to serve him in spirit and in truth, so that they are bound to him by personal decision and not by external force. For he looks to the dignity of the human person, whom he has created and who needs to be guided by his own judgment and enjoy his freedom. This shone out most clearly in Christ Jesus, in whom God fully revealed himself and his ways. For Christ, who is our master and lord,[12] but is also gentle and humble of heart,[13] patiently attracted and invited his disciples.[14] Certainly he illuminated and confirmed his teaching with miracles, to stir up and strengthen the faith of his hearers, though not to exert pressure on them.[15] Certainly, too, he reproved the disbelief of his hearers, but he left the verdict of God to the day of judgment.[16] When he sent his apostles out to the world, he told them: "Whoever believes and is baptised will be saved; whoever does not believe will be condemned" (Mt 16, 16). But, knowing that wheat and cockle were sown together, he ordered that both be allowed to grow till the harvest at the end of time.[17] Refusing to be a political messiah who prevailed by force,[18] he preferred to call himself the Son of man who came "to serve and to give his life as a ransom for many" (Mk 10, 45). He showed himself the perfect servant of God,[19] who "will not break a bruised reed or quench a smouldering wick" (Mt 12, 20). He recognised the civil power and its laws, and ordered that tax be paid to Caesar, but clearly warned that the higher laws of God should be kept: "Render therefore to Caesar the things that are Caesar's, and to God the things that are God's" (Mt 22, 21). Finally, when completing on the cross his work of redemption by which he won salvation and true freedom for humanity, he brought his revelation to perfection. He bore witness to the truth,[20] and would not let force

be used on those who opposed it. For his kingdom is not upheld by the sword,[21] but is founded on hearing and witnessing to the truth, and grows by the love whereby Christ raised on the cross draws people to himself.[22]

The apostles, taught by Christ's word and example, followed the same course. From the very beginnings of the church the followers of Christ strove to convert people to the confession of Christ as Lord, not by any coercive measures or by devices unworthy of the gospel, but chiefly by the power of God's message.[23] They vigorously proclaimed to all the design of God the Saviour, "who desires all to be saved and to come to the knowledge of the truth" (1 Tim 2, 4); but at the same time they respected the weak even though they were caught up in error, thus making plain how "each of us shall give an account of himself to God" (Rm 14, 12)[24] and in the end is bound to obey his own conscience. Like Christ himself, the apostles always strove to give public testimony to God's truth and to speak "the word of God with boldness" (Ac 4, 31)[25] with the greatest daring before people and princes. For they firmly believed that the gospel was in very truth the power of God for salvation to everyone who has faith.[26] So, scorning every kind of "worldly weapon"[27] and following the example of Christ's meekness and moderation, they preached the word of God with full reliance on the divine power of this word to destroy forces hostile to God[28] and to bring people to faith in Christ and allegiance to him.[29] As had the master, so too the apostles acknowledged legitimate civil authority: "For there is no authority except from God," the apostle teaches, and so adds this instruction: "Let every person be subject to the governing authorities . . . anyone who resists the authorities resists what God has appointed" (Rm 13, 1–2).[30] At the same time they were not afraid to confront those in public office when they opposed the holy will of God: "We must obey God rather than men" (Ac 5, 29).[31] Martyrs and faithful without number have trodden this path throughout the ages and throughout the world.

12. Hence the church is being faithful to the truth of the gospel and is following the way of Christ and the apostles, when it sees the principle of religious freedom as in accord with human dignity and the revelation of God, and when it promotes it. Throughout the centuries it has guarded and handed on the teaching received from the master and from the apostles. Although at times in the life of the people of God, as it has pursued its pilgrimage through the twists and turns of human history, there have been ways of acting hardly in tune with the spirit of the gospel, indeed contrary to it, nevertheless the church's teaching that no one's faith should be coerced has held firm.

Thus the leaven of the gospel has long been at work in the minds of people and has played a great part in the course of time in the growing recognition of the dignity of the human person, and in the maturing of the conviction that in religious matters this dignity must be preserved intact in society from any kind of human coercion.

13. Among the values which contribute most to the well-being of the church, as of civil society itself, and which are always to be upheld and safeguarded from all damage, the chief is unquestionably that the church should enjoy all the freedom of action it needs to care for the salvation of humanity.[32] For this is a sacred liberty with which the only-begotten Son of God endowed the church he obtained with his own blood. It is so integral to the church that any who attack it are acting against the will of God. This freedom of the church is a fundamental principle in all relations between the church and both the state and the whole social order.

In human society and in the presence of any civil power the church claims freedom for itself as a spiritual authority, established by Christ the lord, on whom lies the duty by divine command of going into the whole world and preaching the gospel to the whole creation.[33] The church further claims freedom in that it is a human association enjoying the right to live in civil society according to the requirements of christian faith.[34]

Indeed, if the principle of religious freedom prevails, as one not merely set forth in words nor just sanctioned by law, but genuinely put into practice, then the church truly has the solid basis in law and in fact for that independence which is necessary for the fulfilment of its divine mission, and which church authorities more and more insistently claim in today's world.[35] At the same time the faithful, like other people, have the civil right not to be prevented from living their lives as conscience directs. There is therefore a harmony between the freedom of the church and that religious liberty which should be accorded as a right to all individuals and communities, and should be sanctioned by legal enactment.

14. To obey the divine command, "teach all nations" (Mt 28, 19), the catholic church must work unremittingly "that the word of God may speed on and triumph" (2 Th 3, 1).

So the church earnestly begs its children that as a matter of the greatest moment there be made "supplications, prayers, intercessions and thanksgivings for everyone . . . For this is good, and it is acceptable in the sight of God our Saviour, who desires everyone to be saved and to come to the knowledge of the truth" (1 Tm 2, 1–4).

In forming their consciences the christian faithful should give careful attention to the sacred and certain teaching of the church.[36] For the catholic church is by the will of Christ the teacher of truth. Its charge is to announce and authentically teach that truth which is Christ, and at the same time to give authoritative statement and confirmation of the principles of the moral order which derive from human nature itself. In addition, all Christians should find prudent ways in which to spread the light of life to those outside their fold, "by the holy Spirit, genuine love, truthful speech" (2 Cor 6, 6–7), with the confidence[37] and boldness of apostles, even to the shedding of their blood.

For the disciple of Christ owes to his master the serious obligation of absorbing ever more deeply the truth learnt from him, of announcing it loyally and defending it vigorously, but always without recourse to means that go against the spirit of the gospel. At the same time the love of Christ presses the disciple to deal lovingly, prudently and patiently with those who are ignorant or mistaken about the faith.[38] So account must be taken of one's obligations to the proclamation of Christ the life-giving Word, of the rights of the human person, and of the measure of the grace of Christ given to each by God to summon him to the free acceptance and profession of the faith.

15. There is general recognition that people today want to be able to give free expression to their religion in public and in private, and that religious freedom is stated as a civil right in many constitutions and given solemn recognition in international documents.[39]

But there are some regimes in which, though freedom of religious worship has constitutional recognition, the state nonetheless tries to deter its citizens from any religious allegiance and to make life arduous and even dangerous for religious communities.

This holy synod warmly greets the former more positive signs of our times, while it sadly exposes the latter facts and condemns them. It urges Catholics and begs all people to reflect deeply on the degree to which religious freedom is a paramount necessity in the present situation of the human family.

For quite clearly all nations are daily becoming more united, people of different culture and religious belief are bound together by closer ties, and there is a growing awareness of the responsibility of each. To the end, therefore, that relations of peace and harmony may be established and deepened in the human race, it is essential that religious freedom be given adequate legal protection throughout the world, and that the supreme duties and rights of people in regard to the freedom of their religious life in society should be upheld.

May the God and Father of all bring it to pass that the human family, by carefully tending the principle of religious freedom in society, may be led through the grace of Christ and the power of the holy Spirit to the enduring heights of "the glorious liberty of the children of God" (Rm 8, 21).

—December 7, 1965

Declaration on the Church's Relation
to Non-Christian Religions
(Nostra Aetate)

The history of Vatican II's Declaration on the Church's Relation to Non-Christian Religions can be traced back to a half-hour conversation between Pope John XXIII and the Jewish scholar Jules Isaac. In June 1960, Isaac presented the pope with a lengthy memorandum summarizing the legacy of Catholic discrimination toward the Jewish people. He pressed the pope to use the council as an opportunity to move beyond this sad history. Isaac was a historian and an educator who had served as inspector general of public instruction in France until the Nazi occupation forced him out of office. He lost his wife and daughter at Auschwitz. Following the war, Isaac dedicated himself to promoting Jewish-Christian understanding. At age eighty-one, he spoke with great personal authority on a topic close to the heart of John XXIII.

After the audience, Pope John asked Cardinal Augustin Bea to meet with Isaac. By September the pope had commissioned Bea's Secretariat for Promoting Christian Unity to include "the Jewish question" in its preparations for the council.

For centuries, Catholic animosity toward the Jews was fueled by a theology of contempt that portrayed Judaism as a legalistic religion wholly superseded and rendered irrelevant by the New

Covenant in Christ. Christian theologians argued that God continues to punish the Jewish people for rejecting and killing Jesus. According to this view all Jews—past and present—bear the collective
guilt of the crime of deicide ("God murder"). Their only hope is to
accept Jesus as the true Messiah, leave behind their mistaken ways,
and enter into the church.

As Bea would argue again and again, this antisemitic tradition
was a deep distortion of Jesus' own teaching and of St. Paul's claim
that God's covenant with Israel remains (Rm 11). In the months
leading up to the council, the Secretariat for Christian Unity prepared a brief text that condemned antisemitism in all its forms,
clearly stated that the Jewish people are not guilty of deicide, and
stressed the intimate links between the Jewish and Christian faiths.
The draft was scheduled for discussion by the Central Preparatory
Commission in June 1962, its final meeting before the opening of
the council. But at the last minute, the draft "On the Jews" was
dropped from the agenda. The reason was not theological, but political. The Vatican Secretary of State, Cardinal Amleto Cicognani
(who also chaired the Central Preparatory Commission), was feeling intense pressure from several Arab governments who perceived
the statement on the Jews as an indirect endorsement for the State
of Israel. They complained that the church was taking sides in a
political dispute between the Israelis and the Palestinians. Bishops
from Arab nations worried that Christians would suffer reprisals
as a result. A recent announcement coming from the World Jewish
Congress that an official in the Israeli Ministry of Religious Affairs, Dr. Chaim Ward, had been named their "representative" to
the Second Vatican Council only exacerbated the problem.

Though he insisted that the document "On the Jews" was a
theological statement, not a political one, Bea agreed with Cicogani
that it would be better to set it aside for the time being. Between the
council's first and second sessions, however, Bea rescued the text by
including it as chapter 4 in the Decree on Ecumenism. This chapter

was submitted to the bishops for consideration, but not debated. Along with chapter 5 on religious freedom, it was separated from the ecumenism decree, and time ran out before it could be discussed. In his closing remarks at the end of the second session, Cardinal Bea assured the assembly that "what is put off is not put away."

When the text was finally brought before the bishops for debate at the start of the third session, it had been slightly expanded and significantly weakened—and Bea suggested as much in his introduction. The word "deicide"—so important to so many Jewish observers—had been dropped (although the text condemned the concept) and a sentence on Muslims had been added, presumably as an attempt to better balance the text. Although the draft was now titled "On Jews and Non-Christians," it dealt almost exclusively with Judaism. As debate began, objections came from all sides. Cardinal Ernesto Ruffini criticized the excessively laudatory tone of the document and insisted that the content did not match the traditional teaching of the church. We don't need to be told to love Jews, Ruffini argued. They need to be told to love us. The conversion of Jews to Christ ought to be the church's aim here. In a more delicate vein, the Syrian patriarch, Ignace Tappouni, repeated the concerns of many Eastern Catholic bishops from the Middle East, who worried about political reprisals against Arab Christians. He called the document "inopportune" and asked the council to remove it from the agenda. Bishops from Asia and Africa complained that, if the council was going to address Jews, it should also address the other great religions of the world. But the majority of the opposition to the draft text came from those who felt it had become too weak. They asked for the stronger and more positive statement about Judaism that had marked the earlier draft.

When debate ended three days later, the Secretariat for Promoting Christian Unity felt they had received the justification they needed to prepare a stronger text. When the Secretariat received sudden instructions to drop their revisions and fold the material on the Jews into the Dogmatic Constitution on the Church (Lumen Gentium), Bea worried that too much would be lost. His Secretariat decided to consider this request only after they had prepared their larger, revised draft. And within a few short weeks, the basic outline of what would become Nostra Aetate appeared. It consisted of five sections: (1) a statement on the unity of the human family and the innate spiritual impulse of all people; (2) a brief description of various religions, Hinduism, and Buddhism, concluding with the statement that the Catholic Church rejects nothing of what is true and holy in these religions; (3) a positive treatment of Islam; (4) a substantive section on Judaism, which recalls the spiritual ties between Christians and Jews, affirms the ongoing validity of the covenant between God and the people Israel, calls for mutual understanding, and condemns antisemitism unequivocally; and, finally, (5) a rejection of discrimination in all its forms. The new text so impressed the pope and the Coordinating Commission that it was placed before the assembly for a vote as an independent document. It was formally approved at the fourth session of the council, on October 28, 1965, by a vote of 2,221 to 88.

In many ways, the story of the Declaration on the Church's Relation to Non-Christian Religions is a story of setbacks that opened up surprising ways forward. Reflecting later on the troubled history of this declaration, John Oesterreicher (one of the architects of the document) observed that the opposition to this text had a positive result: It forced the council to consider entirely new horizons. In presenting the expanded document to the assembly, Cardinal Bea pointed to a parable. What began as a small mustard seed—a brief statement on the right attitude of Christians to the Jewish people—had grown to become a tree in which all religions could build their nests.

Nostra Aetate
Declaration on the Church's Relation to Non-Christian Religions
TRANSLATED BY LEO ARNOLD, S.J.

1. In our age, when the human race is being daily brought closer together and contacts between the various nations are becoming more frequent, the church is giving closer attention to what is its relation to non-christian religions. In its task of promoting unity and charity among people, indeed also among nations, it now turns its attention chiefly to what things human beings have in common and what things tend to bring them together.

All nations are one community and have one origin, because God caused the whole human race to dwell on the whole face of the earth.[1] They also have one final end, God, whose providence, manifestation of goodness and plans for salvation are extended to all,[2] until the elect be gathered together in the holy city which the bright light of God will illuminate and where the people will walk in his light.[3] Women and men expect from the different religions an answer to the obscure riddles of the human condition which today also, as in the past, profoundly disturb their hearts. What is a human being? What is the meaning and purpose of our life? What is good and what is sin? What origin and purpose do sufferings have? What is the way to attaining true happiness? What are death, judgment and retribution after death? Lastly, what is that final unutterable mystery which takes in our lives and from which we take our origin and towards which we tend?

2. From ancient until modern time there is found among various peoples a certain perception of that unseen force which is present in the course of things and in events in human life, and sometimes even an acknowledgement of a supreme deity or even of a Father. This perception and acknowledgement permeates their lives with a deep religious sense. The religions associated with the development of civilisation, however, strive to answer these questions with more refined ideas and more highly developed language. Thus in Hinduism the divine mystery is explored and propounded with an inexhaustible wealth of myths and penetrating philosophical investigations, and liberation is sought from the distresses of our state either through various forms of ascetical life or deep meditation or taking refuge in God with loving confidence. In Buddhism, according to its various forms, the radical inadequacy of this changeable world is acknowledged and a way is taught whereby those with a devout and trustful spirit may be able to reach either a state of perfect freedom or, relying on their own efforts or on help from a higher source, the highest illumination. In like manner, too, other religions which are to be found throughout the entire world strive in various ways to relieve the anxiety of the human heart by suggesting "ways," that is teachings and rules of life as well as sacred rites.

The catholic church rejects nothing of those things

which are true and holy in these religions. It regards with respect those ways of acting and living and those precepts and teachings which, though often at variance with what it holds and expounds, frequently reflect a ray of that truth which enlightens everyone. Yet, without ceasing it preaches, and is bound to preach, Christ who is "the way, the truth and the life" (Jn 14, 6), in whom people find the fullness of religious life and in whom God has reconciled all things to himself.[4]

It therefore calls upon all its sons and daughters with prudence and charity, through dialogues and cooperation with the followers of other religions, bearing witness to the christian faith and way of life, to recognise, preserve and promote those spiritual and moral good things as well as the socio-cultural values which are to be found among them.

3. The church also looks upon Muslims with respect. They worship the one God living and subsistent, merciful and almighty, Creator of heaven and earth,[5] who has spoken to humanity and to whose decrees, even the hidden ones, they seek to submit themselves whole-heartedly, just as Abraham, to whom the Islamic faith readily relates itself, submitted to God. They venerate Jesus as a prophet, even though they do not acknowledge him as God, and they honour his virgin mother Mary and even sometimes devoutly call upon her. Furthermore they await the day of judgment when God will requite all people brought back to life. Hence they have regard for the moral life and worship God especially in prayer, almsgiving and fasting.

Although considerable dissensions and enmities between Christians and Muslims may have arisen in the course of the centuries, this synod urges all parties that, forgetting past things, they train themselves towards sincere mutual understanding and together maintain and promote social justice and moral values as well as peace and freedom for all people.

4. Reflecting on the mystery of the church, this synod recalls the link where-by the people of the new covenant are spiritually united with the descendants of Abraham.

For the church of Christ recognises that the beginnings of its faith and election are to be found already among the patriarchs, Moses and the prophets in accordance with God's saving mystery. It states its belief that all believers in Christ, children of Abraham according to faith,[6] are included in the same patriarch's calling and that the salvation of the church is mystically prefigured in the exodus of the chosen people from the land of slavery. Hence the church cannot forget that through that people with whom God out of his ineffable mercy deigned to enter into an ancient covenant, it received the revelation of the old Testament and is nourished from the root of the good olive tree, onto which the branches of the wild olive tree of the gentiles have been grafted.[7] For the church believes that Christ our peace reconciled Jews and gentiles and made us both one in himself through the cross.[8]

The church also keeps constantly before its eyes the words of the apostle Paul concerning those of his own race: "and to them belong the adoption as children, the glory, the covenant, the giving of the law, the worship and the promises; to them belong the patriarchs, and of their race, according to the flesh, is Christ" (Rm 9, 4–5), son of the virgin Mary. It also recalls that the apostles, the foundations and pillars of the church, were born out of the Jewish people as were many of those first disciples who proclaimed the gospel of Christ to the world.

As holy scripture is witness, Jerusalem did not know the time of its visitation,[9] and for the most part the Jews did not accept the gospel, indeed many of them opposed its dissemination.[10] Nevertheless, according to the apostle, because of their ancestors the Jews still remain very dear to God, whose gift and call are without regret.[11] Together with the prophets and the same apostle, the church awaits the day known only to God on which all peoples will call upon the Lord with one voice and "will serve him with one arm" (Zp 3, 9).[12]

Since, therefore, the spiritual heritage common to Christians and Jews is so great, this synod wishes to promote and recommend that mutual knowledge and esteem which is acquired especially from biblical and theological studies and from friendly dialogues.

Although the Jewish authorities with their followers pressed for the death of Christ,[13] still those things which were perpetrated during his passion cannot be ascribed indiscriminately to all the Jews living at the time nor to the Jews of today. Although the church is the new people of God, the Jews should not be represented as rejected by God or accursed, as if that follows from holy scripture. All should therefore take care that in holding religious instruction and preaching the word of God, they teach nothing which is not in keeping with the truth of the gospel and the spirit of Christ.

Moreover, the church, which condemns all persecutions against any people, mindful of its common inheritance with the Jews and motivated not by political considerations but by the religious charity of the gospel, deplores feelings of hatred, persecutions and demonstrations of antisemitism directed against the Jews at whatever time and by whomsoever.

Moreover Christ, as the church has always maintained and maintains, went willingly and with immense love to his passion and death because of the sins of all people so that all may obtain salvation. It is the duty of the preaching church, then, to proclaim the cross of Christ as the sign of God's universal love and the source of all grace.

5. We cannot, however, call upon God the Father of all if we refuse to behave like sisters and brothers towards certain

people created to the image of God. The relation of man and woman to God the Father, and their relation to their fellow human beings, are linked to such a degree that scripture says: "Whoever does not love, does not know God" (1 Jn 4, 8).

Therefore the basis is taken away from any theory or practice which draws distinctions between people, between nation and nation, with reference to human dignity and the rights flowing therefrom.

The church therefore condemns as foreign to the mind of Christ any kind of discrimination whatsoever between people, or harassment of them, done by reason of race or colour, class or religion. Consequently, following in the steps of the holy apostles Peter and Paul, this synod earnestly begs the faithful that, "maintaining good conduct . . . among the gentiles" (1 Pt 2, 12), they do what they can to be at peace with all people,[14] so that they may really be children of the Father who is in heaven.[15]

—October 28, 1965

Notes

WHAT HAS BEEN THE RESULT OF THE COUNCIL?

1. *De Spiritu Sancto*, XXX, 77; *PG* 32, 213 A; *SCh* 17 ff., p. 524.
2. *The Documents of Vatican II*, Walter M. Abbott, S.J., p. 715.
3. Cf. ibid.
4. Cf. *Lumen Gentium*, no. 8.

CONSTITUTION ON SACRED LITURGY
(SACROSANCTUM CONCILIUM)
Constitution on Sacred Liturgy

1. *Roman missal*, prayer over the gifts for 9th Sunday after Pentecost.
2. See Heb 13, 14.
3. See Eph 2, 21–22.
4. See Eph 4, 13.
5. See Is 11, 12.
6. See Jn 11, 52.
7. See Jn 10, 16.

Chapter 1. General principles regarding the renewal and encouragement of the liturgy

8. See Is 61, 1; Lk 4, 18.
9. Ignatius of Antioch, *Ad Eph. (To the Ephesians)*, 7, 2: ed. F. X. Funk, *Patres Apostolici*, I, Tübingen 1901, p. 218.
10. See 1 Tm 2, 5.
11. *Sacramentarium Veronense* (Leonine): ed. C. Mohlberg, Rome 1956, no. 1265, p. 162.
12. *Roman missal*, preface of Easter.

13. See Augustine, *Enarr. in Ps. CXXXVIII (Exposition of Psalm 138)*, 2: CChr, 40, Turnhout 1956, p. 1991; and the prayer after the second reading of Holy Saturday, in the *Roman missal*, before the renewal of Holy Week.

14. See Mk 16, 15.

15. See Ac 26, 18.

16. See Rm 6, 4; Eph 2, 6; Col 3, 1; 2 Tm 2, 11.

17. See Jn 4, 23.

18. See 1 Cor 11, 26.

19. Council of Trent, session 13, 11 Oct. 1551, Decree *On the eucharist*, ch. 5: CT, *Diariorum, actorum, epistolarum, tractatuum nova collectio,* ed. Goerresian society, t. VII. *Actorum* part IV, Freiburg im Breisgau 1961, p. 202.

20. Council of Trent, session 22, 17 Sept. 1562, Teaching *On the mass*, ch. 2: CT, *ed. cit.,* t. VIII. *Actorum* part V, Freiburg im Breisgau 1919, p. 960.

21. See Augustine, *In Ioannis Evangelium (On John's gospel),* treatise 6, ch. 1, no. 7: PL 35, 1428; CChr 36, 56–57.

22. See Ap 21, 2; Col 3, 1; Heb 8, 2.

23. See Ph 3, 20; Col 3, 4.

24. See Jn 17, 3; Lk 24, 47; Ac 2, 38.

25. See Mt 28, 20.

26. *Roman missal*, prayer after communion for the Easter vigil and Easter Sunday.

27. Ibid., opening prayer at Mass for Tuesday within the octave of Easter.

28. See 2 Cor 6, 1.

29. See Mt 6, 6.

30. See 1 Th 5, 17.

31. See 2 Cor 4, 10–11.

32. *Roman missal*, prayer over the gifts for Monday within the octave of Pentecost.

33. Cyprian, *De cath. eccl. unitate (On the unity of the catholic church),* 7: ed. G. Hartel, in CSEL, t. III, 1, Vienna 1868, pp. 215–216; CChr 3, 254–255. See *Ep. (Letters),* 66, no. 8, 3: ed. G. Hartel, in CSEL, t. III, 2, Vienna 1871, pp. 732–733.

34. See council of Trent, session 22, 17 Sept. 1562, Teaching *On the mass,* ch. 8: CT, *ed. cit.,* t. VIII, p. 961.

35. See Ignatius of Antioch, *Ad Magn. (To the Magnesians)*, 7; *Ad Philad. (To the Philadelphians)*, 4; *Ad Smyrn. (To the Smyrnaeans)*, 8: ed. F. X. Funk, *op. cit.*, I, pp. 236, 266, 281.

Chapter 2. The holy mystery which is the eucharist

1. See Augustine, *In Ioannis Evangelium (On John's gospel)*, treatise 26, ch. 6, no. 13; PL 35, 1613; CChr 36, 266.
2. *Roman breviary*, feast of Corpus Christi, 2nd vespers, antiphon for Magnificat.
3. See Cyril of Alexandria, *Commentarium in Ioannis Evangelium (Commentary on John's gospel)*, book XI, chs. 11–12: PG 74, 557–565, especially 564–565.
4. See 1 Tm 2, 1–2.
5. Session 21, *Teaching on communion under both kinds and of children*, chs. 1–3, canons 1–3: CT, *ed. cit.*, t. VIII, pp. 698–699.

Chapter 3. The other sacraments, and sacramentals

1. Council of Trent, session 24, Decree *On reform*, ch. 1: CT, *ed. cit.*, t. IX. *Actorum* part VI, Freiburg im Breisgau 1924, p. 969. See *Roman ritual*, tit. VIII, ch. 2, no. 6.

Chapter 6. The music of worship

1. See Eph 5, 19; Col 3, 16.

DOGMATIC CONSTITUTION ON DIVINE REVELATION

(DEI VERBUM)

Introduction

1. See Augustine, *De catechizandis rudibus (On catechizing the uninstructed)*, 4, 8: PL 40, 316; CChr 46, 128.

Chapter 1. Revelation in itself

2. See Mt 11, 27; Jn 1, 14 and 17; 14, 6; 17, 1–3; 2 Cor 3, 16 and 4, 6; Eph 1, 3–14.
3. *Letter to Diognetus*, 7, 4: ed. F. X. Funk, *Patres Apostolici*, Tübingen 1901, I, p. 403. The christian dispensation is the new and definitive covenant. It follows that it will never pass away, and that no new public revelation is to be expected before the glori-

ous manifestation of our lord Jesus Christ (see 1 Tm 6, 14 and Tt 2, 13).

4. Vatican council I, Dogmatic constitution on the catholic faith, *Dei Filius,* ch. 3: D 1789 (3008).

5. Council of Orange II (529), canon 7: D 180 (377); Vatican council I, loc. cit.: D 1791 (3010).

6. Vatican council I, Dogmatic constitution on the catholic faith, *Dei Filius,* ch. 2: D 1786 (3005).

7. Ibid.: D 1785 and 1786 (3004 and 3005).

Chapter 2. The transmission of divine revelation

1. See Mt 28, 19–20 and Mk 16, 15. Council of Trent, Decree *On the canonical Scriptures:* D 783 (1501).

2. See council of Trent, loc. cit.; Vatican council I, Dogmatic constitution on the catholic faith, *Dei Filius,* ch. 2: D 1787 (3006).

3. Irenaeus, *Adv. Haer. (Against Heresies),* III, 3, 1: PG 7, 848; Harvey, 2, p. 9.

4. See council of Nicaea II: D 303 (602). Council of Constantinople IV, session 10, canon 1: D 336 (650–652).

5. See Vatican council I, Dogmatic constitution on the catholic faith, *Dei Filius,* ch. 4: D 1800 (3020).

6. See council of Trent, Decree *On the canonical Scriptures:* D 783 (1501).

7. See Pius XII, Apostolic constitution *Munificentissimus Deus,* 1 Nov. 1950: AAS 42 (1950), p. 756. Compare the words of Cyprian, *Epist. (Letters),* 66, 8: CSEL 3, 2, 733: "The church [is] the people united with the priest, the flock adhering to its shepherd."

8. See Vatican council I, Dogmatic constitution on the catholic faith, *Dei Filius,* ch. 3; D 1792 (3011).

9. See Pius XII, Encyclical *Humani Generis,* 12 Aug. 1950: AAS 42 (1950), pp. 568–569: D 2314 (3886).

Chapter 3. The divine inspiration of holy scripture and its interpretation

1. See Vatican council I, Dogmatic constitution on the catholic faith, *Dei Filius,* ch. 2: D 1787 (3006). Pontifical biblical commission, Decree of 18 June 1915: D 2180 (3629); EB 420. Holy Office, Letter of 22 Dec. 1923: EB 499.

2. See Pius XII, Encyclical *Divino afflante*, 30 Sept. 1943: AAS 35 (1943), p. 314; EB 556.

3. In and *through* human beings: see Heb 1, 1 and 4, 7 (*in*); 2 Kg 23, 2; Mt 1, 22 and passim (*through*); Vatican council I, Schema on catholic doctrine, note 9: Collectio Lacensis, VII, 522.

4. Leo XIII, Encyclical *Providentissimus Deus*, 18 Nov. 1893: D 1952 (3293); EB 125.

5. See Augustine, *De Gen. ad litt. (On the words of Genesis)*, 2, 9, 20: PL 34, 270–271; CSEL 28, 1, 46–47; and *Epist. (Letters)*, 82, 3: PL 33, 277; CSEL 34, 2, 354. Thomas Aquinas, *De Veritate*, quest. 12, art. 2, C. Council of Trent, Decree *On the canonical Scriptures*: D 783 (1501). Leo XIII, Encyclical *Providentissimus Deus*: EB 121, 124, 126–127. Pius XII, Encyclical *Divino afflante*: EB 539.

6. See Augustine, *De Civ. Dei (City of God)*, XVII, 6, 2: PL 41, 537; CSEL 40, 2, 228; CChr 48, 567.

7. See Augustine, *De Doctr. Christ. (Christian Doctrine)*, III, 18, 26: PL 34, 75–76; CSEL 80, 95; CChr 32, 93.

8. See Pius XII, loc. cit.: D 2294 (3829–3830); EB 557–562.

9. See Benedict XV, Encyclical *Spiritus Paraclitus*, 15 Sept. 1920: EB 469. Jerome, *In Gal. (On Galatians)*, 5, 19–21: PL 26, 417 A.

10. See Vatican council I, Dogmatic constitution on the catholic faith, *Dei Filius*, ch. 2: D 1788 (3007).

11. John Chrysostom, *In Gen. (On Genesis)*, 3, 8 (homily 17, 1): PG 53, 134. "Accommodated," Greek συγκατάβασις.

Chapter 4. The old Testament

1. See Pius XI, Encyclical *Mit brennender Sorge*, 14 March 1937: AAS 29 (1937), p. 151.

2. See Augustine, *Quaest. in Hept. (Questions on the Heptateuch)*, 2, 73: PL 34, 623; CChr 33, 106.

3. See Irenaeus, *Adv. Haer. (Against Heresies)*, III, 21, 3: PG 7, 950; (= 25, 1) Harvey, 2, p. 115. Cyril of Jerusalem, *Catech. (Catecheses)*, 4, 35: PG 33, 497. Theodore of Mopsuestia, *In Soph. (On Zephaniah)*, 1, 4–6: PG 66, 452 D–453 A.

Chapter 5. The new Testament

1. See Irenaeus, *Adv. Haer. (Against Heresies)*, III, 11, 8: PG 7, 885; ed. Sagnard, p. 194.

2. See Jn 14, 26; 16, 13.

3. See Jn 2, 22; 12, 16; compare 14, 26; 16, 12–13; 7, 39.

4. See the instruction *Sancta Mater Ecclesia* of the Pontifical biblical commission: AAS 56 (1964), p. 715.

Chapter 6. Holy scripture in the life of the church

1. See Pius XII, Encyclical *Divino afflante:* EB 551, 553, 567. Pontifical biblical commission, *Instructio de S. Scriptura in Clericorum Seminariis et Religiosorum Collegiis recte docenda,* 13 May 1950: AAS 42 (1950), pp. 495–505.

2. See Pius XII, ibid.: EB 569.

3. See Leo XIII, Encyclical *Providentissimus Deus:* EB 114; Benedict XV, Encyclical *Spiritus Paraclitus:* EB 483.

4. Augustine, *Serm. (Sermons),* 179, 1: PL 38, 966.

5. Jerome, *Comm. in Is. (Commentary on Isaiah),* Prologue: PL 24, 17; CChr 73, 1. See Benedict XV, Encyclical *Spiritus Paraclitus:* EB 475–480. Pius XII, Encyclical *Divino afflante:* EB 544.

6. Ambrose, *De officiis ministrorum (Duties of Ministers),* I, 20, 88: PL 16, 50.

7. Irenaeus, *Adv. Haer. (Against Heresies),* IV, 32, 1: PG 7, 1071; (= 49, 2) Harvey, 2, p. 255.

DOGMATIC CONSTITUTION ON THE CHURCH
(LUMEN GENTIUM)

Chapter 1. The mystery of the church

1. See Cyprian, *Epist. (Letters),* 64, 4: PL 3, 1017; CSEL (Hartel), III B, p. 720. Hilary of Poitiers, *In Mt. (On Matthew),* 23, 6: PL 9, 1047. Augustine, passim. Cyril of Alexandria, *Glaph in Gen. (Explanations of Genesis),* 2, 10: PG 69, 110 A.

2. Gregory the Great, *Hom. in Evang. (Homilies on the Gospels),* 19, 1: PL 76, 1154 B. See Augustine, *Serm. (Sermons),* 341, 9, 11: PL 39, 1499 f. John Damascene, *Adv. Iconocl. (Against the Iconoclasts),* 11: PG 96, 1357.

3. See Irenaeus, *Adv. Haer. (Against Heresies),* III, 24, 1: PG 7, 966 B; Harvey 2, 131, ed. Sagnard, SC, p. 398.

4. Cyprian, *De Orat. Dom. (The Lord's Prayer),* 23: PL 4, 553; Hartel, III A, p. 285; CChr 3 A, 105. Augustine, *Serm. (Sermons),* 71, 20,

33: PL 38, 463 f. John Damascene, *Adv. Iconocl. (Against the Icono-clasts),* 12: PG 96, 1358 D.

5. See Origen, *In Mt. (On Matthew),* 16, 21: PG 13, 1443 C; Tertullian, *Adv. Marc. (Against Marcion),* 3, 7: PL 2, 357 C; CSEL 47, 3, p. 386; CChr 1, 516. For the liturgical documents, see *Gregorian Sacramentary:* PL 78, 160 B; or C. Mohlberg, *Liber Sacramentorum Romanae Ecclesiae,* Rome, 1960, p. 111, XC: "God, who from the entire joining together of the saints make for yourself an eternal dwelling . . ." Hymn *Urbs Jerusalem beata* in the monastic breviary, and *Coelestis urbs Jerusalem* in the Roman breviary.

6. See Thomas Aquinas, *Summa Theologiae,* III, quest. 62, art. 5, to 1.

7. See Pius XII, Encyclical *Mystici Corporis,* 29 June 1943: AAS 35 (1943), p. 208.

8. See Leo XIII, Encyclical *Divinum illud,* 9 May 1897: ASS 29 (1896–97), p. 650. Pius XII, Encyclical *Mystici Corporis:* AAS 35 (1943), pp. 219–220: D 2288 (3808). Augustine, *Serm. (Sermons),* 268, 2: PL 38, 1232 and elsewhere. John Chrysostom, *In Eph. (On Ephesians),* homily 9, 3: PG 62, 72. Didymus of Alexandria, *Trin. (The Trinity),* 2, 1: PG 39, 449 f. Thomas Aquinas, *In Col. (On Colossians),* 1, 18, lection 5: ed. Marietti, II, no. 46: "As one body is constituted by the unity of the soul, so is the church by the unity of the Spirit . . ."

9. See Leo XIII, Encyclical *Sapientiae christianae,* 10 Jan. 1890: ASS 22 (1889–90), p. 392. Id., Encyclical *Satis cognitum,* 29 June 1896: ASS 28 (1895–96), pp. 710 and 724 ff. Pius XII, Encyclical *Mystici Corporis,* AAS 35 (1943), pp. 199–200.

10. See Pius XII, Encyclical *Mystici Corporis,* AAS 35 (1943), p. 221 ff. Id., Encyclical *Humani generis,* 12 Aug. 1950: AAS 42 (1950), p. 571.

11. See Leo XIII, Encyclical *Satis cognitum,* ASS 28 (1895–96), p. 713.

12. See *Apostles' creed:* D 6–9 (10–30); *Nicene-Constantinopolitan creed:* D 86 (150); compare *Tridentine profession of faith:* D 994 and 999 (1862 and 1868).

13. It is called "holy (catholic apostolic) Roman church" in *Tridentine profession of faith,* loc. cit., and in Vatican council I,

Dogmatic constitution on the catholic faith, *Dei Filius:* D 1782 (3001).

14. Augustine, *De civ. Dei (The city of God)*, XVIII, 51, 2: PL 41, 614; CChr 48, 650.

Chapter 2. The people of God

1. See Cyprian, *Epist. (Letters)*, 69, 6: PL 3, 1142 B; Hartel, III B, p. 754: "inseparable sacrament of unity."

2. See Pius XII, Allocution *Magnificate Dominum*, 2 Nov. 1954: AAS 46 (1954), p. 669. Encyclical *Mediator Dei*, 20 Nov. 1947: AAS 39 (1947), p. 555.

3. See Pius XI, Encyclical *Miserentissimus Redemptor*, 8 May 1928: AAS 20 (1928), p. 171 f. Pius XII, Allocution *Vous nous avez*, 22 Sept. 1956: AAS 48 (1956), p. 714.

4. See Thomas Aquinas, *Summa Theologiae*, III, quest. 63, art. 2.

5. See Cyril of Jerusalem, *Catech. (Catecheses)*, 17, *de Spiritu sancto*, II, 35–37: PG 33, 1009–1012. Nicholas Cabasilas, *De vita in Christo (Life in Christ)*, book 3, *de utilitate chrismatis*: PG 150, 569–580. Thomas Aquinas, *Summa Theologiae*, III, quest. 65, art. 3 and quest. 72, art. 1 and 5.

6. See Pius XII, Encyclical *Mediator Dei*, 20 Nov. 1947: AAS 39 (1947), especially p. 552 f.

7. 1 Cor 7, 7: "Each has his or her own special gift from God, one of one kind and one of another." See Augustine, *De Dono Persev. (The Gift of Perseverance)*, 14, 37: PL 45, 1015 f.: "Not only is continence a gift of God, but so also is the chastity of married people."

8. Augustine, *De Praed. Sanct. (Predestination of Saints)*, 14, 27: PL 44, 980.

9. John Chrysostom, *In Io. (On John)*, homily 65, 1: PG 59, 361.

10. See Irenaeus, *Adv. Haer. (Against Heresies)*, III, 16, 6; III, 22, 1–3: PG 7, 925 C–926 A and 955 C–958 A; Harvey 2, pp. 87 f. and 120–123; ed. Sagnard, *SC*, pp. 290–292 and 372 ff.

11. See Ignatius of Antioch, *Ad Rom. (To the Romans)*, preface: ed. Funk, I, p. 252.

12. See Augustine, *Bapt. c. Donat. (On Baptism against the Donatists)*, V, 28, 39: PL 43, 197: "It is certainly clear that when we speak of 'within' and 'without' with regard to the church, our con-

sideration should be directed to what is in the heart, not to what is in the body." See ibid., III, 19, 26: col. 152; V, 18, 24: col. 189; *In Io. (On John)*, treatise 61, 2: PL 35, 1800; CChr 36, 481, and frequently elsewhere.

13. Lk 12, 48: "Every one to whom much is given, of him much will be required." See Mt 5, 19–20; 7, 21–22; 25, 41–46; Jas 2, 14.

14. See Leo XIII, Apostolic letter *Praeclara gratulationis*, 20 June 1894: ASS 26 (1893–94), p. 707.

15. See Leo XIII, Encyclical *Satis cognitum*, 29 June 1896; ASS 28 (1895–96), p. 738. Encyclical *Caritatis studium*, 25 July 1898: ASS 31 (1898–99), p. 11. Pius XII, Radio message *Nell'alba*, 24 Dec. 1941: AAS 34 (1942), p. 21.

16. See Pius XI, Encyclical *Rerum Orientalium*, 8 Sept. 1928: AAS 20 (1928), p. 287. Pius XII, Encyclical *Orientalis Ecclesiae*, 9 April 1944: AAS 36 (1944), p. 137.

17. See instruction of the Holy Office, 20 Dec. 1949: AAS 42 (1950), p. 142.

18. See Thomas Aquinas, *Summa Theologiae*, III, quest. 8, art. 3, to 1.

19. See *Letter* of the Holy Office to the archbishop of Boston: D 3869–3872.

20. See Eusebius of Caesarea, *Praeparatio Evangelica (Preparation for the Gospel)*, 1, 1: PG 21, 28 AB; GCS VIII/1, 8.

21. See Benedict XV, Apostolic letter *Maximum illud*: AAS 11 (1919), p. 440, especially p. 451 ff. Pius XI, Encyclical *Rerum Ecclesiae*, 28 Feb. 1926: AAS 18 (1926), pp. 68–69. Pius XII, Encyclical *Fidei Donum*, 21 April 1957: AAS 49 (1957), pp. 236–237.

22. See *Didache*, 14: ed. Funk, I, p. 32. Justin, *Dial. (Dialogue)*, 41: PG 6, 564. Irenaeus, *Adv. Haer. (Against Heresies)*, IV, 17, 5: PG 7, 1023; Harvey, 2, p. 199 f. Council of Trent, session 22, ch. 1: D 939 (1742).

Chapter 3. The hierarchical constitution of the church and in particular the episcopate

1. See Vatican council I, Dogmatic constitution on the church of Christ, *Pastor aeternus*: D 1821 (3050 f.).

2. See council of Florence, *Decree for the Greeks*: D 694 (1307), and Vatican council I, ibid.: D 1826 (3059).

3. See *Gregorian Sacramentary*, prefaces of the birthdays of Matthias and Thomas: PL 78, 51 and 152; see codex Vatican lat. 3548, f. 18. Hilary, *In Ps. (On the Psalms)*, 67, 10: PL 9, 450; CSEL 22, p. 286. Jerome, *Adv. Iovin. (Against Jovinian)*, 1, 26: PL 23, 247 A. Augustine, *In Ps. (On the Psalms)*, 86, 4: PL 37, 1103; CChr 39, 1201. Gregory the Great, *Mor. in Iob (Morals on Job)*, XXVIII, V: PL 76, 455–456; CChr 143 B, 1405–1406. Primasius, *Comm. in Apoc. (Commentary on Apocalypse)*, V: PL 68, 924 BC; CChr 92, 290. Paschasius Radbertus, *In Mt. (On Matthew)*, book 8, ch. 16: PL 120, 561 C. See Leo XIII, Letter *Et sane*, 17 Dec. 1888: ASS 21 (1888), p. 321.

4. See Ac 6, 2–6; 11, 30; 13, 1; 14, 23; 20, 17; 1 Th 5, 12–13; Ph 1, 1; Col 4, 11 and passim.

5. See Ac 20, 25–27; 2 Tm 4, 6 f.; compare 1 Tm 5, 22; 2 Tm 2, 2; Tt 1, 5; Clement of Rome, *Ad Cor. (To the Corinthians)*, 44, 3: ed. Funk, I, p. 156.

6. See Clement of Rome, *Ad Cor. (To the Corinthians)*, 44, 2: ed. Funk, I, p. 154 f.

7. See Tertullian, *Praescr. Haer. (Prescription against Heretics)*, 32: PL 2, 52 f.; CChr 1, 212 f. Ignatius of Antioch, *passim*.

8. See Tertullian, *Praescr. Haer. (Prescription against Heretics)*, 32: PL 2, 53; CChr 1, 212.

9. See Irenaeus, *Adv. Haer. (Against Heresies)*, III, 3, 1: PG 7, 848 A; Harvey 2, p. 8; ed. Sagnard, *SC*, p. 100 f.: "manifested."

10. See Irenaeus, *Adv. Haer. (Against Heresies)*, III, 2, 2: PG 7, 847; Harvey 2, p. 7; ed. Sagnard, *SC*, p. 100: "is safeguarded," see ibid. IV, 26, 2: col. 1053; Harvey 2, p. 236; also IV, 33, 8: col. 1077; Harvey 2, p. 262.

11. See Ignatius of Antioch, *Philad. (To the Philadelphians)*, Preface: ed. Funk, I, p. 264.

12. See Ignatius of Antioch, *Philad. (To the Philadelphians)*, 1, 1; *Magn. (To the Magnesians)*, 6, 1: ed. Funk, I, pp. 264 and 234.

13. Clement of Rome, *Ad Cor. (To the Corinthians)*, 42, 3–4; 44, 3–4; 57, 1–2: ed. Funk, I, pp. 152, 156, 171 f.; Ignatius of Antioch, *Philad. (To the Philadelphians)*, 2; *Smyrn. (To the Smyrnaeans)*, 8; *Magn. (To the Magnesians)*, 3; *Trall. (To the Trallians)*, 7: ed. Funk, I, pp. 265 f., 282, 232, 246 f. etc.; Justin, *Apol. (Apologies)*, 1, 65: PG 6, 428; Cyprian, *Epist. (Letters)*, passim.

14. See Leo XIII, Encyclical *Satis cognitum,* 29 June 1896: ASS 28 (1895–96), p. 732.

15. See council of Trent, Decree *On the sacrament of order,* ch. 4: D 960 (1768); Vatican council I, Dogmatic constitution *Pastor Aeternus,* ch. 3: D 1828 (3061). Pius XII, Encyclical *Mystici Corporis,* 29 June 1943: AAS 35 (1943), pp. 209 and 212. CIC, canon 329 §1.

16. See Leo XIII, Letter *Et sane,* 17 Dec. 1888: ASS 21 (1888), p. 321 f.

17. See Leo the Great, *Serm. (Sermons),* 5, 3: PL 54, 154.

18. Council of Trent, session 23, ch. 3, quotes the words of 2 Tm 1, 6–7, to show that Order is a true sacrament: D 959 (1766).

19. In *Apostolic Tradition,* 3: ed. Botte, *SC,* pp. 27–30, the "primacy of priesthood" is attributed to the bishop. See *Sacramentarium Leonianum,* ed. C. Mohlberg, *Sacramentarium Veronense,* Rome 1955, p. 119: "to the ministry of the high priesthood . . . Complete in your priests the highest point of your mystery." Idem, *Liber Sacramentorum Romanae ecclesiae,* Rome 1960, pp. 121–122: "Give them, Lord, the episcopal throne to rule your church and the whole people." See PL 78, 224.

20. See *Apostolic Tradition,* 2: ed. Botte, p. 27.

21. See council of Trent, session 23, ch. 4, which teaches that the sacrament of Order imprints an indelible character, D 960 (1767). See John XXIII, Allocution *Iubilate Deo,* 8 May 1960: AAS 52 (1960), p. 466. Paul VI, Homily in the Vatican basilica, 20 Oct. 1963: AAS 55 (1963), p. 1014.

22. Cyprian, *Epist. (Letters),* 63, 14: PL 4, 386; Hartel, III B, p. 713: "The priest truly acts in the place of Christ." John Chrysostom, *In 2 Tm. (On 2 Timothy),* homily 2, 4: PG 62, 612: The priest is the "symbol" of Christ. Ambrose, *In Ps. (On the Psalms),* 38, 25–26: PL 14, 1051–1052; CSEL 64, 203–204. Ambrosiaster, *In 1 Tm. (On 1 Timothy),* 5, 19: PL 17, 479 C; CSEL 81, 3, p. 284; and *In Eph. (On Ephesians),* 4, 11–12: PL 17, 387 C; CSEL 81, 3, pp. 98–101. Theodore of Mopsuestia, *Hom. Catech. (Catechetical Homilies),* XV, 21 and 24: ed. Tonneau, pp. 497 and 503. Hesychius of Jerusalem, *In Lev. (On Leviticus),* book 2, 9, 23: PG 93, 894 B.

23. See Eusebius, *Hist. Eccl. (Ecclesiastical History),* V, 24, 10: GCS II,

1, p. 495; ed. Bardy, *SC*, II, p. 69. Denis, in Eusebius, ibid., VII, 5, 2: GCS II, 2, p. 638 f.; Bardy, II, p. 168 f.

24. See for the early councils, Eusebius, *Hist. Eccl. (Ecclesiastical History)*, V, 23–24: GCS II, 1, p. 488 ff.; Bardy, II, p. 66 ff. and passim. Council of Nicaea I, canon 5.

25. See Tertullian, *De Ieiunio (On Fasting)*, 13: PL 2, 972 B; CSEL 20, p. 292, lines 13–16.

26. See Cyprian, *Epist. (Letters)*, 56, 3: Hartel, III B, p. 650; Bayard, p. 154.

27. See the official report of Zinelli at Vatican council I: Msi 52, 1109 C.

28. See Vatican council I, Schema of dogmatic constitution 2, *De Ecclesia Christi*, ch. 4: Msi 53, 310. See the report of Kleutgen on the revised schema: Msi 53, 321 B–322 B; and the statement of Zinelli: Msi 52, 1110 A. See also Leo the Great, *Serm (Sermons)*, 4, 3: PL 54, 151 A.

29. See CIC, canons 222 and 227.

30. See Vatican council I, Dogmatic constitution *Pastor Aeternus:* D 1821 (3050 f).

31. See Cyprian, *Epist. (Letters)*, 66, 8: Hartel, III, 2, p. 733: "The bishop in the church and the church in the bishop."

32. See Cyprian, *Epist. (Letters)*, 55, 24: Hartel, p. 624, line 13: "One church throughout the whole world divided into many members"; *Epist. (Letters)*, 36, 4: Hartel, p. 575, lines 20–21.

33. See Pius XII, Encyclical *Fidei Donum*, 21 April 1957: AAS 49 (1957), p. 237.

34. See Hilary of Poitiers, *In Ps. (On the Psalms)*, 14, 3: PL 9, 206; CSEL 22, p. 86. Gregory the Great, *Moral. (Morals)*, IV, 7, 12: PL 75, 643 C; CChr 143, 170–171. Pseudo-Basil, *In Is. (On Isaiah)*, 15, 296: PG 30, 637 C.

35. See Celestine, *Epist. (Letters)*, 18, 1–2 to the council of Ephesus: PL 50, 505 AB; Schwarz, *Acta Conc. Oec.* I, 1, 1, p. 22. See Benedict XV, Apostolic letter *Maximum illud:* AAS 11 (1919), p. 440. Pius XI, Encyclical *Rerum Ecclesiae*, 28 Feb. 1926: AAS 18 (1926), p. 69. Pius XII, Encyclical *Fidei Donum:* AAS 49 (1957).

36. See Leo XIII, Encyclical *Grande munus*, 30 Sept. 1880: ASS 13 (1880), p. 145. See CIC, canon 1327, canon 1350 §2.

37. For the rights of the patriarchal sees, see council of Nicaea I,

canon 6 for Alexandria and Antioch, and canon 7 for Jerusalem. Lateran council IV, in 1215, constitution 5, *On the dignity of patriarchs*. Council of Ferrara-Florence.

38. See *Codex Iuris Canonici, pro Ecclesiis Orientalibus,* canons 216–314 on patriarchs, canons 324–339 on archbishops, canons 326–391 on other dignitaries, in particular canons 238 §3, 216, 240, 251 and 255 on the nomination of bishops by the patriarch.

39. See council of Trent, Decree *On reform,* session 5, ch. 2, no. 9, and session 24, canon 4.

40. See Vatican council I, Dogmatic constitution *Dei Filius,* 3: D 1792 (3011). See the note added to schema 1 *De Ecclesia* (taken from St. Robert Bellarmine): Msi 51, 579 C; also the revised schema of constitution 2 *De Ecclesia Christi,* together with the commentary of Kleutgen: Msi 53, 313 AB. Pius IX, Letter *Tuas libenter*: D 1683 (2879).

41. See CIC, canons 1322–1323.

42. See Vatican council I, Dogmatic constitution *Pastor Aeternus,* 4: D 1839 (3074).

43. See the explanation of Gasser at Vatican council I: Msi 52, 1213 AC.

44. See Gasser, ibid.: Msi 1214 A

45. See Gasser, ibid.: Msi 1215 CD, 1216–1217 A.

46. See Gasser, ibid.: Msi 1213.

47. See Vatican council I, Dogmatic constitution *Pastor Aeternus,* 4: D 1836 (3070).

48. Prayer of episcopal consecration in the Byzantine rite: *Euchologion to mega,* Rome 1873, p. 139.

49. See Ignatius of Antioch, *Smyrn. (To the Smyrnaeans),* 8, 1: ed. Funk, I, p. 282.

50. See Ac 8, 1; 14, 22–23; 20, 17, and passim.

51. Mozarabic prayer: PL 96, 759 B.

52. See Ignatius of Antioch, *Smyrn. (To the Smyrnaeans),* 8, 1: ed. Funk, I, p. 282.

53. Thomas Aquinas, *Summa Theologiae,* III, quest. 73, art. 3.

54. See Augustine, *C. Faustum (Against Faustus),* 12, 20: PL 42, 265; *Serm. (Sermons),* 57, 7: PL 38, 389, etc.

55. Leo the Great, *Serm. (Sermons),* 63, 7: PL 54, 357 C.

56. See *Apostolic Tradition* of Hippolytus, 2–3: ed. Botte, *SC*, pp. 26–30.

57. See the text of the *Examination* at the beginning of the consecration of a bishop, and the *Prayer* at the end of the mass of the same consecration, after the *Te Deum*.

58. Benedict XIV, Brief *Romana Ecclesia*, 5 Oct. 1752, §1: *Bullarium Benedicti XIV*, tome IV, Rome 1758, 21: "A bishop bears the likeness of Christ and carries out his work." Pius XII, Encyclical *Mystici Corporis*, AAS 35 (1943), p. 211: "Each of them takes care of and rules in the name of Christ the flock assigned to him."

59. See Leo XIII, Encyclical *Satis cognitum*, 29 June 1896: ASS 28 (1895–96), p. 732. Idem, Letter *Officio sanctissimo*, 22 Dec. 1887: ASS 20 (1887), p. 264. Pius IX, Apostolic letter to the bishops of Germany, 12 March 1875, and Consistorial allocution, 15 March 1875: D 3112–3117, only in recent editions.

60. See Vatican council I, Dogmatic constitution *Pastor Aeternus*, 3: D 1828 (3061). See the report of Zinelli: Msi 52, 1114 D.

61. See Ignatius of Antioch, *Ad Ephes. (To the Ephesians)*, 5, 1: ed. Funk, I, p. 216.

62. See Ignatius of Antioch, *Ad Ephes. (To the Ephesians)*, 6, 1: ed Funk, I, p. 218.

63. See council of Trent, *On the sacrament of order*, ch. 2: D 958 (1765); and canon 6: D 966 (1776).

64. See Innocent I, Letter to Decentius: PL 20, 554 A; Msi 3, 1029; D 98 (215): "Presbyters, although they are *priests* of the second rank, do not possess the *summit* of the pontificate." Cyprian, *Epist. (Letters)*, 61, 3: Hartel III B, p. 696.

65. See council of Trent, *On the sacrament of order*: D 956a–968 (1763–1778), especially canon 7: D 967 (1777). Pius XII, Apostolic constitution *Sacramentum Ordinis*: D 2301 (3857–3861).

66. See Innocent I, Letter to Decentius: PL 20, 554 A; Msi 3, 1029; D 98 (215). Gregory of Nazianzen, *Apol. (Apology)*, II, 22: PG 35, 432 B. Pseudo-Denis, *Eccl. Hier. (Ecclesiastical Hierarchy)*, 1, 2: PG 3, 372 D.

67. See council of Trent, session 22: D 940 (1743). Pius XII, Encyclical *Mediator Dei*, 20 Nov. 1947: AAS 39 (1947), p. 553; D 2300 (3850).

68. See council of Trent, session 22: D 938 (1739–1740). Vatican council II, Constitution on the sacred liturgy, *Sacrosanctum Concilium*, nos. 7 and 47: AAS 56 (1964), pp. 100 and 113.

69. See Pius XII, Encyclical *Mediator Dei*: AAS 39 (1947), under no. 67.

70. See Cyprian, *Epist. (Letters)*, 11, 3: PL 4, 242 B; Hartel, II, 2, p. 497.

71. See *Roman Pontifical*, Ordination of priests, at the clothing with vestments.

72. See *Roman Pontifical*, Ordination of priests, Preface.

73. See Ignatius of Antioch, *Philad. (To the Philadelphians)*, 4: ed. Funk, I, p. 266. Cornelius I, in Cyprian, *Epist. (Letters)*, 48, 2: Hartel, III, 2, p. 610.

74. *Constitutiones Ecclesiae Aegyptiacae*, III, 2: ed. Funk, *Didascalia*, II, p. 103. *Statuta Ecclesiae Antiqua*, 37–41: Msi 3, 954.

75. Polycarp, *Ad Phil. (To the Philippians)*, 5, 2: ed. Funk, I, p. 300: It is said that Christ "became the servant of all." See *Didache*, 15, 1: ibid., p. 32. Ignatius of Antioch, *Trall. (To the Trallians)*, 2, 3: ibid., p. 242. *Apostolic Constitutions*, 8, 28, 4: ed. Funk, *Didascalia*, I, p. 530.

Chapter 4. The laity

1. Augustine, *Serm. (Sermons)*, 340, 1: PL 38, 1483.

2. See Pius XI, Encyclical *Quadragesimo anno*, 15 May 1931: AAS 23 (1931), p. 221 f. Pius XII, Allocution *De quelle consolation*, 14 Oct. 1951: AAS 43 (1951), p. 790 f.

3. See Pius XII, Allocution *Six ans se sont écoulés*, 5 Oct. 1957: AAS 49 (1957), p. 927.

4. *Roman Missal*, preface of the feast of Christ the king.

5. See Leo XIII, Encyclical *Immortale Dei*, 1 Nov. 1885: ASS 18 (1885), p. 166 ff. Idem, Encyclical *Sapientiae christianae*, 10 Jan. 1890: ASS 22 (1889–1890), p. 397 ff. Pius XII, Allocution *Alla vostra filiale*, 23 March 1958: AAS 50 (1958), p. 220: "the legitimate and healthy lay nature of the state."

6. See CIC, canon 682.

7. See Pius XII, Allocution *De quelle consolation*: AAS 43 (1951), p. 789: "In decisive battles it happens at times that the best initiatives come from the frontline . . ." Idem, Allocution *L'importance de la presse catholique*, 17 Feb. 1950: AAS 42 (1950), p. 256.

8. See 1 Th 5, 19, and 1 Jn 4, 1.

9. *Letter to Diognetus,* 6: ed. Funk, I, p. 400. See John Chrysostom, *In Mt. (On Matthew),* homily 46 (47), 2: PG 58, 478, on the leaven in the dough.

Chapter 5. The universal call to holiness in the church

1. *Roman Missal,* The Gloria. See Lk 1, 35; Mk 1, 24; Lk 4, 34; Jn 6, 69 (the holy one of God); Ac 3, 14; 4, 27 and 30; Heb 7, 26; 1 Jn 2, 20; Ap 3, 7.

2. See Origen, *Comm. Rom. (Commentary on Romans),* 7, 7: PG 14, 1122 B. Pseudo-Macarius, *De Oratione (On Prayer),* 11: PG 34, 861 AB. Thomas Aquinas, *Summa Theologiae,* II–II, quest. 184, art. 3.

3. See Augustine, *Retract. (Retractations),* II, 18: PL 32, 637 f. Pius XII, Encyclical *Mystici Corporis:* AAS 35 (1943), p. 225.

4. See Pius XI, Encyclical *Rerum omnium,* 26 June 1923: AAS 15 (1923), pp. 50 and 59–60. Idem, Encyclical *Casti Connubii,* 31 Dec. 1930: AAS 22 (1930), p. 548. Pius XII, Apostolic constitution *Provida Mater,* 2 Feb. 1947: AAS 39 (1947), p. 117. Idem, Allocution *Annus sacer,* 8 Dec. 1950: AAS 43 (1951), pp. 27–28. Idem, Allocution *Nel darvi,* 1 July 1956: AAS 48 (1956), p. 574 f.

5. See Thomas Aquinas, *Summa Theologiae,* II–II, quest. 184, art. 5 and 6. Idem, *De perf. vitae spir. (Perfection of the Spiritual Life),* ch. 18. Origen, *In Is. (On Isaiah),* homily 6, 1: PG 13, 239.

6. See Ignatius of Antioch, *Magn. (To the Magnesians),* 13, 1: ed. Funk, I, p. 241.

7. See Pius X, Exhortation *Haerent animo,* 4 Aug. 1908: ASS 41 (1908), p. 560 f. CIC, canon 124. Pius XI, Encyclical *Ad catholici sacerdotii,* 20 Dec. 1935: AAS 28 (1936), p. 22.

8. See *Roman Pontifical,* Ordination of priests, the initial exhortation.

9. See Ignatius of Antioch, *Trall. (To the Trallians),* 2, 3: ed. Funk, I, p. 244.

10. See Pius XII, Allocution *Sous la maternelle protection,* 9 Dec. 1957: AAS 50 (1958), p. 36.

11. See Pius XI, Encyclical *Casti Connubii:* AAS 22 (1930), p. 548 f. John Chrysostom, *In Eph. (On Ephesians),* homily 20, 2: PG 62, 136 ff.

12. See Augustine, *Enchir. (Enchiridion)*, 121, 32: PL 40, 288. Thomas Aquinas, *Summa Theologiae*, II–II, quest. 184, art. 1. Pius XII, Apostolic exhortation *Menti nostrae*, 23 Sept. 1950: AAS 42 (1950), p. 660.

13. On the counsels in general, see Origen, *Comm. Rom. (Commentary on Romans)*, 10, 14: PG 14, 1275 B. Augustine, *De S. Virginitate (Holy Virginity)*, 15, 15: PL 40, 403. Thomas Aquinas, *Summa Theologiae*, I–II, quest. 100, art. 2 C (at end); II–II, quest. 44, art. 4, to 3.

14. On the excellence of holy virginity, see Tertullian, *Exhort. Cast. (Exhortation to Chastity)*, 10: PL 2, 925 C; CChr 2, 1029. Cyprian, *Hab. Virg. (Dress of Virgins)*, 3 and 22: PL 4, 443 B and 461 A f. Athanasius (?), *De Virg. (On Virginity)*: PG 28, 252 ff. John Chrysostom, *De Virg. (On Virginity)*: PG 48, 533 ff.

15. On spiritual poverty, see Mt 5, 3, and 19, 21; Mk 10, 21; Lk 18, 22. With regard to obedience, the example of Christ is given: Jn 4, 34, and 6, 38; Ph 2, 8–10; Heb 10, 5–7.

16. On the effective practice of the counsels which is not imposed on all, see John Chrysostom, *In Mt. (On Matthew)*, homily 7, 7: PG 57, 81 f. Ambrose, *De Viduis (On Widows)*, 4, 23: PL 16, 241 f.

Chapter 6. Religious

1. See Rosweydus, *Vitae Patrum*, Antwerp 1628. *Apophtegmata Patrum*: PG 65. Palladius, *Historia Lausiaca*: PG 34, 995 ff.; ed. C. Butler, Cambridge 1898 (1904). Pius XI, Apostolic constitution *Umbratilem*, 8 July 1924: AAS 16 (1924), pp. 386–387. Pius XII, Allocution *Nous sommes heureux*: AAS 50 (1958), p. 283.

2. See Paul VI, Allocution *Magno gaudio*, 23 May 1964: AAS 56 (1964), p. 566.

3. See CIC, canons 487 and 488, 4°. Pius XII, Allocution *Annus sacer*: AAS 43 (1951), p. 27 f. Pius XII, Apostolic constitution *Provida Mater*: AAS 39 (1947), p. 120 ff.

4. See Paul VI, Allocution *Magno gaudio*: AAS 56 (1964), p. 567.

5. See Thomas Aquinas, *Summa Theologiae*, II–II, quest. 184, art. 3, and quest. 188, art. 2. Bonaventure, Opusc. XI, *Apologia Pauperum*, ch. 3, 3: ed. Opera, Quaracchi, tome 8, 1898, p. 245 a.

6. See Vatican council I, Schema of dogmatic constitution 2, *De*

Ecclesia Christi, ch. 15, and annotation 48: Msi 51, 549 f. and 619 f. Leo XIII, Letter *Au milieu des consolations,* 23 Dec. 1900: ASS 33 (1900–1901), p. 361. Pius XII, Apostolic constitution *Provida Mater:* AAS 39 (1947), p. 114 f.

7. See Leo XIII, Constitution *Romanos Pontifices,* 8 May 1881: ASS 13 (1880–1881), p. 483. Pius XII, Allocution *Annus sacer:* AAS 43 (1951), p. 28 f.

8. See Pius XII, Allocution *Annus sacer:* AAS 43 (1951), p. 28. Pius XII, Apostolic constitution *Sedes Sapientiae,* 31 May 1956: AAS 48 (1956), p. 355. Paul VI, Allocution *Magno gaudio,* 23 May 1964: AAS 56 (1964), pp. 570–571.

9. See Pius XII, Encyclical *Mystici Corporis:* AAS 35 (1943), p. 214 f.

10. See Pius XII, Allocution *Annus sacer:* AAS 43 (1951), p. 30. Idem, Allocution *Sous la protection maternelle,* 9 Dec. 1957: AAS 50 (1958), p. 39 f.

Chapter 7. The eschatological character of the pilgrim church and its union with the heavenly church

1. Council of Florence, *Decree for the Greeks:* D 693 (1305).

2. Besides earlier documents against any kind of evocation of spirits, from the time of Alexander IV (27 Sept. 1258), see the encyclical of the Holy Office, *De magnetismi abusu,* 4 Aug. 1856: ASS (1865), pp. 177–178; D 1653–1654 (2823–2825); the reply of the Holy Office, 24 April 1917: ΛΛS 9 (1917), p. 268; D 2182 (3642).

3. For a synthetic exposition of this Pauline teaching, see Pius XII, Encyclical *Mystici Corporis:* AAS 35 (1943), p. 200 and passim.

4. See, for example, Augustine, *Enarr. in Ps. (Exposition of the Psalms),* 85, 24: PL 37, 1099; CChr 39, 1196. Jerome, *Liber contra Vigilantium (Against Vigilantius),* 6: PL 23, 344. Thomas Aquinas, *In 4m Sentent.,* dist. 45, quest. 3, art. 2. Bonaventure, *In 4m Sentent.,* dist. 45, art. 3, quest. 2; etc.

5. See Pius XII, Encyclical *Mystici Corporis:* AAS 35 (1943), p. 245.

6. See many inscriptions in the Roman catacombs.

7. See Gelasius I, Decretal *De libris recipiendis,* 3: PL 59, 160; D 165 (353).

8. See Methodius, *Symposion (Symposium),* 7, 3: GCS (Bonwetsch), p. 74.

9. See Benedict XV, *Decretum approbationis virtutum in Causa beati-*

ficationis et canonizationis Servi Dei Ioannis Nepomuceni Neumann: AAS 14 (1922), p. 23. Many allocutions of Pius XI on the saints: *Inviti all'eroismo,* in *Discorsi e Radiomessaggi,* tomes I–III, 1941–1942, passim. Pius XII, *Discorsi e Radiomessaggi,* tome X, 1949, 37–43.

10. See Pius XII, Encyclical *Mediator Dei:* AAS 39 (1947), p. 581.

11. See Heb 13, 7; Ecli chs. 44–50; Heb 11, 3–40. See also Pius XII, Encyclical *Mediator Dei:* AAS 39 (1947), pp. 582–583.

12. See Vatican council I, Dogmatic constitution, *Dei Filius,* ch. 3: D 1794 (3013).

13. See Pius XII, Encyclical *Mystici Corporis:* AAS 35 (1943), p. 216.

14. With regard to gratitude to the saints, see E. Diehl, *Inscriptions latinae christianae veteres,* I, Berlin 1925, nos. 2008, 2382 and passim.

15. See council of Trent, Decree *On invocation, veneration and relics of the saints and on sacred images:* D 984 (1821).

16. *Roman Breviary,* Invitatory of the feast of all Saints.

17. See, for example, 2 Th 1, 10.

18. Vatican council II, Constitution on the sacred liturgy, *Sacrosanctum Concilium,* ch. 5, no. 104: AAS 56 (1964), pp. 125–126.

19. See *Roman Missal,* canon of the mass.

20. See council of Nicaea II, session 7: D 302 (600).

21. See council of Florence, *Decree for the Greeks:* D 693 (1304).

22. See council of Trent, Decree *On invocation, veneration and relics of saints and on sacred images:* D 984–988 (1821–1824); Decree *On purgatory:* D 983 (1820); Decree *On justification,* canon 30: D 840 (1580).

23. *Roman Missal,* Preface of saints, granted to dioceses in France.

24. See Peter Canisius, *Catechismus Maior seu Summa Doctrinae christianae,* ch. 3 (critical edn. by F. Streicher), Part 1, pp. 15–16, no. 44 and pp. 100–101, no. 49.

25. See Vatican council II, Constitution on the sacred liturgy, *Sacrosanctum Concilium,* ch. 1, no. 8: AAS 56 (1964), p. 401 (p. 822).

Chapter 8. The blessed virgin Mary, mother of God, in the mystery of Christ and the church

1. Constantinopolitan creed: Msi 3, 566. See council of Ephesus: Msi 4, 1130 (also Msi 2, 665 and 4, 1071); council of Chalcedon:

Msi 7, 111–116; council of Constantinople II: Msi 9, 375–396; *Roman Missal,* creed.

2. *Roman Missal,* canon.

3. Augustine, *De S. Virginitate (Holy Virginity),* 6: PL 40, 399.

4. See Paul VI, Allocution at the council, 4 Dec. 1963: AAS 56 (1964), p. 37.

5. See Germanus of *Constantinople, Hom. in Annunt. Deiparae (Homily on the Annunciation):* PG 98, 328 A; *In Dorm. (On the Dormition),* 2: PG 98, 357. Anastasius of Antioch, *Serm. 2 de Annunt. (Sermon 2 on the Annunciation),* 2: PG 89, 1377 AB; *Serm. (Sermons),* 3, 2: PG 89, 1388 C. Andrew of Crete, *Can. in B.V. Nat. (Canon for the blessed Virgin's Birthday),* 4: PG 97, 1321 B; *In B.V. Nat. (The blessed Virgin's Birthday),* 1: PG 97, 812 A; *Hom. in dorm. (Homily on the Dormition),* 1: PG 97, 1068 C. Sophronius, *Or. 2 in Annunt. (Oration 2 on the Annunciation),* 18: PG 87 (3), 3237 BD.

6. Irenaeus, *Adv. Haer. (Against Heresies),* III, 22, 4: PG 7, 959 A; Harvey 2, 123.

7. Irenaeus, ibid.: Harvey 2, 124.

8. Epiphanius, *Haer. (Heresies),* 78, 18: PG 42, 728 CD–729 AB.

9. Jerome, *Epist. (Letters),* 22, 21: PL 22, 408. See Augustine, *Serm. (Sermons),* 51, 2, 3, and 232, 2: PL 38, 335 and 1108. Cyril of Jerusalem, *Catech. (Catecheses),* 12, 15: PG 33, 741 AB. John Chrysostom, *In Ps. (On the Psalms),* 44, 7: PG 55, 193. John Damascene, *Hom. 2 in dorm. B. M. V. (Homily 2 on the Dormition),* 3: PG 96, 728.

10. See Lateran council in 649, canon 3: Msi 10, 1151. Leo I, *Epist. ad Flav. (Letter to Flavian):* PL 54, 759. Council of Chalcedon: Msi 7, 462. Ambrose, *De instit. virg. (Consecration of a Virgin):* PL 16, 320.

11. See Pius XII, Encyclical *Mystici Corporis:* AAS 35 (1943), pp. 247–248.

12. See Pius IX, Bull *Ineffabilis,* 8 Dec. 1954: *Acta* of Pius IX, 1, I, p. 616; D 1641 (2803).

13. See Pius XII, Apostolic constitution *Munificentissimus,* 1 Nov. 1950: AAS 42 (1950); D 2333 (3903). See John Damascene, *Enc. in dorm. Dei genitricis (Encomium on the Dormition),* homilies 2 and 3: PG 96, 721–761, especially 728 B. Germanus of Constantinople, *In S. Dei gen. dorm. (On the Dormition),* sermons 1

and 3: PG 98 (6), 340–348 and 361. Modestus of Jerusalem, *In dorm. SS. Deiparae (On the Dormition)*: PG 86 (2), 3277–3312.

14. See Pius XII, Encyclical *Ad caeli Reginam*, 11 Oct. 1954: AAS 46 (1954), pp. 633–636; D 3913 ff. See Andrew of Crete, *Hom. 3 in dorm. SS. Deiparae (Homily 3 on the Dormition)*: PG 97, 1089–1109. John Damascene, *De fide orth. (The orthodox Faith)*, 4, 14: PG 94, 1153–1161.

15. See Kleutgen, revised text *De mysterio Verbi incarnati*, ch. 4: Msi 53, 290. See Andrew of Crete, *In nat. Mariae (On Mary's Birthday)*, sermon 4: PG 97, 865 A. Germanus of Constantinople, *In annunt. Deiparae (On the Annunciation)*: PG 98, 321 BC; *In dorm. Deiparae (On the Dormition)*, 3: PG 98, 361 D. John Damascene, *In dorm. B. V. Mariae (On the Dormition)*, homily 1, 8: PG 96, 712 BC–713 A.

16. See Leo XIII, Encyclical *Adiutricem populi*, 5 Sept. 1895: ASS 15 (1895–1896), p. 303. Pius X, Encyclical *Ad diem illum*, 2 Feb. 1904: *Acta* of Pius X, I, p. 154: D 1978 A (3370). Pius XI, Encyclical *Miserentissimus Redemptor*: AAS 20 (1928), p. 178. Pius XII, Radio message of 13 May 1946: AAS 38 (1946), p. 266.

17. See Ambrose, *Epist. (Letters)*, 63: PL 16, 1218.

18. See Ambrose, *Expos. in Lc. (Commentary on Luke)*, 2, 7: PL 15, 1555; CChr 14, 33.

19. See Pseudo-Peter Damian, *Serm. (Sermons)*, 63: PL 144, 861 AB. Godfrey of Saint-Victor, *In nat. B. M. (The birth of blessed Mary)*, Ms. Paris, Mazarin 1002, fol. 109r. Gerhoh of Reichersberg, *De gloria et honore Filii hominis*, 10: PL 194, 1105 AB.

20. See Ambrose, *Expos. in Lc. (Commentary on Luke)*, 2, 7, and 10, 24–25: PL 15, 1555 and 1810; CChr 14, 33 and 353. Augustine, *In Io. (On John)*, treatise 13, 12: PL 35, 1499; CChr 36, 137; see *Serm. (Sermons)*, 191, 2, 3: PL 38, 1010; etc. See also Bede, *Expos. in Lc. (Commentary on Luke)*, 1, ch. 2: PL 92, 330; CChr 120, 47–48. Isaac of Stella, *Serm. (Sermons)*, 51: PL 194, 1863 A.

21. See *Roman Breviary*, antiphon "We fly to your protection" at 1st vespers of the little office of the blessed virgin Mary.

22. See council of Nicaea II, in 787: Msi 13, 378–379; D 302 (600–601). Council of Trent, session 25: Msi 33, 171–172.

23. See Pius XII, Radio message of 24 Oct. 1954: AAS 46 (1954), p. 679. Encyclical *Ad caeli Reginam*: AAS 46 (1954), p. 637.

24. See Pius XI, Encyclical *Ecclesiam Dei,* 12 Nov. 1923: AAS 15 (1923), p. 581. Pius XII, Encyclical *Fulgens corona,* 8 Sept. 1953: AAS 45 (1953), pp. 590–591.

PASTORAL CONSTITUTION ON THE CHURCH IN THE MODERN WORLD (GAUDIUM ET SPES)
Preface
1. *The pastoral constitution "On the church in the world of today" contains two parts which form a unity.*

   The constitution is termed "pastoral" because, while dependent on principles of doctrine, its aim is to express the relationship between the church and the world and people of today. As this pastoral aim is not absent from the first part, so the doctrinal aim is not absent from the second.

   In the first part the church develops its doctrine about humanity, the world in which human beings live, and its own relationship to both. In the second it concentrates on several aspects of modern living and human society, and specifically on questions and problems which seem particularly urgent today. As a result, this latter part comprises material, subject to doctrinal considerations, which contains both permanent and transient features.

   The constitution should therefore be interpreted according to the general norms of theological interpretation and with due regard, especially in the second part, for the naturally changing circumstances of the matters treated.
2. See Jn 18, 37.
3. See Jn 3, 17; Mt 20, 28; Mk 10, 45.

Introduction
4. See Rm 7, 14 ff.
5. See 2 Cor 5, 15.
6. See Ac 4, 12.
7. See Heb 13, 8.
8. See Col 1, 15.

Part 1
Chapter 1. The dignity of the human person
1. See Gn 1, 26; Wis 2, 23.
2. See Ecli 17, 3–10.

3. See Rm 1, 21–25.

4. See Jn 8, 34.

5. See Dn 3, 57–90.

6. See 1 Cor 6, 13–20.

7. See 1 Kg 16, 7; Jer 17, 10.

8. See Ecli 17, 7–8.

9. See Rm 2, 14–16.

10. See Pius XII, Radio message on correctly forming a christian conscience among youths, 23 March 1952: AAS 44 (1952), p. 271.

11. See Mt 22, 37–40; Gal 5, 14.

12. See Ecli 15, 14.

13. See 2 Cor 5, 10.

14. See Wis 1, 13; 2, 23–24; Rm 5, 21; 6, 23; Jas 1, 15.

15. See 1 Cor 15, 56–57.

16. See Pius XI, Encyclical *Divini Redemptoris*, 19 March 1937: AAS 29 (1937), pp. 65–106; Pius XII, Encyclical *Ad Apostolorum Principis*, 29 June 1958: AAS 50 (1958), pp. 601–614; John XXIII, Encyclical *Mater et Magistra*, 15 May 1961: AAS 53 (1961), pp. 451–453; Paul VI, Encyclical *Ecclesiam Suam*, 6 August 1964: AAS 56 (1964), pp. 651–653.

17. See Vatican council II, Dogmatic constitution on the church, *Lumen gentium,* ch. 1, no. 8: AAS 57 (1965), p. 12.

18. See Ph 1, 27.

19. Augustine, *Confess. (Confessions)* I, 1: PL 32, 661; CChr 27, 1.

20. See Rm 5, 14. See Tertullian, *De carnis resurr. (Of the resurrection of the flesh)*, 6: "For in all the shape given to the clay, Christ was intended as the man who was to be": PL 2, 802 (848); CSEL, 47, p. 33, lines 12–13; CChr 2, 928 (971).

21. See 2 Cor 4, 4.

22. See council of Constantinople II, canon 7: "With neither God the Word being changed into the nature of human flesh, nor the human flesh transformed into the nature of the Word": D 219 (428). See also council of Constantinople III: "For, just as his most holy and blameless animate flesh was not destroyed in being made divine (Θεωθε σα οέκ ἀνηρ€θη), but remained in its own limit and category": D 291 (556). See council of Chalcedon: "must be acknowledged in two natures, with-

out confusion or change, without division or separation": D
148 (302).

23. See council of Constantinople III: "so his human will as well
was not destroyed by being made divine": D 291 (556).

24. See Heb 4, 15.

25. See 2 Cor 5, 18–19; Col 1, 20–22.

26. See 1 Pt 2, 21; Mt 16, 24; Lk 14, 27.

27. See Rm 8, 29; Col 1, 18.

28. See Rm 8, 1–11.

29. See 2 Cor 4, 14.

30. See Ph 3, 10; Rm 8, 17.

31. See Vatican council II, Dogmatic constitution on the church,
Lumen gentium, ch. 2, no. 16: AAS 57 (1965), p. 20.

32. See Rm 8, 32.

33. See *Byzantine Easter Liturgy.*

34. See Rm 8, 15; Gal 4, 6; Jn 1, 12 and Jn 3, 1.

Chapter 2. The human community

1. See John XXIII, Encyclical *Mater et Magistra:* AAS 53 (1961), pp.
401–464, and Encyclical *Pacem in terris,* 11 April 1963: AAS 55
(1963), pp. 257–304; Paul VI, Encyclical *Ecclesiam Suam:* AAS 56
(1964), pp. 609–659.

2. See Lk 17, 33.

3. See Thomas Aquinas, *I Ethic. (I Ethics),* Lect. 1.

4. See John XXIII, Encyclical *Mater et Magistra:* AAS 53 (1961), p.
418; Pius XI, Encyclical *Quadragesimo anno,* 15 May 1931: AAS
23 (1931), p. 222 ff.

5. See John XXIII, Encyclical *Mater et Magistra:* AAS 53 (1961), p.
417.

6. See Mk 2, 27.

7. See John XXIII, Encyclical *Pacem in terris:* AAS 55 (1963), p. 266.

8. See Jas 2, 15–16.

9. See Lk 16, 19–31.

10. See John XXIII, Encyclical *Pacem in terris:* AAS 55 (1963), pp.
299–300.

11. See Lk 6, 37–38; Mt 7, 1–2; Rm 2, 1–11; 14, 10–12.

12. See Mt 5, 45–47.

13. Vatican council II, Dogmatic constitution on the church, *Lumen Gentium,* ch. 2, no. 9: AAS 57 (1965), pp. 12–13.
14. See Ex 24, 1–8.

Chapter 3. Human activity throughout the world
 1. See Gn 1, 26–27; 9, 2–3; Wis 9, 2–3.
 2. See Ps 8, 7 and 10.
 3. See John XXIII, Encyclical *Pacem in terris:* AAS 55 (1963), p. 297.
 4. See *Message to all men and women* issued by the fathers at the beginning of Vatican council II, Oct. 1962: AAS 54 (1962), pp. 822–823.
 5. See Paul VI, Allocution to the diplomatic Corps, 7 Jan. 1965: AAS 57 (1965), p. 232.
 6. See Vatican council I, Dogmatic constitution on the catholic faith, *Dei Filius,* ch. 2: D 1785–1786 (3004–3005).
 7. See P. Paschini, *Vita e opera di Galileo Galilei,* 2 vol., Pont. accademia delle scienze, Vatican City, 1964.
 8. See Mt 24, 13; 13, 24–30 and 36–43.
 9. See 2 Cor 6, 10.
10. See Jn 1, 3 and 14.
11. See Eph 1, 10.
12. See Jn 3, 14–16; Rm 5, 8–10.
13. See Ac 2, 36; Mt 28, 18.
14. See Rm 15, 16.
15. See Ac 1, 7.
16. See 1 Cor 7, 31; Irenaeus, *Adv. Haer. (Against Heresies),* V, 36, 1: PG 7, 1222.
17. See 2 Cor 5, 2; 2 Pt 3, 13.
18. See 1 Cor 2, 9; Ap 21, 4–5.
19. See 1 Cor 15, 42 and 53.
20. See 1 Cor 13, 8; 3, 14.
21. See Rm 8, 19–21.
22. See Lk 9, 25.
23. See Pius XI, Encyclical *Quadragesimo anno:* AAS 23 (1931), p. 207.
24. *Roman Missal,* preface for the feast of Christ the king.

Chapter 4. The church's task in today's world

1. See Paul VI, Encyclical *Ecclesiam suam*, III: AAS 56 (1964), pp. 637–659.

2. See Tt 3, 4: "loving kindness."

3. See Eph 1, 3, 5–6, 13–14, 23.

4. See Vatican council II, Dogmatic constitution on the church, *Lumen Gentium*, ch. 1, no. 8: AAS 57 (1965), p. 12.

5. Ibid., ch. 2, no. 9: AAS 57 (1965), p. 14; see no. 8: AAS, same vol., p. 11.

6. Ibid., ch. 1, no. 8: AAS 57 (1965), p. 11.

7. See ibid., ch. 4, no. 38: AAS 57 (1965), p. 43, with note 120.

8. See Rm 8, 14–17.

9. See Mt 22, 39.

10. See Vatican council II, Dogmatic constitution on the church, *Lumen Gentium*, ch. 2, no. 9: AAS 57 (1965), pp. 12–14.

11. See Pius XII, Allocution to historians and artists, 9 March 1956: AAS 48 (1956), p. 212: "Its divine founder, Jesus Christ, gave to the church no mandate or fixed purpose in the cultural order. The end given to it by Christ is strictly religious (. . .). The church ought to lead men and women to God, so that they may unreservedly surrender themselves to him (. . .). The church can never lose sight of this strictly religious and supernatural end. The purpose of all its activities, down to the last canon of its law, can only be to converge directly or indirectly upon this end.

12. Vatican council II, Dogmatic constitution on the church, *Lumen Gentium*, ch. 1, no. 1: AAS 57 (1965), p. 5.

13. See Heb 13, 14.

14. See 2 Th 3, 6–13; Eph 4, 28.

15. See Is 58, 1–12.

16. See Mt 23, 3–33; Mk 7, 10–13.

17. See John XXIII, Encyclical *Mater et Magistra*, IV: AAS 53 (1961), pp. 456–457; and I: same vol., pp. 407, 410–411.

18. See Vatican council II, Dogmatic constitution on the church, *Lumen Gentium*, ch. 3, no. 28: AAS 57 (1965), pp. 34–35.

19. *Ibid.*, no. 28: AAS, same vol., pp. 35–36.

20. See Ambrose, *De virginitate (On virginity)*, ch. 8, no. 48: PL 16, 278.

21. Vatican council II, Dogmatic constitution on the church, *Lumen Gentium*, ch. 2, no. 15: AAS 57 (1965), p. 20.

22. See Vatican council II, Dogmatic constitution on the church, *Lumen Gentium*, ch. 2, no. 13: AAS 57 (1965), p. 17.

23. See Justin, *Dialogus cum Tryphone (Dialogue with Trypho)*, ch. 110: PG 6, 729; ed. Otto, 1897, pp. 391–393: ". . . for the more such persecutions are inflicted on us, the greater the number of others who become devout believers in the name of Jesus." See Tertullian, *Apologeticum (Apologetics)*, ch. 50, 13: PL 1, 534; CChr 1, 171: "We become even more numerous, whenever you mow us down: for the blood of Christians is a seed!" See Dogmatic constitution on the church, *Lumen Gentium*, ch. 2, no. 9: AAS 57 (1965), p. 14.

24. See Vatican council II, Dogmatic constitution on the church, *Lumen Gentium*, ch. 7, no. 48: AAS 57 (1965), p. 53.

25. See Paul VI, Allocution on 3 Feb. 1965: *L'Osservatore Romano*, 4 Feb. 1965. The Lord himself tells us: "Behold, I am coming soon, bringing my recompense, to repay everyone for what he has done. I am the alpha and the omega, the first and the last, the beginning and the end" (Ap 22, 12–13).

Part 2
Chapter 1. Promoting the dignity of marriage and the family

1. See Augustine, *De bono coniugali (The good of marriage)*: PL 40, 375–376 and 394; Thomas Aquinas, *Summa Theol. (Sum of Theology)*, Supplementary question 49, art. 3, to 1; *Decree for the Armenians*: D 702 (1327); Pius XI, Encyclical *Casti Connubii*, 31 Dec. 1930: AAS 22 (1930), pp. 543–555; D 2227–2238 (3703–3714).

2. See Pius XI, Encyclical *Casti Connubii*: AAS 22 (1930), pp. 546–547; D 2231 (3706).

3. See Hos 2; Jer 3, 6–13; Ez 16 and 23; Is 54.

4. See Mt 9, 15; Mk 2, 19–20; Lk 5, 34–35; Jn 3, 29; 2 Cor 11, 2; Eph 5, 27; Ap 19, 7–8; 21, 2 and 9.

5. See Eph 5, 25.

6. See Vatican council II, Dogmatic constitution on the church, *Lumen Gentium*: AAS 57 (1965), pp. 15–16, 40–41, 47.

7. See Pius XI, Encyclical *Casti Connubii*: AAS 22 (1930), p. 583.

8. See 1 Tm 5, 3.

9. See Eph 5, 32.

10. See Gn 2, 22–24; Pro 5, 18–20; 31, 10–31; Tb 8, 4–8; Sg 1, 1–3; 2, 16; 4, 16–5, 1; 7, 8–11; 1 Cor 7, 3–6; Eph 5, 25–33.

11. See Pius XI, Encyclical *Casti Connubii:* AAS 22 (1930), pp. 547–548; D 2232 (3707).

12. See 1 Cor 7, 5.

13. See Pius XII, Allocution *Tra le visite,* 20 Jan. 1958: AAS 50 (1958), p. 91.

14. See Pius XI, Encyclical *Casti Connubii:* AAS 22 (1930), pp. 559–561; D 3716–3718; Pius XII, Allocution to the Congress of the Italian Union of Obstetricians, 29 Oct. 1951: AAS 43 (1951), pp. 835–854; Paul VI, Allocution to their Eminences, 23 June 1964: AAS 56 (1964), pp. 581–589. Some questions requiring further and closer investigation have been remitted by command of the supreme pontiff to the commission for the study of population, the family and birth, so that when it completes its task the supreme pontiff can deliver a judgment. This being the position of the teaching of the magisterium, the council is not aiming immediately to propose specific solutions.

15. See Eph 5, 16; Col 4, 5.

16. See *Gregorian Sacramentary:* PL 78, 262.

17. See Rm 5, 15 and 18; 6, 5–11; Gal 2, 20.

18. See Eph 5, 25–27.

Chapter 2. The proper development of culture

1. See *Introduction* of this constitution, nos. 4–10.

2. See Col 3, 1–2.

3. See Gn 1, 28.

4. See Pro 8, 30–31.

5. See Irenaeus, *Adv. Haer. (Against Heresies),* III, 11, 8: ed. Sagnard, p. 200; see ibid., 16, 6: pp. 290–292; 21, 10–22: pp. 370–372; 22, 3: p. 378; etc.

6. See Eph 1, 10.

7. See Pius XI's words to bishop Roland-Gosselin: "One must never lose sight of the fact that the church's objective is to evangelise and not to civilize. If the church civilizes, it is through evangelisation" (Versailles social week, 1936, pp. 461–462).

8. Vatican council I, Dogmatic constitution on the catholic faith,

Dei Filius, ch. 4: D 1795, 1799 (3015, 3019). See Pius XI, Encyclical *Quadragesimo anno:* AAS 23 (1931), p. 190.

9. See John XXIII, Encyclical *Pacem in Terris:* AAS 55 (1963), p. 260.

10. See John XXIII, Encyclical *Pacem in Terris:* AAS 55 (1963), p. 283; Pius XII, Radio message, 24 Dec. 1941: AAS 34 (1942), pp. 16–17.

11. See John XXIII, Encyclical *Pacem in Terris:* AAS 55 (1963), p. 260.

12. See John XXIII, Allocution on 11 Oct. 1962, at the beginning of the council: AAS 54 (1962), p. 792.

13. See Vatican council II, Constitution on the sacred liturgy, *Sacrosanctum Concilium,* no. 123: AAS 26 (1964), p. 131; Paul VI, Discourse to Roman artists, 7 May 1964: AAS 56 (1964), pp. 439–442.

14. See Vatican council II, Decree on priestly formation, *Optatam Totius,* and Declaration on christian education, *Gravissimum educationis.*

15. See Vatican council II, Dogmatic constitution on the church, *Lumen Gentium,* ch. 4, no. 37: AAS 57 (1965), pp. 42–43.

Chapter 3. Socio-economic life

1. See Pius XII, Message, 23 March 1952: AAS 44 (1952), p. 273; John XXIII, Allocution to A.C.L.I., 1 May 1959: AAS 51 (1959), p. 358.

2. See Pius XI, Encyclical *Quadragesimo anno:* AAS 23 (1931), p. 190 ff.; Pius XII, Message, 23 March 1952: AAS 44 (1952), p. 276 ff.; John XXIII, Encyclical *Mater et Magistra:* AAS 53 (1961), p. 450; Vatican council II, Decree on the mass media, *Inter mirifica,* ch. 1, no. 6: AAS 56 (1964), p. 147.

3. See Mt 16, 26; Lk 16, 1–31; Col 3, 17.

4. See Leo XIII, Encyclical *Libertas praestantissimum,* 20 June 1888: ASS 20 (1887–1888), p. 597 ff.; Pius XI, Encyclical *Quadragesimo anno:* AAS 23 (1931), p. 191 ff.; Id., *Divini Redemptoris:* AAS 29 (1937), p. 65 ff.; Pius XII, Message for Christmas 1941: AAS 34 (1942), p. 10 ff.; John XXIII, Encyclical *Mater et Magistra:* AAS 53 (1961), pp. 401–464.

5. Regarding problems in agriculture, see especially John XXIII, Encyclical *Mater et Magistra:* AAS 53 (1961), p. 341 ff.

6. See Leo XIII, Encyclical *Rerum Novarum:* ASS 23 (1890–1891), pp. 649–662; Pius XI, Encyclical *Quadragesimo anno:* AAS 23 (1931), pp. 200–201; Id., Encyclical *Divini Redemptoris:* AAS 29 (1937), p. 92; Pius XII, Radio message on Christmas eve 1942: AAS 35 (1943), p. 20; Id., Allocution of 13 June 1943: AAS 35 (1943), p. 172; Id., Radio message to Spanish workers, 11 March 1951: AAS 43 (1951), p. 215; John XXIII, Encyclical *Mater et Magistra:* AAS 53 (1961), p. 419.

7. See John XXIII, Encyclical *Mater et Magistra:* AAS 53 (1961), pp. 408, 424, 427; the word "undertaking" was taken from the text of the encyclical *Quadragesimo anno:* AAS 23 (1931), p. 199. For the development of the question see also: Pius XII, Allocution of 3 June 1950: AAS 42 (1950), pp. 485–488; Paul VI, Allocution of 8 June 1964: AAS 56 (1964), pp. 574–579.

8. See Pius XII, Encyclical *Sertum laetitiae:* AAS 31 (1939), p. 642; John XXIII, Consistorial allocution: AAS 52 (1960), pp. 5–11; Id., Encyclical *Mater et Magistra:* AAS 53 (1961), p. 411.

9. See Thomas Aquinas, *Summa Theol. (Sum of Theology)* II–II, quest. 32, art. 5, to 2; Ibid. quest. 66, art. 2; see the explanation in Leo XIII, Encyclical *Rerum Novarum:* ASS 23 (1890–1891), p. 651; see also Pius XII, Allocution of 1 June 1941: AAS 33 (1941), p. 199; Id., Radio message for Christmas 1954: AAS 47 (1955), p. 27.

10. See Basil, *Hom. in illud Lucae "Destruam horrea mea" (Homily on the text of Luke "I will pull down my barns"),* no. 2: PG 31, 263; Lactantius, *Divinarum Institutionum (The Divine Institutes),* book 5, on justice: PL 6, 565 B; Augustine, *In Ioann. Ev. (Commentary on John's Gospel),* tract 50, no. 6: PL 35, 1760; CChr 36, 435; Id., *Enarratio in Ps. (Exposition of the Psalms),* 147, 12: PL 37, 1922; CChr 40, 2148; Gregory the Great, *Homiliae in Ev. (Homilies on the Gospels),* homily 20, 12: PL 76, 1165; Id., *Regulae Pastoralis liber (Pastoral Care),* part 3, ch. 21: PL 77, 87; Bonaventure, *In III Sent. (Commentary on III Sentences),* dist. 33, query 1: ed. Quaracchi III, 728; Id., *In IV Sent. (Commentary on IV Sentences),* dist. 15, part II, art. 2, quest. 1: Ibid. IV, 371 B; *Quaest. de superfluo (Questions on superfluity):* MS Assisi, Communal library 186, ff. 112ª–113ª; Albert the Great, *In III Sent. (Commentary on III Sentences),* dist. 33, art. 3, sol. 1: ed. Borgnet XXVIII, 611;

Id., *In IV Sent. (Commentary on IV Sentences),* dist. 15, art. 16: Ibid. XXIX, 494–497. Regarding the definition of superfluity in modern times, see John XXIII, Radio and television message 11 Sept. 1962: AAS 54 (1962), p. 682: "The duty of everybody, the compelling duty of a Christian, is to consider superfluity by the measure of the needs of others, and to take care that the administration and distribution of created goods benefits all."

11. In this situation the old principle holds: "In extreme need all goods are common, that is, to be shared." On the other hand, for the nature, scope and manner of applying the principle, see Thomas Aquinas, *Summa Theol. (Sum of Theology)* II–II, quest. 66, art.

12. See Gratian, *Decrees,* ch. 21, dist. 86: ed. Friedberg I, 302. This saying is already found in PL 54, 491 A and PL 56, 1132 B. See in *Antonianum* 27 (1952), pp. 349–366.

13. See Leo XIII, Encyclical *Rerum Novarum:* ASS 23 (1890–1891), pp. 643–646; Pius XI, Encyclical *Quadragesimo anno:* AAS 23 (1931), p. 191; Pius XII, Radio message of 1 June 1941: AAS 35 (1941), p. 199; Id., Radio message on Christmas eve 1942: AAS 35 (1943), p. 17; Id., Radio message of 1 Sept. 1944: AAS 36 (1944), p. 253; John XXIII, Encyclical *Mater et Magistra:* AAS 53 (1961), pp. 428–429.

14. See Pius XI, Encyclical *Quadragesimo anno:* AAS 23 (1931), p. 214; John XXIII, Encyclical *Mater et Magistra:* AAS 53 (1961), p. 429.

15. See Pius XII, Radio message at Pentecost 1941: AAS 44 (1941), p. 199; John XXIII, Encyclical *Mater et Magistra:* AAS 53 (1961), p. 430.

16. For the right use of goods according to the teaching of the new Testament, see Lk 3, 11; 10, 30 ff.; 11, 41; 1 Pt 5, 3; Mk 8, 36; 12, 29–31; Jas 5, 1–6; 1 Tm 6, 8; Eph 4, 28; 2 Cor 8, 13 ff.; 1 Jn 3, 17–18.

Chapter 4. Life in the political community
1. See John XXIII, Encyclical *Mater et Magistra:* AAS 53 (1961), p. 417.
2. See Ibid.
3. See Rm 13, 1–5.
4. See Rm 13, 5.

5. See Pius XII, Radio message, 24 Dec. 1942: AAS 35 (1943), pp. 9–24; 24 Dec. 1944: AAS 37 (1945), pp. 11–17; John XXIII, Encyclical *Pacem in terris:* AAS 55 (1963), pp. 263, 271, 277–278.

6. See Pius XII, Radio message, 1 June 1941: AAS 33 (1941), p. 200; John XXIII, Encyclical *Pacem in terris:* AAS 55 (1963), pp. 273–274.

7. See John XXIII, Encyclical *Mater et Magistra:* AAS 53 (1961), pp. 415–418.

8. See Pius XI, Allocution to the directors of the Federation of Catholic Universities: *Discorsi di Pio XI,* ed. Bertetto, Turin, vol. 1 (1960), p. 743.

9. See Vatican council II, Dogmatic constitution on the church, *Lumen Gentium,* no. 13: AAS 57 (1965), p. 17.

10. See Lk 2, 14.

Chapter 5. Promoting peace and encouraging the community of nations

1. See Eph 2, 16; Col 1, 20–22.

2. See John XXIII, Encyclical *Pacem in terris:* AAS 55 (1963), p. 291: "Therefore in this age of ours, which prides itself on its atomic power, it is irrational to think that war is a proper way to obtain justice for violated rights."

3. See Pius XII, Allocution of 30 Sept. 1954: AAS 46 (1954), p. 589; Radio message, 24 Dec. 1954: AAS 47 (1955), p. 15 ff.; John XXIII, Encyclical *Pacem in terris:* AAS 55 (1963), pp. 286–291; Paul VI, Allocution to the assembly of the United Nations, 4 Oct. 1965: AAS 57 (1965), pp. 877–885.

4. See John XXIII, Encyclical *Pacem in terris,* where the reduction of arms is spoken of: AAS 55 (1963), p. 287.

5. See 2 Cor 6, 2.

Conclusion

1. See John XXIII, Encyclical *Ad Petri Cathedram,* 29 June 1959: AAS 55 (1959), p. 513.

2. See Mt 7, 21.

DECLARATION ON RELIGIOUS FREEDOM
(DIGNITATIS HUMANAE)

1. See John XXIII, Encyclical *Pacem in terris,* 11 April 1963: AAS 55 (1963), p. 279; Ibid., p. 265; Pius XII, Radio message, 24 Dec. 1944: AAS 37 (1945), p. 14.

2. See John XXIII, Encyclical *Pacem in terris,* 11 April 1963: AAS 55 (1963), pp. 260–261; Pius XII, Radio message, 24 Dec. 1942: AAS 35 (1943), p. 19; Pius XI, Encyclical *Mit brennender Sorge,* 14 March 1937: AAS 29 (1937), p. 160; Leo XIII, Encyclical *Libertas praestantissimum,* 20 June 1888: *Acta* of Leo XIII, 8 (1888), pp. 237–238.

3. See Thomas Aquinas, *Summa Theologiae,* I–II, quest. 91, art. 1; quest. 93, art. 1–2.

4. See John XXIII, Encyclical *Pacem in terris,* 11 April 1963: AAS 55 (1963), p. 270; Paul VI, Radio message, 22 Dec. 1964: AAS 57 (1965), pp. 181–182; Thomas Aquinas, *Summa Theologiae,* I–II, quest. 91, art. 4 c.

5. See John XXIII, Encyclical *Mater et Magistra,* 15 May 1961: AAS 53 (1961), p. 417; idem, Encyclical *Pacem in terris,* 11 April 1963: AAS 55 (1963), p. 273.

6. See John XXIII, Encyclical *Pacem in terris,* 11 April 1963: AAS 55 (1963), pp. 273–274; Pius XII, Radio message, 1 June 1942: AAS 33 (1941), p. 200.

7. See Leo XIII, Encyclical *Immortale Dei,* 1 Nov. 1885: AAS 18 (1885), p. 161.

8. See Lactantius, *Divinarum Institutionum (The Divine Institutes),* book 5, 19: CSEL 19, pp. 463–465; PL 6, 614 and 616 (chapter 20); Ambrose, *Epistola ad Valentinianum Imp. (Letter to Emperor Valentinian),* Letter 21: PL 16, 1005; Augustine, *Contra litteras Petiliani (Against the letter of Petilian),* book 2, ch. 83: CSEL 52, p. 112; PL 43, 315; see C.23, quest. 5, canon 33 (ed. Friedberg, 1, 939); idem, Letter 23: PL 33, 98; idem, Letter 34: PL 33, 132; Idem, Letter 35: PL 33, 135; Gregory the Great, *Epistola ad Virgilium et Theodorum Episcopos Massiliae Galliarum (Letter to Bishops Virgilius and Theodore),* Registrum epistolarum, I, 45: MGH Ep. 1, p. 72; PL 77, 510–511 (book 1, letter 47); CChr 140, 59; Idem, *Epistola ad Iohannem Episcopum Constantinopolitanum (Letter to John, bishop of Constantinople),* Registrum epistolarum,

III, 52: MGH Ep. I, p. 210; PL 77, 649 (book 3, letter 53); CChr 140, 199; see D.45, canon 1 (ed. Friedberg, 1, 160); council of Toledo IV (633), canon 57: Msi 10, 633; see D.45, canon 5 (ed. Friedberg, 1, 161–162); Clement III: *Decretals*, V, 6, 9 (ed. Friedberg, 2, 774); Innocent III, *Epistola ad Arelatensem Archiepiscopum (Letter to the archbishop of Arles): Decretals*, III, 42, 3 (ed. Friedberg, 2, 646).

9. See CIC, canon 1351; Pius XII, Allocution to the prelate auditors and other officials and administrators of the Roman Rota, 6 Oct. 1946: AAS 38 (1946), p. 394; idem, Encyclical *Mystici Corporis*, 29 June 1943: AAS (1943), p. 243.

10. See Eph 1, 5.

11. See Jn 6, 44.

12. See Jn 13, 13.

13. See Mt 11, 29.

14. See Mt 11, 28–30; Jn 6, 67–68.

15. See Mt 9, 28–29; Mk 9, 23–24; 6, 5–6; Paul VI, Encyclical *Ecclesiam suam*, 6 Aug. 1964: AAS 56 (1964), pp. 642–643.

16. See Mt 11, 20–24; Rm 12, 19–20; 2 Th 1, 8.

17. See Mt 13, 30, 40–42.

18. See Mt 4, 8–10; Jn 6, 15.

19. See Is 42, 1–4.

20. See Jn 18, 37.

21. See Mt 26, 51–53; Jn 18, 36.

22. See Jn 12, 32.

23. See 1 Cor 2, 3–5; 1 Th 2, 3–5.

24. See Rm 14, 1–23; 1 Cor 8, 9–13; 10, 23–33.

25. See Eph 6, 19–20.

26. See Rm 1, 16.

27. See 2 Cor 10, 4; 1 Th 5, 8–9.

28. See Eph 6, 11–17.

29. See 2 Cor 10, 3–5.

30. See 1 Pt 2, 13–17.

31. See Ac 4, 19–20.

32. See Leo XIII, Letter *Officio sanctissimo*, 22 Dec. 1887: ASS 20 (1887), p. 269; Idem, Letter *Ex litteris*, 7 April 1887: ASS 19 (1886), p. 465.

33. See Mk 16, 15; Mt 28, 18–20; Pius XII, Encyclical *Summi Pontificatus,* 20 Oct. 1939: AAS 31 (1939), pp. 445–446.

34. See Pius XI, Letter *Firmissimam constantiam,* 28 March 1937: AAS 29 (1937), p. 196.

35. See Pius XII, Allocution *Ci riesce,* 6 Dec. 1953: AAS 45 (1953), p. 802.

36. See Pius XII, Radio message, 23 March 1952: AAS 44 (1952), pp. 270–278.

37. See Ac 4, 29.

38. See John XXIII, Encyclical *Pacem in terris,* 11 April 1963: AAS 55 (1963), pp. 299–300.

39. *Ibid.,* pp. 295–296.

DECLARATION ON THE CHURCH'S RELATION
TO NON-CHRISTIAN RELIGIONS (NOSTRA AETATE)

1. See Ac 17, 26.

2. See Wis 8, 1; Ac 14, 17; Rm 2, 6–7; 1 Tm 2, 4.

3. See Ap 21, 23–24.

4. See 2 Cor 5, 18–19.

5. See Gregory VII, *Epist. III, 21 ad Anazir (Al–Nasir) regem Mauritaniae,* ed. E. Caspar in MGH, *Ep. sel. II,* 1920, I, p. 288, 11–15; PL 148, 451 A.

6. See Gal 3, 7.

7. See Rm 11, 17–24.

8. See Eph 2, 14–16.

9. See Lk 19, 44.

10. See Rm 11, 28.

11. See Rm 11, 28–29; Vatican council II, Dogmatic constitution on the church, *Lumen Gentium,* AAS 57 (1965), p. 20.

12. See Is 66, 23; Ps 65, 4; Rm 11, 11–32.

13. See Jn 19, 6.

14. See Rm 12, 18.

15. See Mt 5, 45.

Abbreviations

Bible

The Latin abbreviation, if different, is given in brackets.

Ac	Acts
Am	Amos
Ap	Apocalypse / Revelation
Bar	Baruch
1 Chr (1 Par)	1 Chronicles
2 Chr (2 Par)	2 Chronicles
Col	Colossians
1 Cor	1 Corinthians
2 Cor	2 Corinthians
Dn	Daniel
Dt	Deuteronomy
Ec	Ecclesiastes
Ecli	Ecclesiasticus
Eph	Ephesians
1 Es	1 Esdras
2 Es	2 Esdras
Est	Esther
Ex	Exodus
Ez	Ezechiel
Gal	Galatians
Gn	Genesis
Hab	Habakkuk

Hag	Haggai
Heb	Hebrews
Hos (Os)	Hosea
Is	Isaiah
Jas (Ic)	James
Jdt (Idt)	Judith
Jer (Ir)	Jeremiah
Jg (Id)	Judges
Jl (Il)	Joel
Jn (Io)	John
1 Jn (1 Io)	1 John
2 Jn (2 Io)	2 John
3 Jn (3 Io)	3 John
Jnh (In)	Jonah
Job (Ib)	Job
Jos (Ios)	Joshua
Ju (Iu)	Jude
1 Kg (1 Rg)	1 Kings / 1 Samuel
2 Kg (2 Rg)	2 Kings / 2 Samuel
3 Kg (3 Rg)	3 Kings / 1 Kings
4 Kg (4 Rg)	4 Kings / 2 Kings
Lk (Lc)	Luke
Lm	Lamentations
Lv	Leviticus
1 Mc	1 Maccabees
2 Mc	2 Maccabees
Mic	Micah
Mk (Mr)	Mark
Ml	Malachi
Mt	Matthew
Nh	Nahum
Nm	Numbers
Ob (Ab)	Obadiah

Ph	Philippians
Phl	Philemon
Pro	Proverbs
Ps	Psalms
1 Pt	1 Peter
2 Pt	2 Peter
Rm	Romans
Rt	Ruth
Sg (Cn)	Song of Songs
Tb	Tobit
1 Th	1 Thessalonians
2 Th	2 Thessalonians
1 Tm	1 Timothy
2 Tm	2 Timothy
Tt	Titus
Wis (Sap)	Wisdom
Zc	Zechariah
Zp	Zephaniah

Others

AAS   *Acta Apostolicae Sedis.*

ACO   E. Schwartz, *Acta Conciliorum Oecumenicorum:* tome I *Concilium universale Ephesinum* (5 vols.); tome II *Concilium universale Chalcedonense* (6 vols.), Berlin and Leipzig 1927–1932.

Asd   *Acta scitu dignissima docteque concinnata Constantiensis concilii celebratissimi,* ed. Jerome of Croaria, Hagenau 1500.

ASS   *Acta Sedis Sanctae.*

Benešević   W. Benešević, *Sinagoga v 50 titulov i drugie iuridičeskie zborniki Joana Scholastika,* St. Petersburg 1914.

Bettenson[2]   H. Bettenson, *Documents of the Christian Church,* Oxford [2]1967.

Bl   S. Baluze (Balutius), *Nova collectio conciliorum . . . ,* tome I Paris 1683.

Bn/BN[1 2 3]   S. Binius, *Concilia generalia et provincialia* . . . , 5 vols. Cologne 1606; 9 vols. ibid. [2]1618; 11 vols. Paris [3]1636.

Br   C. Baronius (continued by O. Raynaldi), *Annales ecclesiastici*, ed. J. D. Mansi, 38 vols. Lucca 1728–1759.

BR   *Bullarum, diplomatum et privilegiorum sanctorum Romanorum pontificum* [Bullarium Taurinense], 25 vols. Turin 1857–1872; Naples 1867–1885.

Bruns   *Canones apostolorum et conciliorum saeculorum IV. V. VI. VII*, ed. H. T. Bruns, Berlin 1839 (facsimile ed. Turin 1959).

CChr   *Corpus Christianorum*, Turnhout 1953–.

CCO   *Les canons des conciles oecuméniques*, ed. P-P. Jouannou (Pontificia commissione per la redazione del codice di diritto canonico orientale. Fonti. Fasc. IX: *Discipline générale antique [IIe–IXe s.]* tome I, part I), Grottaferrata 1962.

CF   *Concilium Florentinum. Documenta et scriptores*, ed. Pontifical Oriental Institute, Rome 1940–.

CIC   *Codex Iuris Canonici*, 1917.

Cl   N. Coleti, *Sacrosancta concilia ad regiam editionem exacta quae olim quarta parte prodiit . . . longe locupletior et emendatior exhibetur . . .* , 23 vols. Venice 1728–1733.

Clem.   *Clementis Papae V. Constitutiones.*

Clementines   see Clem.

COD   *Conciliorum Oecumenicorum Decreta*, ed. G. Alberigo and others, Bologna [3]1973.

CPG   *Les canons des pères Grecs*, ed. P-P. Jouannou (Pontificia commissione per la redazione del codice di diritto canonico orientale. Fonti. Fasc. IX: *Discipline générale antique [IIe–IXe s.]* tome II), Grottaferrata 1963.

Cr[1 2]   P. Crabbe, *Concilia omnia, tam generalia, quam particularia . . .* , 2 vols. Cologne 1538; 3 vols. ibid. [2]1551.

CSEL   *Corpus Scriptorum Ecclesiasticorum Latinorum*, Vienna 1866–.

CSP   *Les canons des synodes particuliers*, ed. P-P. Jouannou

(Pontificia commissione per la redazione del codice di diritto canonico orientale. Fonti. Fasc. IX: *Discipline générale antique* [*II*ᵉ–*IX*ᵉ s.] tome I, part II), Grottaferrata 1962.

CT   *Concilium Tridentinum. Diariorum, actorum, epistularum, tractatuum nova collectio,* ed. Goerresian Society, 13 vols. so far, Freiburg 1901–.

D   H. Denzinger and A. Schönmetzer, *Enchiridion symbolorum, definitionum et declarationum de rebus fidei et morum,* Barcelona and Freiburg ³³1965.

Dc   *Decreta concilii Basileensis,* Basel 1499.

DDrC   *Dictionnaire de droit canonique,* Paris 1935–1965.

Decretals   see *X.*

DHGE   *Dictionnaire d'histoire et géographie ecclésiastique,* Paris 1912–.

Dölger   F. Dölger, *Regesten der Kaiserurkunden des Oströmischen. Reiches von 565–1453,* 5 vols. Munich 1924–1963.

DThC   *Dictionnaire de théologie catholique,* Paris 1903–1950.

EB   *Enchiridion Biblicum,* Naples and Rome ⁴1961.

EC   *Enciclopedia Cattolica,* Rome 1949–1954.

ER   *Conciliorum omnium generalium et provincialium collectio* [Editio Regia], 37 vols. Paris 1644.

Extrav. comm.   *Extravagantes communes.*

Extrav. Ioann. XXII   *Extravagantes Ioannis Papae XXII.*

Fr/Friedberg   *Corpus Iuris Canonici,* ed. E. Friedberg, 2 vols. Leipzig 1879 (facsimile ed. Graz 1955).

Funk   *Patres Apostolici,* ed. F. X. Funk, 2 vols. Tübingen ²1901.

GCS   *Die griechischen christlichen Schriftsteller der ersten Jahrhunderte,* Leipzig and Berlin 1897–.

Grumel   V. Grumel, *Les regestes des actes du patriarcat de Constantinople;* vol. I *Les actes des patriarches:* fasc. I *Les registes de 381 à 715,* fasc. II *Les registes de 715 à 1043,* Kadiköy–Istanbul 1932–1936.

Hahn

Hahn   A. Hahn, *Bibliothek der Symbole und Glaubensregeln der Alten Kirche,* Breslau ³1897.

Hardt   H. von der Hardt, *Magnum oecumenicum Constantiense concilium,* 6 vols. Frankfurt and Leipzig 1696–1700.

HC   *History of the Church,* ed. H. Jedin, 10 vols. London 1980.

Hinschius   *Decretales Pseudo-Isidorianae et capitula Angilramni,* ed. P. Hinschius, Leipzig 1863.

H–L   K. J. Hefele, *Histoire des conciles d'après les documents originaux,* trans. and continued by H. Leclerq, 11 vols. 1907–1952.

Hrd   J. Hardouin, *Conciliorum collectio regia maxima ad p. Philippi Labbei et p. Gabrielis Cossartii e Societate Jesu labores haud modica accessione facta et emendationibus pluribus additis . . . ,* 12 vols. Paris 1714–1715.

Jaffé   P. Jaffé, *Regesta pontificum Romanorum ab condita ecclesia ad annum post Christum natum MCXCVIII,* 2 vols. Leipzig ²1885–1888 (facsimile ed. Graz 1956).

JThS   *Journal of Theological Studies.*

Kirch   C. Kirch, *Enchiridion fontium historiae ecclesiasticae antiquae,* ed. L. Ueding, Barcelona and Freiburg ⁸1950.

Lauchert   F. Lauchert, *Die Kanones der wichtigsten altkirchlichen Concilien nebst den apostolischen Kanones,* Freiburg and Leipzig 1896 (facsimile ed. Frankfurt 1961).

LC   P. Labbe and G. Cossart, *Sacrosancta concilia ad regiam editionem exacta quae nunc quarta parte prodit auctior studio Philippi Labbei et Gabrielis Cossartii . . . ,* 17 vols. Paris 1671–1672.

Le concile   *Le concile et les conciles. Contribution à l'histoire de la vie conciliaire de l'église,* [ed. O. Rousseau], Chevetogne 1960.

LThK   *Lexicon für Theologie und Kirche, Freiburg* ²1957–1968.

Martin   J. B. Martin, *Conciles et bullaire du diocèse de Lyon . . . ,* Lyons 1905.

MD   E. Martène and U. Durand, *Thesaurus novus anecdotorum seu collectio monumentorum . . .*, 5 vols. Paris 1717.

MGH   *Monumenta Germaniae Historica*, Hannover and Berlin 1826–.

Mr[1 2 3]   J. Merlin, *Tomus primus quatuor conciliorum generalium, quadraginta septem conciliorum provincialium . . . Secundus tomus conciliorum generalium . . .*, 2 vols. Paris 1524; Cologne [2]1530; Paris [3]1535.

Msi   J. D. Mansi (continued by J. B. Martin and L. Petit), *Sacrorum conciliorum nova et amplissima collectio . . .*, 53 vols. Florence, Venice, Paris and Leipzig 1759–1927.

Msi[1]   J. D. Mansi, *Sanctorum conciliorum et decretorum collectio nova seu collectionis conciliorum a pp. Ph. Labbeo et G. Cossartio . . . amplioris opera N. Coleti sacerdotis Venetiae recusae supplementum*, 6 vols. Lucca 1748–1752.

Mxv   *Monumenta conciliorum generalium sec. XV.*, 4 vols. Vienna 1857–1935.

NCE   *New Catholic Encyclopedia*, New York 1967.

N–D   J. Neuner and J. Dupuis, *The Christian Faith*, Bangalore and London [4]1983.

Opitz, *Urkunden*   H. G. Opitz, *Athanasius Werke 3.1, Urkunden zur Geschichte des Arianischen Streites*, Berlin and Leipzig 1934–1935.

Pastor   L. Pastor, *History of the Popes*, trans. L. Autrobus and others, 40 vols. London 1899–1953.

Percival   H. R. Percival, *The Seven Ecumenical Councils of the Undivided Church*, New York and Oxford 1900.

PG   J. P. Migne, *Patrologia Graeca*, 162 vols. Paris 1857–1866.

Pitra   J. B. Pitra, *Iuris ecclesiastici Graecorum historia et monumenta*, 2 vols. Rome 1864–1868.

PL   J. P. Migne, *Patrologia Latina*, 221 vols. Paris 1844–1864.

Potthast   *Regesta pontificum Romanorum inde ab a. post Chris-*

tum natum MCXCVIII ad a. MCCIV, ed. A. Potthast, 2 vols. Berlin 1874–1875 (facsimile ed. Graz 1957).

RE *Realencyklopädie für protestantische Theologie und Kirche,* ed. A. Hauck, Leipzig ³1896–1913.

RGG *Die Religion in Geschichte und Gegenwart,* ed. K. Galling, 7 vols. Tübingen ³1957–1965.

Rm Τάν ἐγίων οἀχουμενικάν συνόδων της χαθολιχης ἀχχλησίας απαντα. *Concilia generalia Ecclesiae catholicae* [Editio Romana], 4 vols. Rome 1608–1612.

SC *Sources chrétiennes,* Paris 1942–.

Sext see *VI°*.

Strewe A. Strewe, *Die Canonessammlung des Dionysius Exiguus in der ersten Redaktion,* Berlin 1931.

Su L. Surius, *Tomus primus conciliorum omnium, tum generalium, tum provincialium atque particularium . . . ,* 4 vols. Cologne 1567.

Su–Bo D. Bollani and D. Nicolini, *Conciliorum omnium tam generalium quam provincialium . . . quibus novissima hac editione post Surianam accessere praesertim Nicaenum et Ephesinum . . . ,* 5 vols. Venice 1587.

ThLZ *Theologische Literaturzeitung.*

TU *Texte und Untersuchungen,* Leipzig and Berlin 1882–.

Turner C. H. Turner, *Ecclesiae occidentalis monumenta iuris antiquissimi. Canonum et conciliorum Graecorum interpretationes Latinae,* 2 vols. Oxford 1899–1939.

VI° *Liber Sextus Decretalium Bonifacii Papae VIII.*

X *Decretales Gregorii Papae IX.*

ZKG *Zeitschrift für Kirchengeschichte.*

Note on Text

The English-language translations of the Vatican II Council Documents which appear in this volume originally appeared in *Decrees of the Ecumenical Councils, Vol. II* [Trent—Vatican II], published by Sheed & Ward/Georgetown University Press in 1990. These texts were edited by Norman P. Tanner, S.J., and are the work of a team of Jesuits from, or working in, the British Isles, each of whom is identified at the start of the document which he translated.